FLASHMAPS NEW YORK

Editor
Steven K. Amsterdam

Creative Director
Fabrizio La Rocca

Cartographer
David Lindroth

Designer
Tigist Getachew

Editorial Contributors
Robert Blake
Martha Schulman
Jason Tougaw

Cartographic Contributors
Edward Faherty
Aaron Flacke
Sheila Levin
Page Lindroth
Eric Rudolph

Contents

PARKS & RECREATION MAP

SHOPPING MAP

DINING & LODGING MAP

NIGHTLIFE MAP

Special Sales

Fodor's Travel Publications are available at special discounts for bulk purchases for sales promotions or premiums. Special editions, including personalized covers, excerpts of existing guides, and corporate imprints, can be created in large quantities for special needs. For more information, contact your local bookseller or write to Special Markets, Fodor's Travel Publications, 201 East 50th St., New York, NY 10022. Inquiries from Canada should be directed to your local Canadian bookseller or sent to Random House of Canada, Ltd., Marketing Dept., 2775 Matheson Blvd. East, Mississauga, Ontario L4W4P7. Inquiries from the United Kingdom should be sent to Fodor's Travel Publications, 20 Vauxhall Bridge Rd., London, England SW1V 2SA. **ISBN 0-679-00008-9**

PRINTED IN THE UNITED STATES OF AMERICA 10 9 8 7 6 5 4 3 2 1

Important Telephone Numbers

Area Codes: Manhattan (212); Bronx, Brooklyn, Queens, Staten Island (718); Nassau & Suffolk (516); Northern NJ (201). All (212) unless otherwise noted.

EMERGENCIES

AAA Emergency Road Service ☎ 800/222-4357

Ambulance, Fire, Police ☎ 911

Animal Bites ☎ 676-2483

Animal Medical Center ☎ 838-8100

Arson Hotline ☎ 718/722-3600

Battered Women ☎ 800/942-6908

Child Abuse ☎ 800/342-3720

Deaf Emergency ☎ 718/899-8800

Dental Emergency ☎ 677-2510

Domestic Violence ☎ 800/942-6908

Drug Abuse ☎ 800/395-3400

Hospital Patient Location Information ☎ 718/416-7000

Lesbian and Gay Anti-Violence Project ☎ 807-0197

Park Emergencies ☎ 800/201-5722

Poison Control ☎ 340-4494

Rape Hotline ☎ 577-7777

Runaway Hotline ☎ 966-8000

Sex Crimes Reports ☎ 267-7273

Suicide Prevention ☎ 673-3000

Victim Services Hotline ☎ 577-7777

SERVICES

AAA ☎ 757-2000

AIDS Hotline ☎ 800/342-2437

Alcoholics Anonymous ☎ 870-3400

All Night Pharmacy ☎ 541-9078

Amex Lost Travelers Checks ☎ 800/221-7282

ASPCA ☎ 876-7700

Better Business Bureau ☎ 533-6200

Borough President ☎ 669-8300

Bridges & Tunnels ☎ 360-3000

Central Park Events ☎ 360-8126

Chamber of Commerce ☎ 493-7400

Chequepoint USA ☎ 869-6281

City Sanitation ☎ 219-8090

Consumer Affairs ☎ 487-4444

Convention & Visitor's Bureau ☎ 397-8222

Department of Aging ☎ 442-1000

Disabilities Information ☎ 788-2830

Foreign Exchange Rates ☎ 883-0400

Foreign Newspapers ☎ 840-1868

Gay and Lesbian Switchboard ☎ 777-1800

Health Department ☎ 442-1999

Health Information (24 hr.) ☎ 434-2986

Housing Authority ☎ 306-3000

Immigration/Naturalization ☎ 800/375-5283

Legal Aid Society ☎ 577-3300

Mayor's Office ☎ 788-7585

Medicaid ☎ 718/291-1900

Medicare ☎ 800/638-6833

New York Post Office ☎ 967-8585

NY Public Library Information ☎ 340-0849

Passport Information ☎ 399-5290

Planned Parenthood ☎ 541-7800

Potholes ☎ 768-4653

Salvation Army ☎ 337-7200

Sidewalks ☎ 442-7942

Social Security ☎ 800/772-1213

Supreme Court ☎ 374-4585

Taxi Complaints ☎ 302-8294

Telegrams ☎ 800/325-6000

Time ☎ 976-2928

Towaways ☎ 869-2929

Traffic Information ☎ 787-3387

Traveler's Aid ☎ 944-0013

UN Information ☎ 963-1234

US Customs (24 hr.) ☎ 800/697-3662

Weather ☎ 970-1212

24-Hour Locksmith ☎ 247-6747

TOURS

Adventure on a Shoestring ☎ 265-2663

Art Tours ☎ 239-4160

Circle Line ☎ 563-3200

Doorways to Design ☎ 718/339-1542

Ellis Island Ferry ☎ 269-5755

Express Navigation ☎ 800/262-8743

Gray Line ☎ 397-2600

Harlem Renaissance ☎ 862-7200

Island Helicopter ☎ 564-9290

New York City Walking Tours ☎ 979-2388

The Petrel (1938) ☎ 825-1976

Seaport Line ☎ 608-9840

Short Line ☎ 736-4700

Spirit Cruises of NY ☎ 727-2789
Statue of Liberty Ferry ☎ 269-5755
World Yacht Cruises ☎ 630-8100

PARKS AND RECREATION

Acqueduct Race Track ☎ 718/641-4700
Belmont Raceway ☎ 718/641-4700
Brendan Byrne Arena ☎ 201/935-3900
Bryant Park ☎ 983-4142
Giants Stadium ☎ 201/935-8222
Jets Information ☎ 516/560-8200
Madison Square Garden ☎ 465-6000
Meadowlands Arena ☎ 201/935-3900
Meadowlands Race Track ☎ 201/935-8500
Nassau Coliseum ☎ 516/794-9300
NY Knicks Hot Line ☎ 465-5867
NY Islanders ☎ 516/784-4100
NY Liberty ☎ 465-6216
NY Mets ☎ 718/507-8499
NYC Marathon ☎ 860-2280
Parks Events ☎ 360-3456
Parks & Recreation ☎ 408-0100
Shea Stadium ☎ 718/507-8499
Sports Phone ☎ 976-1313
US Open Tennis ☎ 516/354-2590
Yankee Stadium ☎ 718/293-6000
Yonkers Raceway ☎ 914/968-4200
Zoo/Central Park ☎ 861-6030
Zoo/Bronx ☎ 718/367-1010

TRANSPORTATION

Adirondack Pine Hill Trailways ☎ 800/225-6815
Airport Bus Transportation ☎ 718/632-0500; 964-6233
Amtrak ☎ 800/872-7245; 800/523-8720
Bonanza Bus Lines ☎ 800/556-3815
Bus & Subway ☎ 718/330-1234
Bus & Subway Access ☎ 718/596-8585
George Washington Bridge Bus Station ☎ 564-1114
Greyhound Bus Lines ☎ 800/231-2222; 971-6300
Hoboken Ferry (NJ) ☎ 201/420-4422
JFK Airport ☎ 718/244-4444
JFK Bus Transportation ☎ 718/632-0506
JFK Express (train to plane) ☎ 718/858-7272
JFK Parking ☎ 718/656-5699
LaGuardia Airport ☎ 718/533-3850
LaGuardia Bus Transportation ☎ 718/476-5353
LaGuardia Ferry ☎ 800/54-FERRY
LaGuardia Parking ☎ 718/533-3850
Long Island Railroad (LIRR) ☎ 718/217-5477
Manhattan Helicopter ☎ 967-6464
Martz Trailways ☎ 800/233-8604
Metro North ☎ 532-4900
Newark Airport ☎ 201/961-6000
Newark Bus Transportation ☎ 201/762-5100
Newark Parking ☎ 201/761-4750
NJ Transit ☎ 800/626-7433; 201/762-5100
New York Helicopter ☎ 800/645-3494
PATH ☎ 800/234-7284
Passenger Ship Terminal ☎ 246-5451
Peter Pan Bus Lines ☎ 413/781-2900
Port Authority Bridges and Tunnels ☎ 360-3000
Port Authority Bus Information ☎ 564-8484
Port Authority Heliport ☎ 248-7240
Roosevelt Island Tram ☎ 832-4543
Staten Island Ferry ☎ 718/390-5253
Vermont Transit ☎ 802/862-9671

ENTERTAINMENT

Alliance of Resident Theatres ☎ 989-5257
The Big Apple Circus ☎ 268-2500
Carnegie Hall ☎ 247-7800
City Center ☎ 581-7907
Jazz Line ☎ 479-7888
League of American Theatres ☎ 764-1122
Lincoln Center ☎ 875-5000
Movie Phone ☎ 777-FILM
NYC On Stage ☎ 725-1174
Parents League of NY ☎ 737-7385
Radio City Music Hall ☎ 247-4777
Reduced Price Theatre Tickets (TKTS) ☎ 768-1818
Telecharge ☎ 239-6200
Ticket Central ☎ 279-4200
Ticketmaster ☎ 307-7171

Metropolitan Area

Monksville Reservoir
511
Suffern
59
Westbrook Rd.
Mahwah
PASSAIC
287
Ramsey
Upper Saddle River
Montvale
513
Macopin Rd.
Wanaque Reservoir
202
Allendale
17
Woodcliff Lake
Park Ridge
Wanaque
Oakland
Franklin Lakes
23
511
Wyckoff
Ho-Ho-Kus
Garden State Pkwy
Hillsdale
513
503
Bloomingdale
208
Waldwick
Butler
Pompton Lakes
Ridgewood
Emerson
Kinnelon
23
BERGEN
Riverdale
Glen Rock
North Haledon
Oradell
Kinnelon Rd.
Hamburg Tnpk.
511
287
Hawthorne
208
Paramus
Meriden Rd.
Boonton Twp.
Fairlawn
Lincoln Park
Wayne
Rochelle Park
4
202
4
Boulevard
Paterson
Towaco
Totowa
20
23
Hackensack
80
Mountain Lakes
Boonton
80
Little Falls
46
Lodi
46
46
Garden State Pkwy.
Fairfield
527
Clifton
80
Teterboro
80
23
17
Passaic Ave.
Cedar Grove
Passaic
Woodridge
53
202
Parsippany
3
Valley Rd.
21
Caldwell
506
Moonachie
NEW JERSEY
287
280
577
527
Rutherford
Hanover
Montclair
Eagle Rock Rd.
Bloomfield
NJ Tnpk. (Western Spur)
3
Eisenhower Pkwy.
Bloomfield Ave.
21
Lyndhurst
24
10
Livingston
Glen Ridge
MORRIS
ESSEX
280
West Orange
510
527
Kearny
124
Florham Park
Orange
New Jersey Tnpk.
Union City
508
Madison
East Orange
HUDSON
South Orange
510
24
Newark
Chatham
527
Maplewood
1/9
Short Hills
577
Springfield Ave.
Millburn
124
24
Jersey City
New Providence
78
440
78
Summit
Union
Bay
501
New Jersey Tnpk.
Murray Hill
Springfield
27
Newark
95
Elizabeth
512
Berkeley Heights
Scotch Plains
22
UNION
Roselle Park
1/9
Bayonne
28
Cranford
Bayonne Bridge
Westfield
Roselle
Richmond Tr.
Goethals Bridge
Garwood
78
527
Clifton
Fanwood
Winfield
278
North Plainfield
Clark
Garden State Pkwy.
27
514
Linden
Staten Island Expwy.
509
Verrazano-Narrows Bridge
22
28
Plainfield
Rahway
Richmond Ave.
STATEN ISLAND (RICHMOND CO.)
1/9
Carteret
Dunellen
27
Avenel
440
New Dorp
South Plainfield
581
Menlo Park
Iselin
95
Amboy Rd.
Metuchen
Woodbridge
Eltingville
287
95
535
Outerbridge Crossing
Hylan Blvd.
Piscataway
Fords
95
440
Richmond Valley
Edison
529
27
514
Tottenville
Highland Park
Perth Amboy
New Brunswick
South Amboy
Raritan Bay

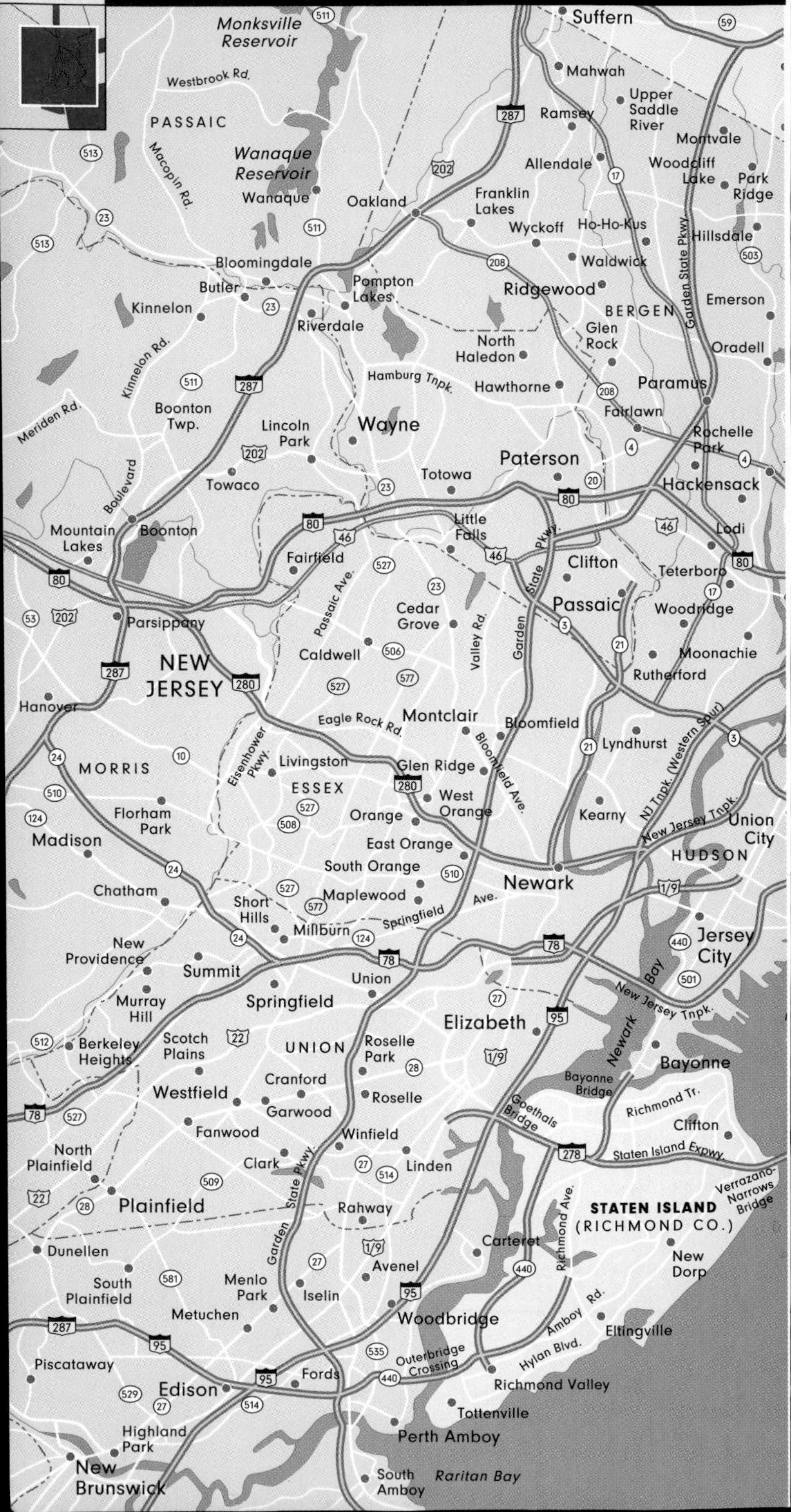

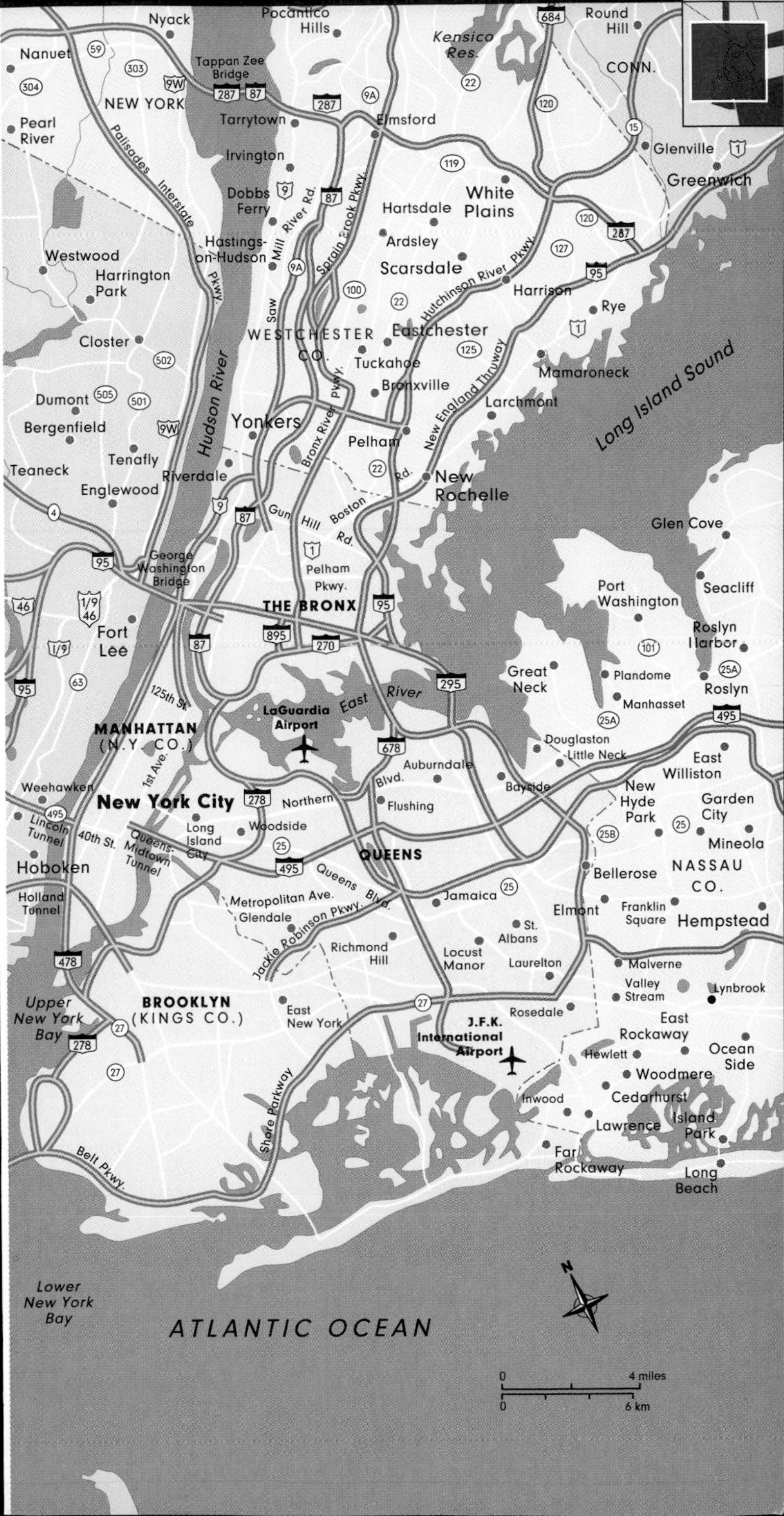

Nyack
Pocantico Hills
Kensico Res.
Round Hill
Nanuet
Tappan Zee Bridge
CONN.
NEW YORK
Pearl River
Tarrytown
Elmsford
Glenville
Palisades Interstate Pkwy.
Irvington
Greenwich
Dobbs Ferry
White Plains
Mill River Rd.
Sprain Brook Pkwy.
Hartsdale
Ardsley
Hastings-on-Hudson
Westwood
Scarsdale
Harrington Park
Hutchinson River Pkwy.
Harrison
Saw
Rye
WESTCHESTER CO.
Eastchester
Closter
Tuckahoe
Mamaroneck
Bronxville
New England Thruway
Long Island Sound
Dumont
Hudson River
Larchmont
Bergenfield
Yonkers
Bronx River Pkwy.
Pelham
Tenafly
Teaneck
Riverdale
Rd.
New Rochelle
Englewood
Gun Hill Rd.
Boston
Glen Cove
George Washington Bridge
Pelham Pkwy.
Port Washington
Seacliff
THE BRONX
Fort Lee
Roslyn Harbor
125th St.
Great Neck
Plandome
East River
Roslyn
LaGuardia Airport
Manhasset
MANHATTAN (N.Y. CO.)
Douglaston
Little Neck
1st Ave.
Auburndale
East Williston
Weehawken
Bayside
Blvd.
New Hyde Park
New York City
Northern
Flushing
Garden City
Lincoln Tunnel
Long Island City
Woodside
40th St.
Queens-Midtown Tunnel
Mineola
QUEENS
NASSAU CO.
Hoboken
Queens Blvd.
Bellerose
Holland Tunnel
Metropolitan Ave.
Jamaica
Franklin Square
Elmont
Glendale
Jackie Robinson Pkwy.
Hempstead
St. Albans
Richmond Hill
Locust Manor
Laurelton
Malverne
Valley Stream
Lynbrook
Upper New York Bay
BROOKLYN (KINGS CO.)
East New York
Rosedale
East Rockaway
J.F.K. International Airport
Hewlett
Ocean Side
Woodmere
Shore Parkway
Inwood
Cedarhurst
Lawrence
Island Park
Belt Pkwy.
Far Rockaway
Long Beach
Lower New York Bay
ATLANTIC OCEAN
N
0 4 miles
0 6 km

MAP 2

New York City

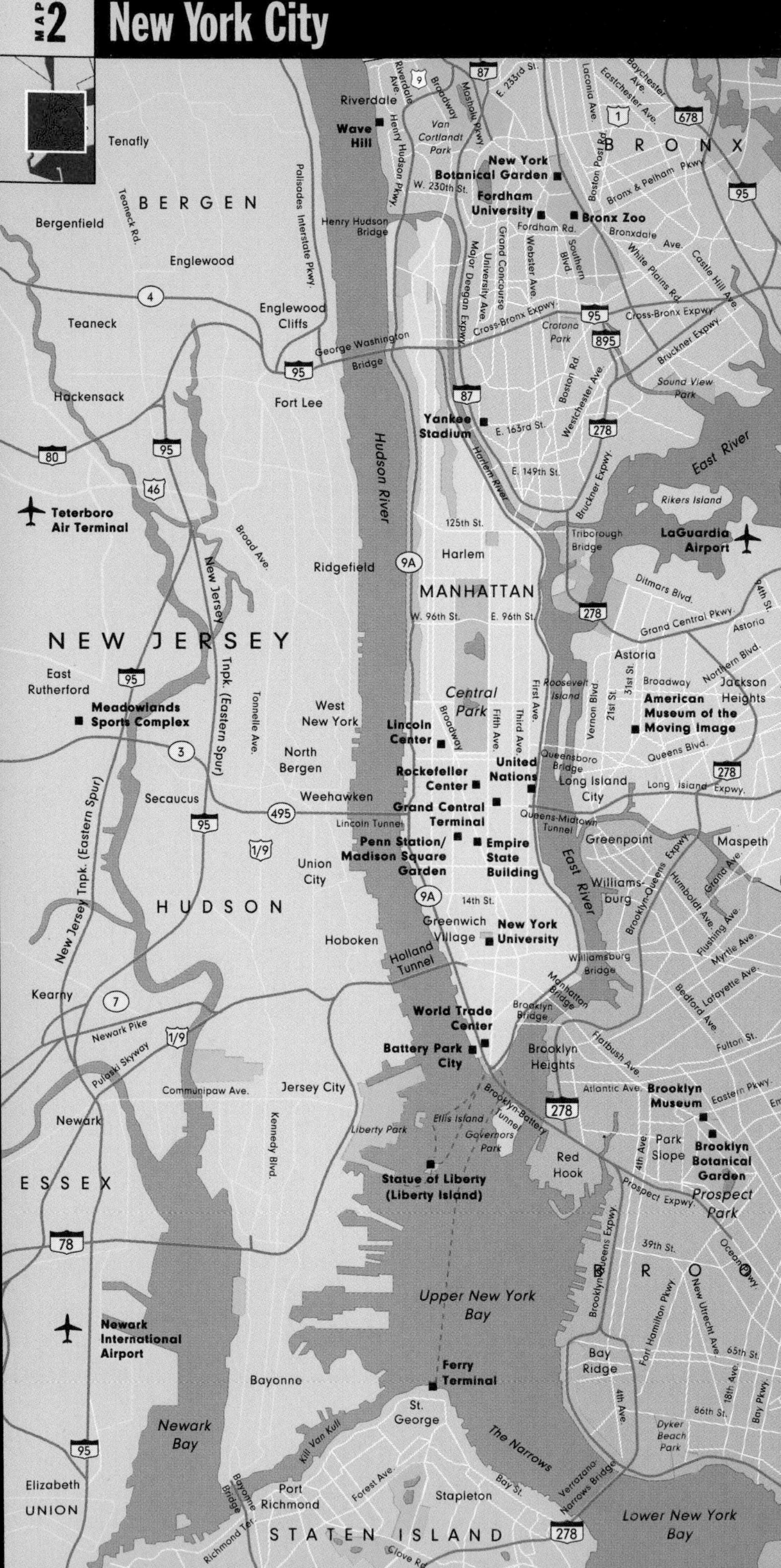

Long Island Sound
Port Washington
Manhasset Bay
Eastchester Bay
City Island
Kings Point
Great Neck
Great Neck Estates
NASSAU
Little Neck Bay
North New Hyde Park
Little Neck
Bayside
College Point
Flushing Bay
Throgs Neck
Floral Park
Belmont Park
Queens Village
Shea Stadium
USTA National Tennis Center
Queens College
St. John's University
Flushing Meadows-Corona Park
St. Albans
QUEENS
Forest Hills
Jamaica
Springfield Gardens
Valley Stream
Forest Park
Brookville Park
Ridgewood
Woodhaven
Ozone Park
South Ozone Park
Aqueduct Race Track
John F. Kennedy International Airport
Bushwick
East New York
Wildlife Refuge (Gateway National Recreation Area)
Canarsie
Jamaica Bay
Flatbush
Brooklyn College
Flatlands
Floyd Bennett Field (Gateway Natl. Rec. Area)
Marine Park
Bensonhurst
Manhattan Beach
Rockaway Inlet
Jacob Riis Park (Gateway National Recreation Area)
Brighton Beach
Coney Island
New York Aquarium
ATLANTIC OCEAN
0 2 miles
0 3 km
N

MAP 3 Manhattan/Uptown

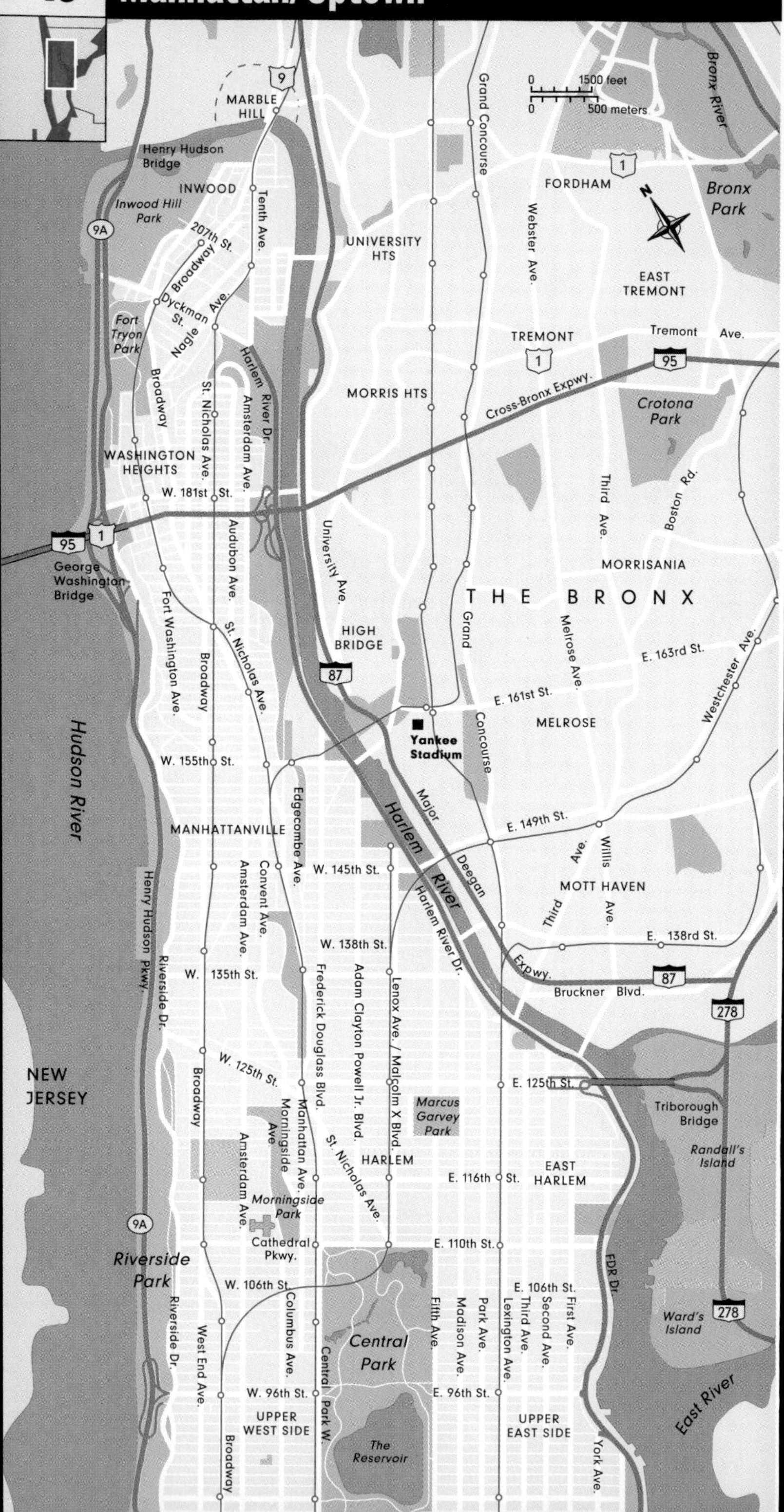

MARBLE HILL
Henry Hudson Bridge
INWOOD
Inwood Hill Park
207th St.
Broadway
Tenth Ave.
Dyckman St.
Nagle Ave.
Fort Tryon Park
Harlem River Dr.
St. Nicholas Ave.
Amsterdam Ave.
WASHINGTON HEIGHTS
W. 181st St.
George Washington Bridge
Audubon Ave.
Fort Washington Ave.
Hudson River
W. 155th St.
Edgecombe Ave.
MANHATTANVILLE
W. 145th St.
Convent Ave.
Henry Hudson Pkwy.
W. 138th St.
W. 135th St.
Riverside Dr.
Frederick Douglass Blvd.
Adam Clayton Powell Jr. Blvd.
Lenox Ave. / Malcolm X Blvd.
W. 125th St.
NEW JERSEY
Morningside Ave
Manhattan Ave.
St. Nicholas Ave.
Marcus Garvey Park
HARLEM
E. 116th St.
EAST HARLEM
Morningside Park
Cathedral Pkwy.
E. 110th St.
Riverside Park
W. 106th St.
E. 106th St.
Columbus Ave.
West End Ave.
Central Park W.
Central Park
Fifth Ave.
Madison Ave.
Park Ave.
Lexington Ave.
Third Ave.
Second Ave.
First Ave.
W. 96th St.
E. 96th St.
UPPER WEST SIDE
UPPER EAST SIDE
The Reservoir
York Ave.
FDR Dr.
East River
Ward's Island
Randall's Island
Triborough Bridge
E. 125th St.
Grand Concourse
1500 feet
500 meters
Bronx River
Bronx Park
FORDHAM
Webster Ave.
UNIVERSITY HTS
EAST TREMONT
TREMONT
Tremont Ave.
Cross-Bronx Expwy.
MORRIS HTS
Crotona Park
Third Ave.
Boston Rd.
University Ave.
MORRISANIA
THE BRONX
HIGH BRIDGE
Melrose Ave.
E. 163rd St.
Westchester Ave.
E. 161st St.
Yankee Stadium
MELROSE
Harlem River
Major Deegan Expwy.
E. 149th St.
Willis Ave.
MOTT HAVEN
E. 138rd St.
Bruckner Blvd.
Harlem River Dr.

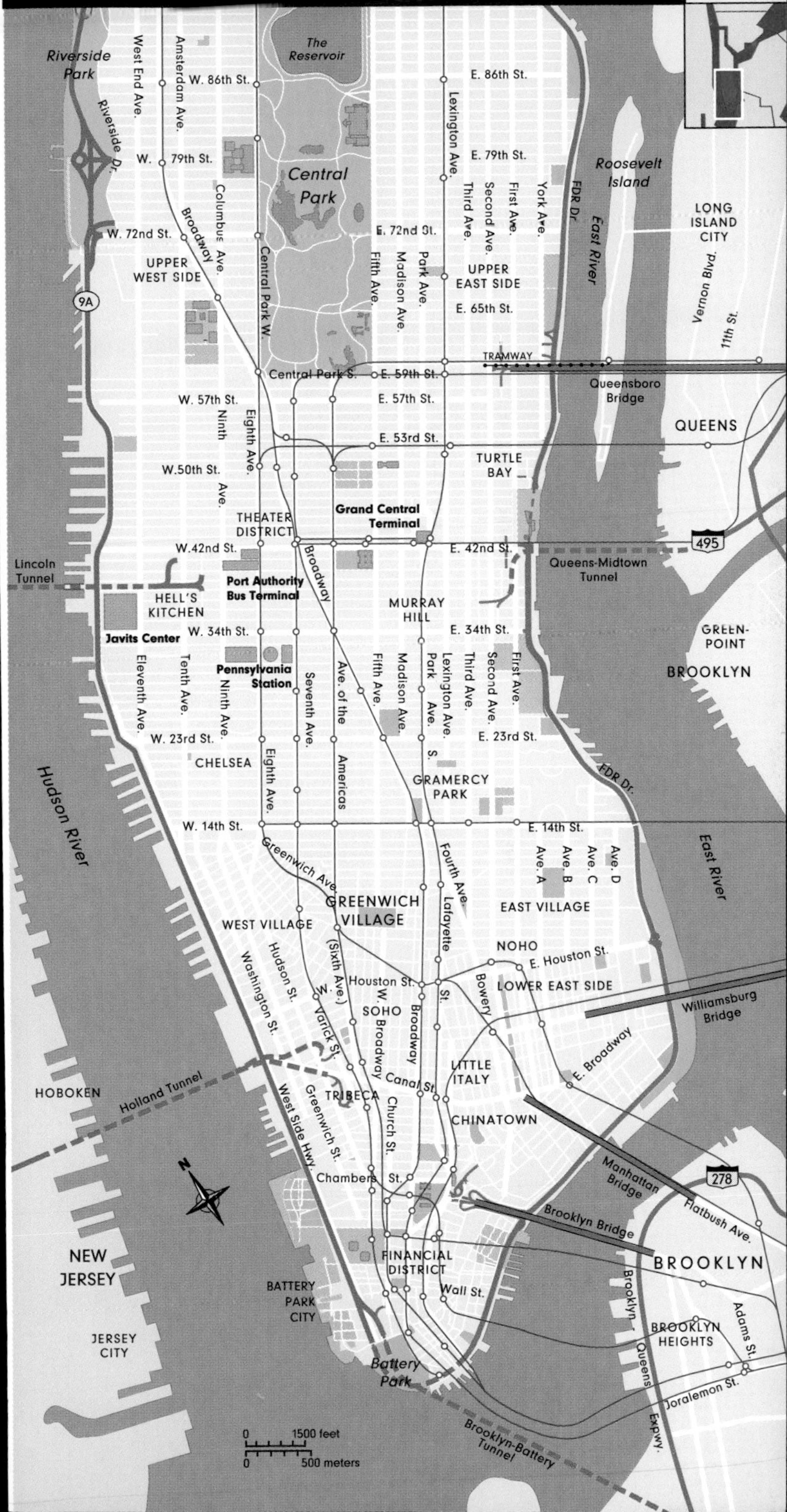

Manhattan/Downtown

The Reservoir
Riverside Park
Riverside Dr.
West End Ave.
Amsterdam Ave.
W. 86th St.
E. 86th St.
Lexington Ave.
W. 79th St.
E. 79th St.
Central Park
Roosevelt Island
Columbus Ave.
Broadway
Third Ave.
Second Ave.
First Ave.
York Ave.
FDR Dr.
East River
LONG ISLAND CITY
W. 72nd St.
E. 72nd St.
UPPER WEST SIDE
Central Park W.
Fifth Ave.
Madison Ave.
Park Ave.
UPPER EAST SIDE
E. 65th St.
9A
Vernon Blvd.
11th St.
TRAMWAY
Central Park S.
E. 59th St.
Queensboro Bridge
W. 57th St.
E. 57th St.
Ninth Ave.
Eighth Ave.
E. 53rd St.
QUEENS
W.50th St.
TURTLE BAY
THEATER DISTRICT
Grand Central Terminal
W.42nd St.
E. 42nd St.
495
Lincoln Tunnel
Queens-Midtown Tunnel
Port Authority Bus Terminal
HELL'S KITCHEN
MURRAY HILL
Javits Center
W. 34th St.
E. 34th St.
GREEN-POINT
Pennsylvania Station
BROOKLYN
Eleventh Ave.
Tenth Ave.
Seventh Ave.
Ave. of the Americas
Park Ave. S.
W. 23rd St.
E. 23rd St.
CHELSEA
Hudson River
GRAMERCY PARK
FDR Dr.
W. 14th St.
E. 14th St.
Ave. A
Ave. B
Ave. C
Ave. D
East River
Greenwich Ave.
Fourth Ave.
GREENWICH VILLAGE
EAST VILLAGE
WEST VILLAGE
Lafayette St.
NOHO
E. Houston St.
Hudson St.
(Sixth Ave.)
Washington St.
Houston St.
W. Houston St.
Bowery
LOWER EAST SIDE
Williamsburg Bridge
Varick St.
SOHO
W. Broadway
LITTLE ITALY
E. Broadway
Canal St.
HOBOKEN
Holland Tunnel
West Side Hwy.
Greenwich St.
TRIBECA
Church St.
CHINATOWN
Manhattan Bridge
N
Chambers St.
278
Flatbush Ave.
Brooklyn Bridge
NEW JERSEY
FINANCIAL DISTRICT
BROOKLYN
BATTERY PARK CITY
Wall St.
Brooklyn-Queens Expwy.
BROOKLYN HEIGHTS
Adams St.
JERSEY CITY
Battery Park
Joralemon St.
0 1500 feet
0 500 meters
Brooklyn-Battery Tunnel

MAP 5

Manhattan Neighborhoods

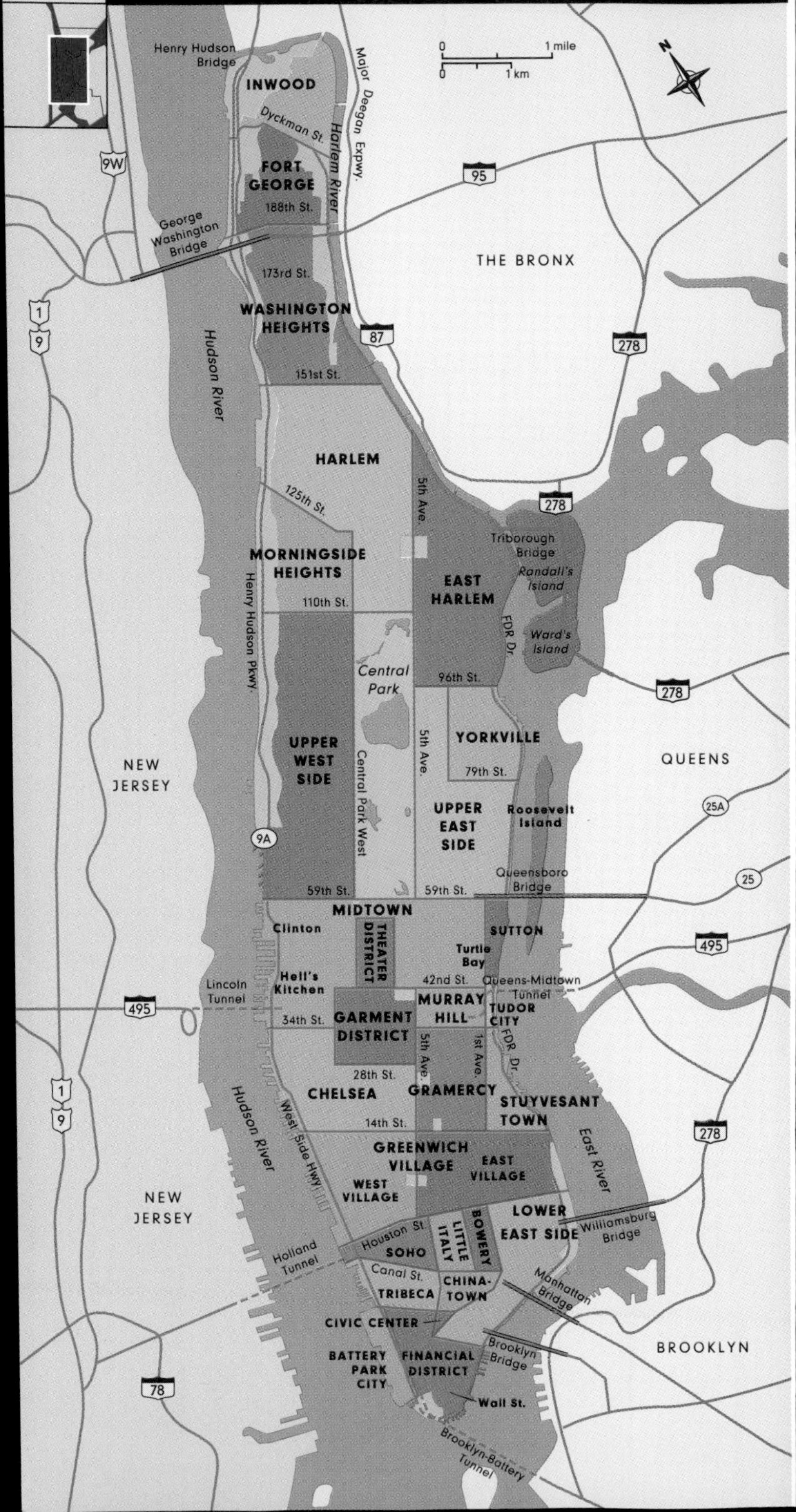

0 1 mile
0 1 km
N

Henry Hudson Bridge
INWOOD
Dyckman St.
Harlem River
Major Deegan Expwy.
9W
95
FORT GEORGE
188th St.
George Washington Bridge
THE BRONX
173rd St.
1
9
WASHINGTON HEIGHTS
87
278
Hudson River
151st St.
HARLEM
125th St.
5th Ave.
278
Triborough Bridge
Randall's Island
MORNINGSIDE HEIGHTS
EAST HARLEM
Henry Hudson Pkwy.
110th St.
FDR Dr.
Ward's Island
Central Park
96th St.
278
UPPER WEST SIDE
Central Park West
5th Ave.
YORKVILLE
QUEENS
NEW JERSEY
79th St.
UPPER EAST SIDE
Roosevelt Island
25A
9A
59th St.
59th St.
Queensboro Bridge
25
MIDTOWN
Clinton
THEATER DISTRICT
SUTTON
Turtle Bay
495
Hell's Kitchen
Lincoln Tunnel
42nd St.
Queens-Midtown Tunnel
495
34th St.
GARMENT DISTRICT
MURRAY HILL
TUDOR CITY
5th Ave.
1st Ave.
FDR Dr.
1
9
Hudson River
28th St.
CHELSEA
GRAMERCY
West Side Hwy.
STUYVESANT TOWN
14th St.
East River
278
GREENWICH VILLAGE
EAST VILLAGE
NEW JERSEY
WEST VILLAGE
LOWER EAST SIDE
Williamsburg Bridge
Houston St.
SOHO
LITTLE ITALY
BOWERY
Holland Tunnel
Canal St.
CHINA-TOWN
Manhattan Bridge
TRIBECA
CIVIC CENTER
BROOKLYN
BATTERY PARK CITY
FINANCIAL DISTRICT
Brooklyn Bridge
78
Wall St.
Brooklyn-Battery Tunnel

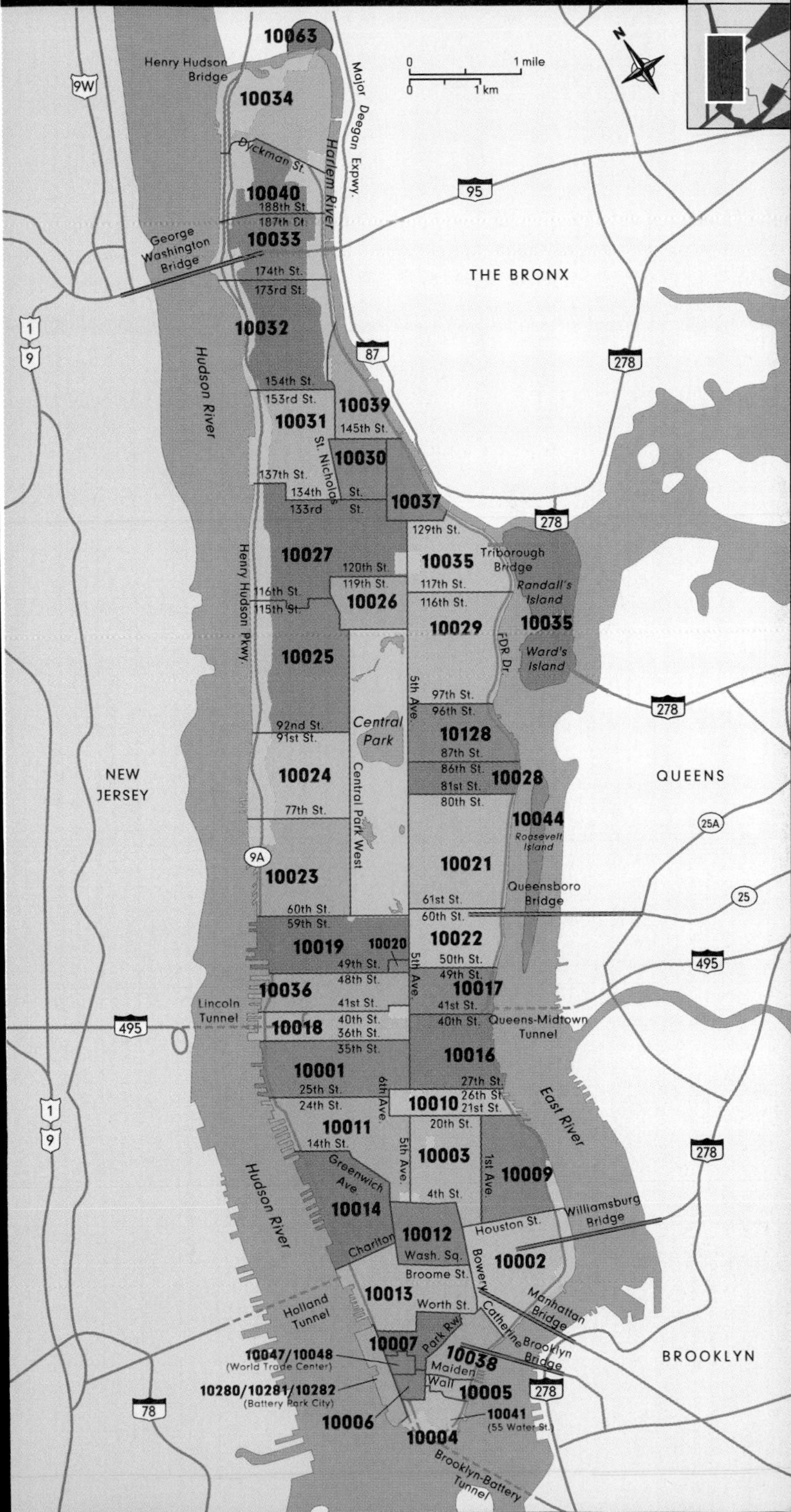

10063
Henry Hudson Bridge
9W
10034
Major Deegan Expwy.
0 1 mile
0 1 km
N
Dyckman St.
Harlem River
95
10040
188th St.
187th St.
George Washington Bridge
10033
174th St.
173rd St.
THE BRONX
1
9
10032
87
278
Hudson River
154th St.
153rd St.
10039
10031
145th St.
St. Nicholas
10030
137th St.
134th St.
133rd St.
10037
278
129th St.
Henry Hudson Pkwy.
10027
10035
Triborough Bridge
120th St.
119th St.
117th St.
Randall's Island
116th St.
115th St.
10026
116th St.
10035
10029
FDR Dr.
10025
Ward's Island
5th Ave.
97th St.
96th St.
278
92nd St.
91st St.
Central Park
10128
87th St.
86th St.
10028
81st St.
NEW JERSEY
10024
QUEENS
80th St.
77th St.
10044
Roosevelt Island
25A
Central Park West
9A
10021
10023
Queensboro Bridge
25
60th St.
61st St.
59th St.
60th St.
10022
10019
10020
495
50th St.
49th St.
49th St.
48th St.
10036
10017
5th Ave.
41st St.
41st St.
Lincoln Tunnel
40th St.
Queens-Midtown Tunnel
495
10018
40th St.
36th St.
35th St.
10016
10001
27th St.
26th St.
25th St.
6th Ave.
10010
21st St.
East River
24th St.
20th St.
1
9
10011
14th St.
10003
278
Greenwich Ave.
5th Ave.
1st Ave.
10009
Hudson River
4th St.
10014
Williamsburg Bridge
Houston St.
10012
Charlton
Wash. Sq.
Bowery
10002
Broome St.
10013
Manhattan Bridge
Holland Tunnel
Worth St.
Catherine
10007
Park Rw.
Brooklyn Bridge
BROOKLYN
10047/10048
(World Trade Center)
10038
Maiden
Wall
10280/10281/10282
(Battery Park City)
10005
278
78
10041
(55 Water St.)
10006
10004
Brooklyn-Battery Tunnel

MAP 7 Avenue Address Finder

Streets	West End Ave.	Broadway	Amsterdam Ave.	Columbus Ave.	Central Park West
94–96	700-737	2520–2554	702–733	701–740	350–360
92–94	660–699	2476–2519	656–701	661–700	322–336
90–92	620–659	2440–2475	620–655	621–660	300–320
88–90	578–619	2401–2439	580–619	581–620	279–295
86–88	540–577	2361–2400	540–579	541–580	262–275
84–86	500–539	2321–2360	500–539	501–540	241–257
82–84	460–499	2281–2320	460–499	461–500	212–239
80–82	420–459	2241–2280	420–459	421–460	211
78–80	380–419	2201–2240	380–419	381–420	American Museum of Natural History
76–78	340–379	2161–2200	340–379	341–380	
74–76	300–339	2121–2160	300–339	301–340	145–160
72–74	262–299	2081–2114	261–299	261–300	121–135
70–72	221–261	2040–2079	221–260	221–260	101–115
68–70	176–220	1999–2030	181–220	181–220	80–99
66–68	122–175	1961–1998	140–180	141–180	65–79
64–66	74–121	1920–1960	100–139	101–140	50–55
62–64	44–73	Lincoln Center	60–99	61–100	25–33
60–62	20–43	1841–1880	20–59	21–60	15
58–60	2–19	Columbus Circle	1–19	2–20	Columbus Circle

Central Park

Streets	11th Ave.	Broadway	10th Ave.	9th Ave.	8th Ave.	7th Ave.	6th Ave.
56–58	823–854	1752–1791	852–889	864–907	946–992	888–921	1381–1419
54–56	775–822	1710–1751	812–851	824–863	908–945	842–887	1341–1377
52–54	741–774	1674–1709	772–811	782–823	870–907	798–841	1301–1330
50–52	701–740	1634–1673	737–770	742–781	830–869	761–797	1261–1297
48–50	665–700	1596–1633	686–735	702–741	791–829	720–760	1221–1260
46–48	625–664	1551–1595	654–685	662–701	735–790	701–719	1180–1217
44–46	589–624	1514–1550	614–653	622–661	701–734	Times Square	1141–1178
42–44	553–588	1472–1513	576–613	582–621	661–700		1100–1140
40–42	503–552	1440–1471	538–575	Port Authority	620–660	560–598	1061–1097
38–40	480–502	1400–1439	502–537		570–619	522–559	1020–1060
36–38	431–471	1352–1399	466–501	468–501	520–569	482–521	981–1019
34–36	405–430	Macy's	430–465	432–467	480–519	442–481	Herald Square
32–34	360–404	1260–1282	380–429	412–431	442–479	Penn Station	
30–32	319–359	1220–1279	341–379	Post Office	403–441	362–399	855–892
28–30	282–318	1178–1219	314–340	314–351	362–402	322–361	815–844
26–28	242–281	1135–1177	288–313	262–313	321–361	282–321	775–814
24–26	202–241	1100–1134	239–287	230–261	281–320	244–281	733–774
22–24	162–201	940–1099	210–238	198–229	236–280	210–243	696–732
20–22	120–161	902–939	162–209	167–197	198–235	170–209	656–695
18–20	82–119	873–901	130–161	128–166	162–197	134–169	613–655
16–18	54–81	860–872	92–129	92–127	126–161	100–133	574–612
14–16	26–53	Union Square	58–91	91–44	80–125	64–99	573–530

Crosstown Street Address Finder

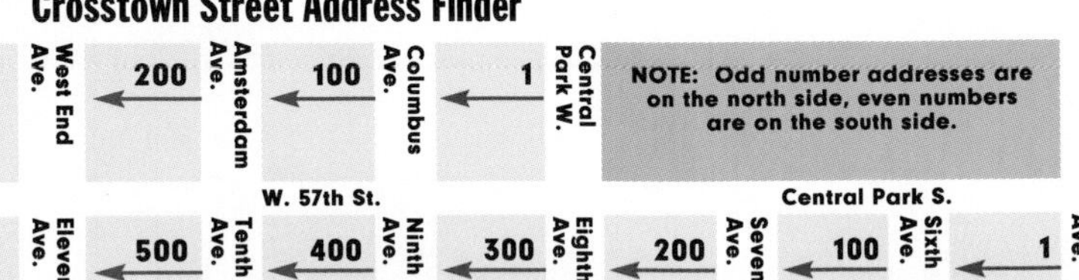

5th Ave.	Madison Ave.	Park Ave.	Lexington Ave.	3rd Ave.	2nd Ave.	1st Ave.	Streets
1130–1148	1340–1379	1199–1236	1449–1486	1678–1709	1817–1868	1817–1855	**94–96**
1109–1125	1295–1335	1160–1192	1400–1444	1644–1677	1766–1808	1780–1811	**92–94**
1090–1107	1254–1294	1120–1155	1361–1396	1601–1643	1736–1763	1740–1779	**90–92**
1070–1089	1220–1250	1080–1114	1311–1355	1568–1602	1700–1739	1701–1735	**88–90**
1050–1069	1178–1221	1044–1076	1280–1301	1530–1566	1660–1698	1652–1689	**86–88**
1030–1048	1130–1171	1000–1035	1248–1278	1490–1529	1624–1659	1618–1651	**84–86**
1010–1028	1090–1128	960–993	1210–1248	1450–1489	1584–1623	1578–1617	**82–84**
990–1009	1058–1088	916–959	1164–1209	1410–1449	1538–1583	1540–1577	**80–82**
970–989	1012–1046	878–911	1120–1161	1374–1409	1498–1537	1495–1539	**78–80**
950–969	974–1006	840–877	1080–1116	1330–1373	1456–1497	1462–1494	**76–78**
930–947	940–970	799–830	1036–1071	1290–1329	1420–1454	1429–1460	**74–76**
910–929	896–939	760–791	1004–1032	1250–1289	1389–1417	1344–1384	**72–74**
895–907	856–872	720–755	962–993	1210–1249	1328–1363	1306–1343	**70–72**
870–885	813–850	680–715	926–961	1166–1208	1296–1327	1266–1300	**68–70**
850–860	772–811	640–679	900–922	1130–1165	1260–1295	1222–1260	**66–68**
830–849	733–771	600–639	841–886	1084–1129	1222–1259	1168–1221	**64–66**
810–828	690–727	560–599	803–842	1050–1083	1180–1221	1130–1167	**62–64**
790–807	654–680	520–559	770–802	1010–1049	1140–1197	1102–1129	**60–62**
755–789	621–649	476–519	722–759	972–1009	**Queensborough Bridge**		**58–60**
720–754	572–611	434–475	677–721	942–968	1066–1101	1026–1063	**56–58**
680–719	532–568	408–430	636–665	894–933	1028–1062	985–1021	**54–56**
656–679	500–531	360–399	596–629	856–893	984–1027	945–984	**52–54**
626–655	452–488	320–350	556–593	818–855	944–983	889–944	**50–52**
600–625	412–444	280–300	518–555	776–817	902–943	860–888	**48–50**
562–599	377–400	240–277	476–515	741–775	862–891	827	**46–48**
530–561	346–375	**Met Life** (200)	441–475	702–735	824–860	785 **United Nations**	**44–46**
500–529	316–345	**Grand Central**	395–435	660–701	793–823		**42–44**
460–499	284–315		354–394	622–659	746–773	**Tudor City**	**40–42**
424–459	250–283	68–99	314–353	578–621	707–747	666–701	**38–40**
392–423	218–249	40–67 **Park Ave.**	284–311	542–577	666–700	**Midtown Tunnel**	**36–38**
352–391	188–217	5–35	240–283	508–541	622–659	599–626	**34–36**
320–351	152–184	1–4	196–239	470–507	585–621	556–598	**32–34**
284–319	118–150	444–470 **Park Ave. S.**	160–195	432–469	543–581	**Kips Bay**	**30–32**
250–283	79–117	404–431	120–159 **Lexington Ave.**	394–431	500–541	**NYU Hosp.**	**28–30**
213–249	50–78	364–403	81–119	358–393	462–499	446–478	**26–28**
201–212	11–37	323–361	40–77	321–355	422–461	411–445	**24–26**
172–200	1–7	286–322	9–39	282–318	382–421	390–410	**22–24**
154–170		251–285	1–8	244–281	344–381	315–389	**20–22**
109–153		221–250	70–78 **Irving Pl.**	206–243	310–343	310–314	**18–20**
85–127		184–220	40–69	166–205	301–309	280–309	**16–18**
69–108		Union Square	2–30	126–165	230–240	240–279	**14–16**

Fifth Ave.	**Madison Ave.**	**Park Ave.**	**Lexington Ave.**	**Third Ave.**	**Second Ave.**	**First Ave.**
1 →	→	**100** →	**140** →	**200** →	**300** →	**400** →

MAP 8 Streetfinder/The Village & Downtown

Union Sq. Park
W. 15th St.
A,C,E,L
1,2,3,9
F,L,Q
L,N,R, 4,5,6
W. 14th St.
W. 13th St.
W. 12th St.
W. 11th St.
W. 10th St.
W. 9th St.
W. 8th St.
Seventh Ave. S.
Avenue of the Americas
Fifth Ave.
University Pl.
Broadway
Little W. 12th St.
Gansevoort St.
Horatio St.
Jane St.
W. 12th St.
Bethune St.
Bank St.
W. 11th St.
Abingdon Square
Eighth Ave.
Greenwich Ave.
W. 4th St.
Waverly Pl.
Milligan Pl.
Patchin Pl.
Perry St.
Charles St.
W. 10th St.
Christopher St.
Grove St.
Gay St.
MacDougal St.
MacDougal Alley
Washington Mews
Greene St.
N,R
Sheridan Square
1,9
Waverly Pl.
W. Washington Pl.
Washington Sq. N.
Washington Square Park
E. Washington Pl.
Washington Sq. S.
A,B,C,D, E,F,Q
New York University
W. 3rd St.
Jones St.
Cornelia St.
Bleecker St.
Commerce St.
Minetta La.
Father Demo Sq.
LaGuardia Pl.
Bleecker St.
Bedford St.
Carmine St.
Downing St.
Barrow St.
Morton St.
St. Luke's Pl.
Leroy St.
Clarkson St.
W. Houston St.
W. Houston St.
B,D,F,Q
Hudson St.
Washington St.
Greenwich St.
West St.
West Side Highway
Ave. of the Americas
MacDougal St.
Sullivan St.
N,R
King St.
Charlton St.
Vandam St.
Varick St.
Spring St.
Dominick St.
C,E
(Sixth Ave.)
Thompson St.
West Broadway
Wooster St.
Greene St.
Mercer St.
Broadway
Hudson River
Broome St.
Holland Tunnel Entrance
Grand St.
1,9
A,C,E
Canal St.
N,R
Watts St.
Holland Tunnel
Holland Tunnel Exit
Desbrosses St.
Vestry St.
Laight St.
Hubert St.
Beach St.
Ericsson Pl.
Church St.
Lispenard St.
Walker St.
White St.
Franklin St.
1,9
N. Moore St.
Franklin St.
Leonard St.
Catherine La.
Worth St.
Thomas St.
Federal Plaza
Manhattan Community College
Harrison St.
Jay St.
Staple St.
Duane St.
Reade St.
Independence Plaza
Chambers St.
Chambers St.
1,2,3,9
A,C
Warren St.
Warren St.
N,R
City Hall Park
Park Pl.
Murray St.
Murray St.
River Terrace
North End Ave.
Washington St.
Park Pl.
2,3
Barclay St.
N,R
Vesey St.
Vesey St.
C,E
Park Row
World Trade Center
Fulton St.
A,C
4,5
World Financial Center
Dey St.
1,9
N,R
Cortlandt St.
Liberty St.
Liberty St.
Cedar St.
Thames St.
Albany St.
Albany St.
South End Ave.
Carlisle St.
Rector St.
Pine St.
Wall St.
Exchange Pl.
Trinity Pl.
BATTERY PARK CITY
West Thames St.
Morris St.
New St.
Bowling Green
Whitehall St.
Beaver St.
3rd Pl.
2nd Pl.
1st Pl.
Battery Place
Battery Pl.
Bridge St.
State St.
Battery Park
0 1200 feet
0 400 meters
N
A B C
1 2 3 4 5 6

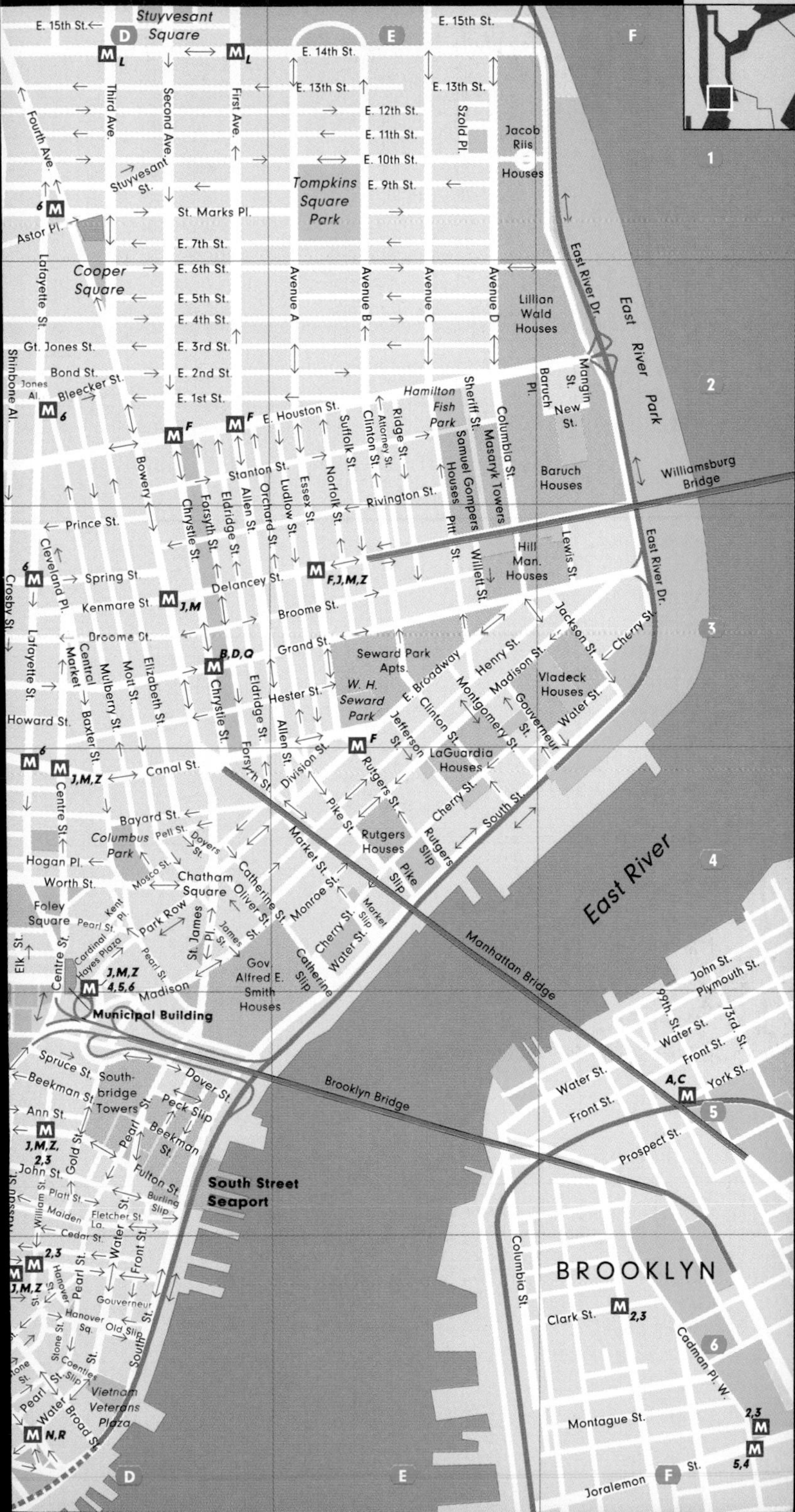

D E F

1 2 3 4 5 6

Stuyvesant Square
E. 15th St.
E. 14th St.
E. 13th St.
E. 12th St.
E. 11th St.
E. 10th St.
E. 9th St.
St. Marks Pl.
E. 7th St.
E. 6th St.
E. 5th St.
E. 4th St.
E. 3rd St.
E. 2nd St.
E. 1st St.
E. Houston St.
Third Ave.
Second Ave.
First Ave.
Fourth Ave.
Stuyvesant St.
Szold Pl.
Jacob Riis Houses
Tompkins Square Park
Astor Pl.
Cooper Square
Lafayette St.
Avenue A
Avenue B
Avenue C
Avenue D
Lillian Wald Houses
East River Dr.
East River Park
Gt. Jones St.
Bond St.
Jones Al.
Bleecker St.
Shinbone Al.
Hamilton Fish Park
Baruch Pl.
Mangin St.
New St.
Sheriff St.
Columbia St.
Samuel Gompers Houses
Masaryk Towers
Baruch Houses
Williamsburg Bridge
Attorney St.
Ridge St.
Clinton St.
Suffolk St.
Norfolk St.
Essex St.
Ludlow St.
Orchard St.
Allen St.
Eldridge St.
Forsyth St.
Chrystie St.
Bowery
Stanton St.
Rivington St.
Pitt St.
Willett St.
Hill Man. Houses
Lewis St.
Prince St.
Spring St.
Cleveland Pl.
Crosby St.
Kenmare St.
Delancey St.
Broome St.
Grand St.
Jackson St.
Cherry St.
Seward Park Apts.
W. H. Seward Park
E. Broadway
Henry St.
Madison St.
Montgomery St.
Gouverneur St.
Vladeck Houses
Water St.
Hester St.
Mott St.
Mulberry St.
Elizabeth St.
Central Market
Baxter St.
Howard St.
Centre St.
Canal St.
Division St.
Jefferson St.
LaGuardia Houses
Rutgers St.
Pike St.
Rutgers Houses
Rutgers Slip
Pike Slip
South St.
East River
Bayard St.
Pell St.
Doyers St.
Columbus Park
Hogan Pl.
Worth St.
Mosco St.
Chatham Square
Catherine St.
Oliver St.
Market St.
Monroe St.
Market Slip
Foley Square
Kent Pl.
Pearl St.
Park Row
St. James Pl.
James St.
Cherry St.
Water St.
Catherine Slip
Manhattan Bridge
Elk St.
Cardinal Hayes Plaza
Gov. Alfred E. Smith Houses
Madison
Municipal Building
Spruce St.
South-bridge Towers
Dover St.
Beekman St.
Peck Slip
Ann St.
Gold St.
Pearl St.
Beekman St.
Fulton St.
John St.
Platt St.
William St.
Maiden La.
Fletcher St.
Burling Slip
Cedar St.
South Street Seaport
Brooklyn Bridge
Water St.
Front St.
Hanover St.
Gouverneur La.
Hanover Sq.
Old Slip
South St.
Stone St.
Coenties Slip
Broad St.
Vietnam Veterans Plaza
N,R
John St.
Plymouth St.
99th St.
73rd St.
Water St.
Front St.
York St.
A,C
Prospect St.
Columbia St.
BROOKLYN
Clark St.
2,3
Cadman Pl. W.
Montague St.
Joralemon St.
5,4

Streetfinder/The Village & Downtown

Letter codes refer to grid sectors on preceding map

Abingdon Sq. B1
Albany St. B6, C5
Allen St. D2, D3
Ann St. C5, D5
Astor Pl. D1
Attorney St. E2
Ave. A E1, E2
Ave. B E1, E2
Ave. C E1, E2
Ave. D E1, E2
Ave. of the Americas (Sixth Ave.) C1, C4
Bank St. A2, B1
Barclay St. C5
Barrow St. B2
Baruch Pl. F2
Battery Pl. C6
Baxter St. D3, D4
Bayard St. D4
Beach St. B4
Beaver St. C6, D6
Bedford St. B2, C2
Beekman St. D5
Bethune St. A1, B1
Bleecker St. B1, D2
Bond St. D2
Bowery D2, D4
Bowling Green C6
Bridge St. C6, D6
Broadway C1, C6
Brooklyn Battery Tunnel C6, D6
Brooklyn Bridge D5, F5
Broome St. B3, E3
Burling Slip D5
Canal St. C3, E3
Cardinal Hayes Plaza D4
Carlisle St. C6
Carmine St. B2
Catherine La. C4
Catherine Slip E4
Catherine St. D4, E4
Cedar St. C5, D5
Central Market D3
Centre St. D3, D5
Chambers St. B4, D4
Charles St. B1, B2
Charlton St. B3, C3
Chatham Sq. D4
Cherry St. E4, F3
Christopher St. B2, C1
Chrystie St. D2, D3
Church St. C4, C5
Clarkson St. B2, B3
Cleveland Pl. D3
Clinton St. E2, E4
Coenties Slip D6
Columbia St. E2, E3
Commerce St. B2
Cooper Sq. D1, D2
Cornelia St. B2
Cortlandt St. C5
Crosby St. C2, C3
Delancey St. D3, E3
Depyster St. D6
Desbrosses St. B3
Dey St. C5
Division St. D4, E4
Dominick St. B3, C3
Dover St. D5
Downing St. B2, C2
Doyers St. D4
Duane St. C4, D4
East Broadway D4, E3
East Houston St. D2, F2
East River Drive F1, F3
East Washington Pl. C2
Eighth Ave. B1
Eldridge St. D2, D3
Elizabeth St. D2, D4
Elk St. D4
Ericsson Pl. C4
Essex St. E2, E3
Exchange Pl. C6, D6
FDR Dr. F1, F3
Father Demo Sq. C2
Federal Plaza C4, D4
Fifth Ave. C1
First Ave. D1, D2
Fletcher St. D5
Foley Sq. D4
Forsyth St. D4, E4
Fourth Ave. D1
Franklin St. C4
Front St. D6
Fulton St. C5, D5
Gansevoort St. A1, B1
Gay St. B1, C1
Gold St. D5
Gouverneur La. D6
Gouverneur St. E3
Grand St. C3, F3
Great Jones St. D2
Greene St. C1, C3
Greenwich Ave. B1, C1
Greenwich St. B1, C6
Grove St. B2
Hanover Sq. D6
Hanover St. D6
Harrison St. B4, C4
Henry St. D4, E3
Hester St. D3, E3
Hogan Pl. D4
Holland Tunnel A4, C3
Horatio St. A1, B1
Hubert St. B4
Hudson St. B1, C4
Independence Plaza B4, C4
Jackson St. F3
James St. D4
Jane St. A1, B1
Jay St. C4
Jefferson St. E3
John St. C5, D5
Jones Alley D2
Jones St. B2
Kenmare St. D3
Kent Pl. D4
King St. B3, C3
Lafayette St. D1, D4
LaGuardia Pl. C2
Laight St. B4
Leonard St. C4
Leroy St. B2
Lewis St. F3
Liberty St. C5
Lispenard St. C4
Little W. 12th St. A1
Ludlow St. E2, E3
MacDougal Alley C1
MacDougal St. C1, C3

Letter codes refer to grid sectors on preceding map

Madison St. D4, F3
Maiden La. D5
Mangin St. F2
Manhattan Bridge D4, F5
Market Slip E4
Market St. E4
Mercer St. C1, C3
Milligan Pl. B1, C1
Minetta La. C2
Monroe St. E4
Montgomery St. E3, E4
Morris St. C6
Morton St. B2
Mosco St. D4
Mott St. D2, D4
Mulberry St. D2, D4
Murray St. B5, D5
Nassau St. C6, D5
New St. F2
Ninth Ave. A1
Norfolk St. E2, E3
North End Ave. B5
N. Moore St. B4, C4
Old Slip D6
Oliver St. D4
Orchard St. D2, E3
Park Pl. B5, C5
Park Row C5, D4
Patchin Pl. B1
Pearl St. C6, D5
Peck Slip D5
Pell St. D4
Perry St. B1, B2
Pike Slip E4
Pike St. E4
Pine St. C6, D6
Pitt St. E2, E3
Platt St. D5
Prince St. C3, D3
Reade St. C4, D4
Rector St. C6
Ridge St. E2, E3
River Ter. B5
Rivington St. D3, E2
Rutgers Slip E4
Rutgers St. E4
St. James Pl. D4, D5
St. Luke's Pl. B2
St. Mark's Pl. D1
Second Ave. D1, D2
Seventh Ave. B1
Seventh Ave. S. B1, B2
Sixth Ave. (Ave. of the Americas) C1, C4
Sheridan Sq. B2
Sheriff St. E2
Shinbone Alley D2
South St. D6, F3
South End Ave. C6
South William St. D6`
Spring St. B3, D3
Spruce St. D5
Stanton St. D2, E2
Staple St. C4
State St. C6, D6
Stone St. D6
Stuyvesant St. D1
Suffolk St. E2, E3
Sullivan St. C2, C3
Szold Pl. E1
Tenth Ave. A1
Thames St. C5
Third Ave. D1, D2
Thomas St. C4
Thompson St. C2, C3
Trinity Pl. C5, C6
University Pl. C1
Vandam St. B3, C3
Varick St. B3, C4
Vesey St. B5, C5
Vestry St. B3, B4
Vietnam Veterans Plaza D6
Walker St. C4, D4
Wall St. C6, D6
Warren St. B5, C5
Washington Mews C1
Washington Sq. E. C2
Washington Sq. N. C1
Washington Sq. S. C2
Washington Sq. W. C2
Washington St. A1, C6
Water St. D6, F3
Watts St. B3, C3
Waverly Pl. B1, C1
West St. A1, C6
West Broadway C3, C5
West Houston St. B3, C2
West Side Hwy. A1, C6
West Thames St. C6
W. Washington Pl. B2, C2
White St. C4, D4
Whitehall St. C6, D6
Willet St. E3
William St. D5
Williamsburg Br. E3, F2
Wooster St. C2, C3
Worth St. C4

NUMBERED STREETS

1st Pl. C6
2nd Pl. C6
3rd Pl. C6
E. 1st St. D2, E2
E. 2nd St. D2, E2
E. 3rd St. D2, E2
E. 4th St. D2, E2
E. 5th St. D2, E2
E. 6th St. D2, E2
E. 7th St. D1, E1
E. 8th St. C1, E1
E. 9th St. C1, E1
E. 10th St. C1, E1
E. 11th St. C1, E1
E. 12th St. C1, E1
E. 13th St. C1, E1
E. 14th St. C1, E1
E. 15th St. C1, E1
W. 3rd St. C2
W. 4th St. B1, C2
W. 8th St. C1
W. 9th St. C1
W. 10th St. B2, C1
W. 11th St. A2, C1
W. 12th St. A1, C1
W. 13th St. A1, C1
W. 14th St. A1, C1
W. 15th St. C1, E1

Hospitals & Late-Night Pharmacies

Listed by Site Number

1 Columbia Presbyterian
2 NY Orthopedic
3 Babies Hospital
4 Sloane (Women)
5 Harkness Eye Institute
6 Harlem Center
7 Sydenham (NFCC)
8 St. Luke's
9 Cooke Health Care Center
10 Mount Sinai
11 Metropolitan
12 Irmat Pharmacy
13 Beth Israel North
14 Coler Memorial
15 Star Pharmacy
16 Lenox Hill
17 Nicolas Institute (Sports)
18 Payne Whitney (Psychiatric)
19 Strang Center
20 Gracie Square
21 Cornell Med Center
22 Special Surgery
23 Sloan-Kettering
24 Eye, Ear, & Throat
25 Medical Arts Center
26 Roosevelt
27 Pollack Bailey
28 St Clare's
29 Metropolis Drug Co
30 Kaufman Pharmacy
31 Goldwater Memorial
32 NYU Med Center
33 Bellevue Med Center
34 Veterans Admin
35 Joint Diseases
36 Beth Israel Med Center
37 Cabrini Med Center
38 CVS Pharmacy
39 St Vincent's
40 Bigelow Pharmacy
41 Village Apothecary
42 Chung Wah
43 Gouverneurs
44 Beekman Downtown

Listed Alphabetically

HOSPITALS

Babies Hospital, 3. 622 W 168th St ☎ 305-2500

Beekman Downtown, 44. 170 William St ☎ 312-5000

Bellevue Med Center, 33. 462 First Ave ☎ 562-4141

Beth Israel Med Center, 36. 281 First Ave ☎ 420-2000

Beth Israel North, 13. 170 East End Ave ☎ 870-9000

Cabrini Med Center, 37. 227 E 19th St ☎ 995-6000

Coler Memorial, 14. Roosevelt Island ☎ 848-6000

Columbia Presbyterian, 1. 622 W 168th St ☎ 305-2500

Cooke Health Care Center, 9. 1249 Fifth Ave ☎ 360-1000

Cornell Med Center, 21. 525 E 68th St ☎ 746-5454

Eye, Ear, & Throat, 24. 210 E 64th St ☎ 838-9200

Goldwater Memorial, 31. Roosevelt Island ☎ 318-8000

Gouverneurs, 43. 227 Madison St ☎ 238-7000

Gracie Square, 20. 421 E 75th St ☎ 988-4400

Harkness Eye Institute, 5. 630 W 165th St ☎ 305-2500

Harlem Hospital Center, 6. 506 Lenox Ave ☎ 939-1000

Joint Diseases, 35. 301 E 17th St ☎ 598-6000

Lenox Hill, 16. 100 E 77th St ☎ 434-2000

Medical Arts Center, 25. 57 W 57th St ☎ 755-0200

Metropolitan, 11. 1901 First Ave ☎ 423-6262

Mount Sinai, 10. 1 Gustav Levi Pl ☎ 241-6500

Nicolas Institute (Sports), 17. 130 E 77th St ☎ 434-2700

NY Orthopedic, 2. 622 W 168th St ☎ 305-5974

NYU Med Center, 32. 550 First Ave ☎ 263-7300

Payne Whitney (Psychiatric), 18. 420 E 76th St ☎ 746-3800

Roosevelt, 26. 428 W 59th St ☎ 523-4000

Sloane (Women), 4. 622 W 168th St ☎ 305-5222

Sloan-Kettering (Cancer), 23. 1275 York Ave ☎ 639-2000

Special Surgery, 22. 535 E 70th St ☎ 606-1000

St Clare's, 28. 415 W 51st St ☎ 586-1500

St Luke's, 8. 419 W 114th St ☎ 523-4000

St Vincent's, 39. 153 W 11th St ☎ 604-7000

Strang Cancer Prevention Center, 19. 428 E 72nd ☎ 794-4900

Sydenham (Neighborhood Family Care Center), 7. 215 W 125th St ☎ 932-6520

Veterans Admin, 34. 408 First Ave ☎ 686-7500

LATE-NIGHT PHARMACIES

Bigelow Pharmacy, 40. 414 Sixth Ave ☎ 533-2700

Chung Wah Pharmacy, 42. 65 Mott St ☎ 587-4160

CVS Pharmacy, 38. 272 Eighth Ave ☎ 255-2592

Irmat Pharmacy, 12. 531 Columbus Ave ☎ 362-2350

Kaufman Pharmacy, 30. 557 Lexington Ave ☎ 755-2266

Metropolis Drug Co, 29. 721 Ninth Ave ☎ 246-0168

Pollack-Bailey Pharmacy, 27. 405 E 57th St ☎ 355-6094

Star Pharmacy, 15. 1540 First Ave ☎ 737-4324

Village Apothecary, 41. 346 Bleecker St ☎ 807-7566

MAP 10 Universities, Colleges & Schools

Listed by Site Number

1 Yeshiva University
2 Columbia Physicians/Surgeons
3 City College of NY
4 Manhattan School of Music
5 Jewish Theological
6 Union Theological
7 Barnard College
8 Columbia University
9 Teachers College
10 Columbia School of Social Work
11 Bank St College
12 Mt Sinai Sch of Med
13 Mannes Col of Music
14 Marymount College
15 NY School of Int Design
16 NY Inst of Tech
17 Hunter College
18 Cornell Medical Ctr
19 Rockefeller Univ
20 Martha Graham Sch
21 Juilliard
22 School of American Ballet
23 Fordham University
24 Fordham Sch of Law
25 Art Students' League
26 John Jay College
27 Circle in the Square
28 CUNY Graduate Sch
29 NYU Medical Center
30 American Academy of Dramatic Arts
31 Fashion Inst of Tech
32 Baruch College
33 School of Visual Arts
34 Cardozo Law
35 Parsons Design
36 New School
37 Cooper Union
38 Leonard N. Stern Sch of Business at NYU
39 Hebrew Union
40 NYU Law School
41 NYU
42 Stella Adler Cons
43 Pratt Institute
44 French Culinary Inst
45 NY Law School
46 Borough of Manhattan Community College
47 Pace University

Listed Alphabetically

American Academy of Dramatic Arts, 30. 120 Madison Ave ☎ 686-9244

Art Students' League, 25. 215 W 57th St ☎ 247-4510

Bank St College, 11. 610 W 112th St ☎ 875-4400

Barnard College, 7. 3009 Broadway & 120th St ☎ 854-5262

Baruch College, 32. 17 Lexington Ave ☎ 802-2000

Borough of Manhattan Community College, 46. 199 Chambers Street ☎ 346-8000

Cardozo Law, 34. 55 Fifth Ave ☎ 790-0200

Circle in the Square, 27. 1633 Broadway ☎ 307-0388

City College of NY, 3. Convent Ave & 138th St ☎ 650-7000

CUNY Graduate Sch and Univ Ctr, 28. 33 W 42nd St ☎ 642-1600

Columbia Physicians/Surgeons, 2. 630 W 168th St ☎ 305-2500

Columbia School of Social Work, 10. 622 W 113th St ☎ 854-4088

Columbia University, 8. B'way & 116th St ☎ 854-1754

Cooper Union, 37. 30 Cooper Sq ☎ 353-4100

Cornell Medical Center, 18. 1300 York Ave ☎ 746-5454

Fashion Institute of Technology, 31. 227 W 27th St ☎ 217-7675

Fordham University School of Law, 24. 140 W 62nd St ☎ 636-6810

Fordham University, 23. 113 W 60th St ☎ 636-6000

The French Culinary Institute, 44. 462 B'way ☎ 219-8890

Hebrew Union, 39. 1 W 4th St ☎ 674-5300

Hunter College, 17. 695 Park Ave ☎ 772-4000

Jewish Theological Seminary, 5. Broadway & 122nd St ☎ 678-8000

John Jay College, 26. 445 W 59th St ☎ 237-8000

Juilliard School of Music, 21. Lincoln Center, 144 W 66th St ☎ 799-5000

Leonard N. Stern School of Business at NYU, 38. 44 W 4th St ☎ 998-0600

Manhattan School of Music, 4. 120 Claremont Ave ☎ 749-2802

Mannes College of Music, 13. 150 W 85th St ☎ 580-0210

Martha Graham School, 20. 316 E 63rd St ☎ 838-5886

Marymount College, 14. 221 E 71st St ☎ 517-0400

Mount Sinai School of Medicine, 12. Fifth Ave & 100th St ☎ 241-6696

New School, 36. 66 W 12th St ☎ 229-5600

NY Institute of Technology, 16. 1855 Broadway ☎ 261-1500

NY Law School, 45. 47 Worth St ☎ 431-2100

NY School of Interior Design, 15. 170 E 70th St ☎ 753-5365

NYU, 41. Washington Sq ☎ 998-1212

NYU Law School, 40. 110 W 3rd St ☎ 998-6060

NYU Medical Center, 29. 550 First Ave ☎ 263-5290

Pace University, 47. 1 Pace Plaza ☎ 346-1200

Parsons School of Design, 35. 66 Fifth Ave ☎ 229-8900

Pratt Institute, 43. 259 Lafayette St ☎ 925-8481

Rockefeller University, 19. York Ave & 66th St ☎ 327-8000

School of American Ballet, 22. 165 W 65th St ☎ 877-0600

School of Visual Arts, 33. 209 E 23rd St ☎ 592-2000

Stella Adler Conservatory, 42. 419 Lafayette St ☎ 260-0525

Teachers College, 9. 525 W 120th St ☎ 678-3000

Union Theological Seminary, 6. Broadway & 120th St ☎ 662-7100

Yeshiva University, 1. Amsterdam Ave & 185th St ☎ 960-5400

MAP **11**

Libraries

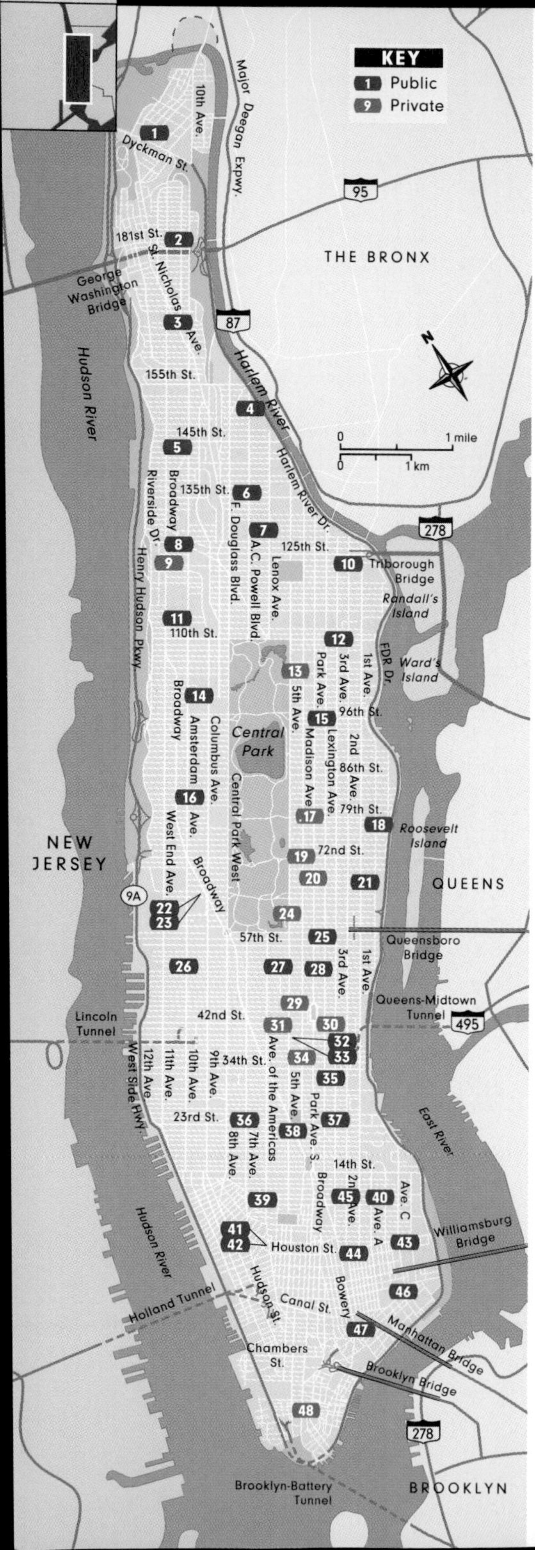

Listed by Site Number

1 Inwood
2 Fort Washington
3 Washington Heights
4 Macomb's Bridge
5 Hamilton Grange
6 Schomburg Center
7 Countee Cullen
8 George Bruce
9 Jewish Theological Seminary
10 125th St
11 Columbia Univ
12 Aguila
13 NY Academy of Medicine
14 Bloomingdale
15 96th St
16 St Agnes
17 NY Society
18 Webster
19 Frick Art
20 Italian Institute
21 67th St
22 Riverside
23 Lincoln Center
24 Alliance Francaise
25 58th St
26 Columbus
27 Donnell
28 Cathedral
29 Mercantile
30 Goethe House
31 NY Bar Assoc
32 NY Public (Main)
33 Mid-Manhattan
34 Pierpont Morgan
35 Kips Bay
36 Muhlenberg
37 Epiphany
38 Andrew Heiskell
39 Jefferson Market
40 Tompkins Square
41 Early Childhood
42 Hudson Park
43 Hamilton Fish Park
44 Archive Contemporary Music
45 Ottendorfer
46 Seward Park
47 Chatham Square
48 NY Law

Listed Alphabetically

PUBLIC

Aguila, 12. 174 E 110th St ☎ 534-2930

Andrew Heiskell Library For the Blind and Physically Handicapped, 38. 40 W 20th St ☎ 206-5400

Bloomingdale, 14. 150 W 100th St ☎ 222-8030

Cathedrale, 28. 560 Lexington Ave ☎ 752-3824

Chatham Square, 47. 33 E Broadway ☎ 964-6598

Columbia Univ, 11. 573 W 113th St ☎ 864-2530

Columbus, 26. 742 Tenth Ave ☎ 586-5098

Countee Cullen, 7. 104 W 136th St ☎ 491-2070

Donnell, 27. 20 W 53rd St ☎ 621-0618

Early Childhood, 41. 66 Leroy St ☎ 929-0815

Epiphany, 37. 228 E 23rd St ☎ 679-2645

58th St, 25. 127 E 58th St ☎ 759-7358

Fort Washington, 2. 535 W 179th St ☎ 927-3533

George Bruce, 8. 518 W 125th St ☎ 662-9727

Hamilton Fish Park, 43. 415 E Houston St ☎ 673-2290

Hamilton Grange, 5. 503 W 145th St ☎ 926-2147

Hudson Park, 42. 66 Leroy St ☎ 243-6876

Inwood, 1. 4790 Broadway ☎ 942-2445

Jefferson Market, 39. 425 Sixth Ave ☎ 243-4334

Kips Bay, 35. 446 Third Ave ☎ 683-2520

Library for the Performing Arts, 23. 111 Amsterdam Ave ☎ 870-1630

Macomb's Bridge, 4. 2650 Seventh Ave ☎ 281-4900

Mid-Manhattan, 33. 455 Fifth Ave ☎ 340-0849

Muhlenberg, 36. 209 W 23rd St ☎ 924-1585

NY Public (Main), 32. Fifth Ave & 42nd St ☎ 930-0800

96th St, 15. 112 E 96th St ☎ 289-0908

125th St, 10. 224 E 125th St ☎ 534-5050

Ottendorfer, 45. 135 Second Ave ☎ 674-0947

Riverside, 22. 127 Amsterdam Ave ☎ 870-1810

St Agnes, 16. 444 Amsterdam Ave ☎ 877-4380

Schomburg Center, 6. 515 W 135th St ☎ 491-2200

Seward Park, 46. 192 E Broadway ☎ 477-6770

67th St, 21. 328 E 67th St ☎ 734-1717

Tompkins Square, 40. 331 E 10th St ☎ 228-4747

Washington Heights, 3. 1000 St Nicholas Ave ☎ 923-6054

Webster, 18. 1465 York Ave ☎ 288-5049

PRIVATE

Alliance Francaise, 24. 22 E 60th St ☎ 355-6100

Archive of Contemporary Music, 44. 132 Crosby ☎ 226-6967

Frick Art, 19. 10 E 71st St ☎ 288-8700

Goethe House, 30. 1014 Fifth Ave ☎ 439-8700

Italian Institute, 20. 686 Park Ave ☎ 879-4242

Jewish Theological Seminary, 9. 3080 Broadway ☎ 678-8080

Mercantile, 29. 17 E 47th St ☎ 755-6710

NY Academy of Medicine, 13. 2 E 103rd St ☎ 822-7200

NY Bar Association, 31. 42 W 44th St ☎ 382-6600

NY Law, 48. 120 Broadway ☎ 732-8720

NY Society, 17. 53 E 79th St ☎ 288-6900

Pierpont Morgan, 34. 29 E 36th St ☎ 685-0008

Consulates & Missions

Listed by Site Number

1 Czech
2 Greece
3 Iraq
4 Mongolia
5 Myanmar
6 Lebanon
7 France
8 Cameroon
9 Burkina Faso
10 Italy
11 Austria
12 Indonesia
13 Senegal
14 Belarus
14 Russia
14 Ukraine
15 Palestine Liberation Organization (PLO)
16 Congo
17 Pakistan
18 India
19 Somalia
20 Egypt
21 Spain
22 Germany
23 Korea
24 Belgium
25 Argentina
26 Hungary
27 Thailand
28 Switzerland
29 Venezuela
30 Canada
31 Belgium
32 Australia
32 Estonia
33 Brazil
33 Portugal
34 Ireland
35 Laos
36 Great Britain
36 Monaco
37 Norway
38 Niger
39 Tunisia
40 Luxembourg
41 Iceland
42 Peru
43 New Zealand
44 Sierra Leone
45 Netherlands
46 Kenya
47 Japan
48 Afghanistan
48 Chile
48 Ethiopia
48 Finland
48 Guyana
48 Jordan
48 Oman
48 Panama
48 Saudi Arabia
48 Yemen
49 Slovakia
50 Gambia
50 Ghana
51 Sweden
52 Qatar
52 United Arab Emirates
52 Uruguay
53 Trinidad & Tobago
54 Bahamas
55 Jamaica
56 Philippines
57 Colombia
58 Denmark
59 Bangladesh
59 Turkey
60 USA
61 Bahrain
61 Bhutan
62 Fiji
62 New Zealand
62 Surinam
63 Kuwait
64 Nigeria
65 Grenada
65 Liberia
65 Nepal
65 Nicaragua
65 St Lucia
65 Syria
66 Malaysia
67 Barbados
67 Zambia
67 Equador
67 Israel
68 Bolivia
68 Mauritania
68 Mauritius
69 Madagascar
69 St Vincent
70 Tanzania
71 Croatia
72 Dominican Republic
73 China
74 Costa Rica
74 Honduras
75 Haiti
76 Mexico
77 Gabon
78 Morocco
79 Cyprus
80 Afghanistan
81 Paraguay
82 Sudan
83 Sri Lanka
84 Iran
85 Lesotho
86 Slovenia
87 Romania
88 South Africa
89 Malta
90 Cuba
91 Guinea
92 El Salvador
93 Botswana
94 Guatemala
95 Poland
96 Lithuania

Consulates & Missions

Listed Alphabetically

CONSULATES

Afghanistan, 80. 360 Lexington Ave ☎ 972-2277

Argentina, 25. 12 W 56th St ☎ 603-0400

Australia, 32. 630 Fifth Ave ☎ 408-8400

Austria, 11. 31 E 69th St ☎ 737-6400

Bahamas, 54. 231 E 46th St ☎ 421-6420

Bahrain, 61. 2 UN Plaza ☎ 223-6200

Bangladesh, 59. 211 E 43rd St ☎ 867-3434

Barbados, 67. 800 Second Ave ☎ 867-8431

Belgium, 31. 1330 Avenue of the Americas ☎ 586-5110

Bhutan, 61. 2 UN Plaza ☎ 826-1919

Bolivia, 68. 211 E 43rd St ☎ 687-0530

Brazil, 33. 630 Fifth Ave ☎ 757-3085

Canada, 30. 1251 Sixth Ave ☎ 596-1700

Chile, 48. 866 UN Plaza ☎ 980-3366

China, 73. 520 Twelfth Ave ☎ 868-7752

Colombia, 50. 10 E 46th St ☎ 949-9898

Costa Rica, 74. 80 Wall St ☎ 425-2620

Cyprus, 79. 13 E 40th St ☎ 686-6016

Denmark, 58. 885 Second Ave ☎ 223-4545

Dominican Republic, 72. 1501 Broadway ☎ 768-2480

Ecuador, 67. 800 Second Ave ☎ 808-0170

Egypt, 20. 1110 Second Ave ☎ 759-7120

El Salvador, 92. 46 Park Ave ☎ 889-3608

Estonia, 32. 630 Fifth Ave ☎ 247-7634

Fiji, 62. 630 Third Ave ☎ 687-4130

Finland, 48. 866 UN Plaza ☎ 750-4400

France, 7. 934 Fifth Ave ☎ 606-3688

Germany, 22. 460 Park Ave ☎ 308-8700

Ghana, 48. 19 E 47th St ☎ 832-1300

Great Britain, 36. 845 Third Ave ☎ 745-0202

Greece, 2. 69 E 79th St ☎ 988-5500

Grenada, 65. 820 Second Ave ☎ 599-0301

Guatemala, 94. 57 Park Ave ☎ 686-3837

Guyana, 48. 866 UN Plaza ☎ 527-3215

Haiti, 75. 271 Madison Ave ☎ 697-9767

Honduras, 74. 80 Wall St ☎ 269-3611

Hungary, 26. 223 E 52nd St ☎ 752-0661

Iceland, 41. 800 Third Ave ☎ 593-2700

India, 18. 3 E 64th St ☎ 774-0600

Indonesia, 12. 5 E 68th St ☎ 879-0600

Ireland, 34. 345 Park Ave ☎ 319-2555

Israel, 67. 800 Second Ave ☎ 499-5000

Italy, 10. 690 Park Ave ☎ 737-9100

Jamaica, 55. 767 Third Ave ☎ 935-9000

Japan, 47. 299 Park Ave ☎ 371-8222

Kenya, 46. 424 Madison Ave ☎ 486-1300

Korea, 23. 460 Park Ave ☎ 752-1700

Lebanon, 6. 9 E 76th St ☎ 744-7905

Liberia, 65. 820 Second Ave ☎ 687-1033

Lithuania, 96. 420 Fifth Ave ☎ 354-7840

Luxembourg, 40. 17 Beekman Pl ☎ 888-6664

Malaysia, 66. 313 E 43rd St ☎ 490-2722

Mexico, 76. 8 E 41 St ☎ 689-0456

Monaco, 36. 565 Fifth Ave ☎ 286-3330

Morocco, 78. 10 E 40th St ☎ 758-2625

Nepal, 65. 820 Second Ave ☎ 370-4188

Netherlands, 45. 1 Rockefeller Plaza ☎ 246-1429

New Zealand, 43. 780 Third Ave ☎ 832-4038

Nigeria, 64. 828 Second Ave ☎ 808-0301

Norway, 37. 825 Third Ave ☎ 421-7333

Pakistan, 17. 12 E 65th St ☎ 879-5800

Paraguay, 81. 675 Third Ave ☎ 682-9441

Peru, 42. 215 Lexington Ave ☎ 481-7410

Poland, 95. 233 Madison Ave ☎ 889-8360

Portugal, 33. 630 Fifth Ave ☎ 765-2980

Listed Alphabetically (cont.)

Romania, 87. 200 E 38th St ☎ 682-9120

Saudi Arabia, 48. 866 UN Plaza ☎ 752-2740

South Africa, 88. 333 E 38th St ☎ 213-4880

Spain, 21. 150 E 58th St ☎ 355-4080

Sweden, 51. 885 Second Ave ☎ 583-2550

Switzerland, 28. 665 Fifth Ave ☎ 758-2560

Thailand, 27. 351 E 52nd St ☎ 754-1770

Trinidad & Tobago, 53. 733 Third Ave ☎ 682-7272

Turkey, 59. 821 UN Plaza ☎ 949-0160

Uruguay, 52. 747 Third Ave ☎ 753-8191

Venezuela, 29. 7 E 51st St ☎ 826-1660

MISSIONS

Belarus, 14. 136 E 67th St ☎ 535-3420

Botswana, 93. 103 E 37th St ☎ 889-2277

Burkina Faso, 9. 115 E 73rd St ☎ 288-7515

Cameroon, 8. 22 E 73rd St ☎ 794-2295

Congo, 16. 14 E 65th St ☎ 744-7840

Croatia, 71. 820 Second Ave ☎ 986-1585

Cuba, 90. 315 Lexington Ave ☎ 689-7215

Czech Republic, 1. 1109 Madison Ave ☎ 535-8814

Ethiopia, 48. 866 UN Plaza ☎ 421-1830

Gabon, 77. 18 E 41st St ☎ 686-9720

Gambia, 50. 820 Second Ave ☎ 949-6640

Guinea, 91. 140 E 39th St ☎ 687-8115

Iran, 84. 622 Third Ave ☎ 687-2020

Iraq, 3. 14 E 79th St ☎ 737-4433

Jordan, 48. 866 UN Plaza ☎ 752-0135

Kuwait, 63. 321 E 44th St ☎ 973-4300

Laos, 35. 317 E 51st St ☎ 832-2734

Lesotho, 85. 204 E 39th St ☎ 661-1690

Madagascar, 69. 801 Second Ave ☎ 687-1033

Malta, 89. 249 E 35th St ☎ 725-2345

Mauritania, 68. 211 E 43rd St ☎ 986-7963

Mauritius, 68. 211 E 43rd St ☎ 949-0190

Mongolia, 4. 6 E 77th St ☎ 861-9460

Myanmar, 5. 10 E 77th St ☎ 535-1310

New Zealand, 62. 1 UN Plaza ☎ 826-1960

Nicaragua, 65. 820 Second Ave ☎ 490-7997

Niger, 38. 417 E 50th St ☎ 421-3260

Oman, 48. 866 UN Plaza ☎ 355-3505

Panama, 48. 866 UN Plaza ☎ 421-5420

Palestine Liberation Organization (PLO), 15. 115 E 65th St ☎ 288-8500

Phillippines, 56. 556 Fifth Ave ☎ 764-1300

Qatar, 52. 747 Third Ave ☎ 486-9335

Republic of Slovakia, 49. 866 UN Plaza ☎ 980-1558

Romania, 87. 573-577 Third Ave ☎ 682-3274

Russia Federation, 14. 136 E 67th St ☎ 861-4900

Senegal, 13. 238 E 68th St ☎ 517-9030

Sierra Leone, 44. 245 E 49th St ☎ 688-1656

Slovenia, 86. 600 Third Ave ☎ 370-3007

Somalia, 19. 425 E 61st St ☎ 688-9410

Sri Lanka, 83. 630 Third Ave ☎ 986-7040

St Lucia, 65. 820 Second Ave ☎ 697-9360

St Vincent, 69. 801 Second Ave ☎ 687-4490

Sudan, 82. 655 Third Ave ☎ 573-6033

Surinam, 62. 1 UN Plaza ☎ 826-0660

Syria, 65. 820 Second Ave ☎ 661-1313

Tanzania, 70. 205 E 42nd St ☎ 972-9160

Tunisia, 39. 31 Beekman Pl ☎ 751-7503

Ukraine, 14. 136 E 67th St ☎ 535-3418

United Arab Emirates, 52. 747 Third Ave ☎ 371-0480

USA, 60. 799 UN Plaza ☎ 415-4000

Yemen, 48. 866 UN Plaza ☎ 355-1730

Zambia, 67. 800 Second Ave ☎ 758-1110

MAP 13 Airport Access

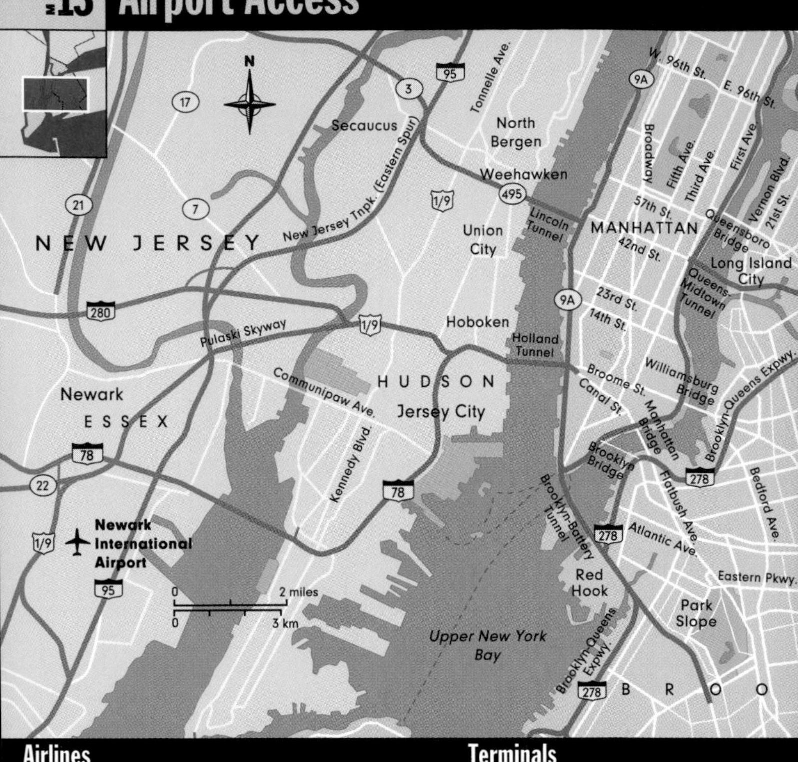

Airlines / Terminals

	JFK	LaGUARDIA	NEWARK
Aer Lingus ☎ 212/557-1110	4E		A, B
Aeroflot ☎ 212/332-1050	3		
Aerolineas Argentinas ☎ 800/333-0276	4E		
AeroMexico ☎ 800/237-6639	2		B
Air Afrique ☎ 800/237-2747	4W		
Air Aruba ☎ 800/882-7822			B
Air Canada ☎ 800/776-3000		CTB-A	C
Air China ☎ 212/371-9898	3		
Air France ☎ 800/237-2747	4W		B
Air India ☎ 212/751-6200	4W		
Air Jamaica ☎ 800/523-5585	4W		B
Air Nova ☎ 800/776-3000			C
Air Ontario ☎ 800/776-3000			C
Alitalia ☎ 800/223-5730	4W		B, C
ALIA-Royal Jordanian ☎ 212/949-0050	4E		
All Nippon Airways ☎ 800/235-9262	3		
American ☎ 800/433-7300	8, 9	CTB-D	A
American Eagle ☎ 800/433-7300	9		
American Trans Air ☎ 800/435-9282	2		
America West ☎ 800/235-9292	2	CTB-A	C
Asiana Airlines ☎ 800/227-4262	4E		
Austrian Airlines ☎ 800/843-0002	3		
Avianca ☎ 800/284-2622	3		B
Balkan Bulgarian ☎ 800/796-5706	4E		
Biman Bangladesh ☎ 888/702-4626	4W		
British Airways ☎ 800/247-9297	7		B
Business Express ☎ 800/345-3400			B
BWIA ☎ 800/538-2942	8		
Canadian Airlines ☎ 800/426-7000	9	CTB-D	
Carnival ☎ 800/437-2110	4E	CTB-C	B
Cathay Pacific ☎ 800/233-2742	3		
China Airlines ☎ 800/227-5118	3		
Colgan Air ☎ 800/272-5488		CTB-B	A

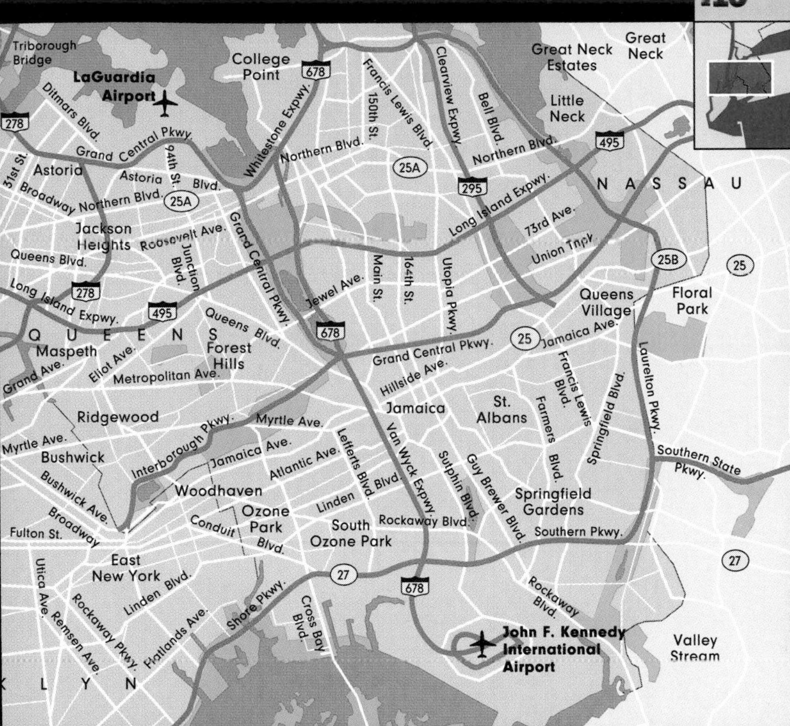

Airlines

Terminals (cont.)

	JFK	LaGUARDIA	NEWARK
Continental ☎ 800/525-0280		**CTB-A**	**C**
Continental Express ☎ 800/525-0280	**2**	**CTB-A**	**C**
Czech Airlines ☎ 212/765-6022			**B**
Delta International ☎ 800/241-1414	**3**	**Delta**	**B**
Delta Domestic ☎ 800/221-1212	**3**	**Delta**	**B**
Delta Shuttle ☎ 212/239-0700		**MAT**	
Ecuatoriana ☎ 800/328-2367	**3**		
Egypt Air ☎ 212/315-0900	**4W**		
El-Al ☎ 800/223-6700	**4W**		**B**
EVA Airways ☎ 800/695-1188	**4E**		**B**
Finnair ☎ 212/499-9026	**2**		
Ghana Airways ☎ 800/404-4262	**4W**		
Guyana ☎ 718/657-7474	**4E**		
Iberia ☎ 800/772-4642	**4E**		
Icelandair ☎ 800/223-5500	**4E**		
Japan ☎ 800/525-3663	**4E**		
KIWI ☎ 800/538-5494			**A**
KLM ☎ 212/759-3600; 800/374-7747	**4E**		**B**
Korean ☎ 800/438-5000	**4W**		**B**
Kuwait ☎ 212/308-5454	**4E**		
Lacsa Airlines ☎ 800/225-2272	**7**		
Lan Chile ☎ 800/488-0070	**8**		
LOT Polish ☎ 800/223-0593	**8**		**B**
LTU ☎ 800/888-0200	**4E**		
Lufthansa ☎ 800/645-3880	**4E**		
Malev Hungarian ☎ 212/757-6446	**3**		**B**
Mexicana ☎ 800/531-7921	**4W**		
Midway ☎ 800/446-4392		**CTB-D**	**A**
Midwest Express ☎ 800/452-2022		**CTB-C**	**B**
North American ☎ 718/656-3289	**5**	**Delta**	**B**
Northwest International ☎ 800/447-4747	**4E**	**Delta**	**B**
Northwest Domestic ☎ 800/225-2525	**4E**	**Delta**	**B**
Northwest Airlink ☎ 800/225-2525	**4E**		

MAP 14 New York Area Airports

Airlines

Terminals (cont.)

Airlines	JFK	LaGUARDIA	NEWARK
Olympic ☎ 212/838-3600	4E		
Pakistan ☎ 212/370-9158	4W		
Pan Am ☎ 800/359-7262	4E		
Philippine Airlines ☎ 800/435-9725			B
Precision Airlink ☎ 888/635-5293		Delta	
Qantas ☎ 800/227-4500	4		
Royal Air Maroc ☎ 212/750-6071	4E		
SAS ☎ 800/221-2350	7		C
Sabena ☎ 800/955-2000	3		
SAETA ☎ 212/302-0004	7		
Singapore Airlines ☎ 800/742-3333	3		
South African Airways ☎ 212/826-0995	8		
Sun Country ☎ 800/359-5786	6		
Sun Jet ☎ 800/478-6538			A
Swissair ☎ 800/221-4750	3		B
Tarom-Romanian ☎ 212/687-6013	3		
TACA International ☎ 800/535-8780	2		
TAP Air Portugal ☎ 800/221-7370	3		B
Tower Air ☎ 718/553-8500	Tower		
TransBrasil ☎ 800/872-3153	4W		
TWA ☎ 212/290-2141; 201/643-3339	5, 6	CTB-B	A
Turkish Airlines ☎ 212/339-9650			B
TW Express ☎ 212/290-2141;201/643-3339	5		A
United ☎ 800/241-6522	7	CTB-C	A
United Express ☎ 800/241-6522	7	CTB-C	A
USAir ☎ 800/428-4322	7	USAir	A
USAir Express ☎ 800/428-4322	7	USAir	A
USAir Shuttle ☎ 800/428-4322		USAir Shuttle	
Uzbekistan Airways ☎ 212/489-3954	4W		
Varig ☎ 212/682-3100	2		
VASP ☎ 718/955-0540	4W		
Virgin Atlantic ☎ 800/862-8621	2		B

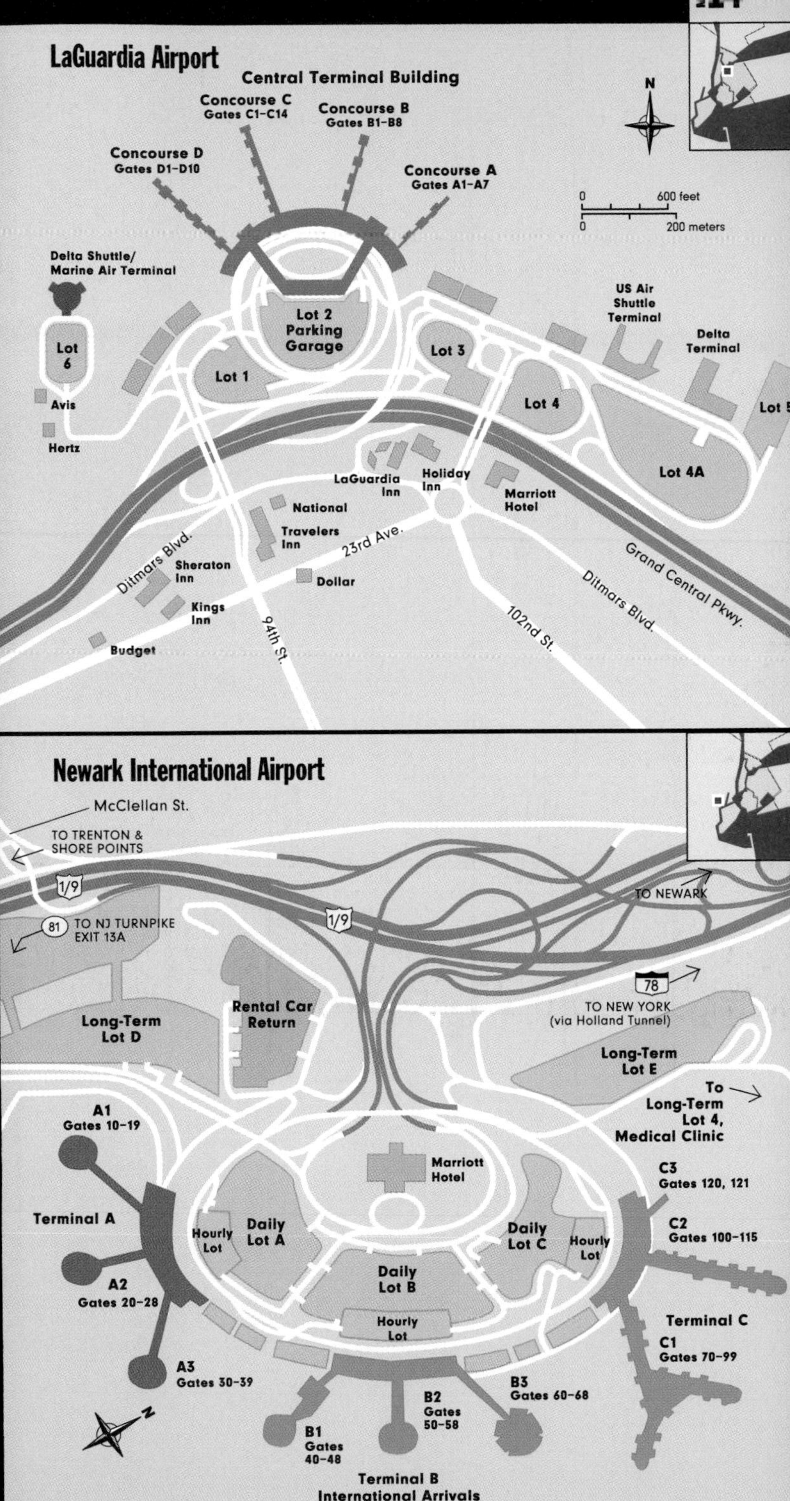
LaGuardia Airport
Central Terminal Building
Concourse C
Gates C1–C14
Concourse B
Gates B1–B8
Concourse D
Gates D1–D10
Concourse A
Gates A1–A7
N
0
600 feet
0
200 meters
Delta Shuttle/
Marine Air Terminal
Lot 6
Lot 2
Parking
Garage
Lot 1
Lot 3
US Air
Shuttle
Terminal
Delta
Terminal
Lot 4
Lot 5
Lot 4A
Avis
Hertz
LaGuardia
Inn
Holiday
Inn
Marriott
Hotel
National
Travelers
Inn
23rd Ave.
Ditmars Blvd.
Sheraton
Inn
Dollar
Kings
Inn
Budget
94th St.
102nd St.
Ditmars Blvd.
Grand Central Pkwy.
Newark International Airport
McClellan St.
TO TRENTON &
SHORE POINTS
1/9
81
TO NJ TURNPIKE
EXIT 13A
1/9
TO NEWARK
78
TO NEW YORK
(via Holland Tunnel)
Rental Car
Return
Long-Term
Lot D
Long-Term
Lot E
To
Long-Term
Lot 4,
Medical Clinic
A1
Gates 10–19
Terminal A
Marriott
Hotel
C3
Gates 120, 121
Hourly
Lot
Daily
Lot A
Daily
Lot C
Hourly
Lot
C2
Gates 100–115
A2
Gates 20–28
Daily
Lot B
Hourly
Lot
Terminal C
C1
Gates 70–99
A3
Gates 30–39
B3
Gates 60–68
B2
Gates
50–58
N
B1
Gates
40–48
Terminal B
International Arrivals

Passenger Rail Network

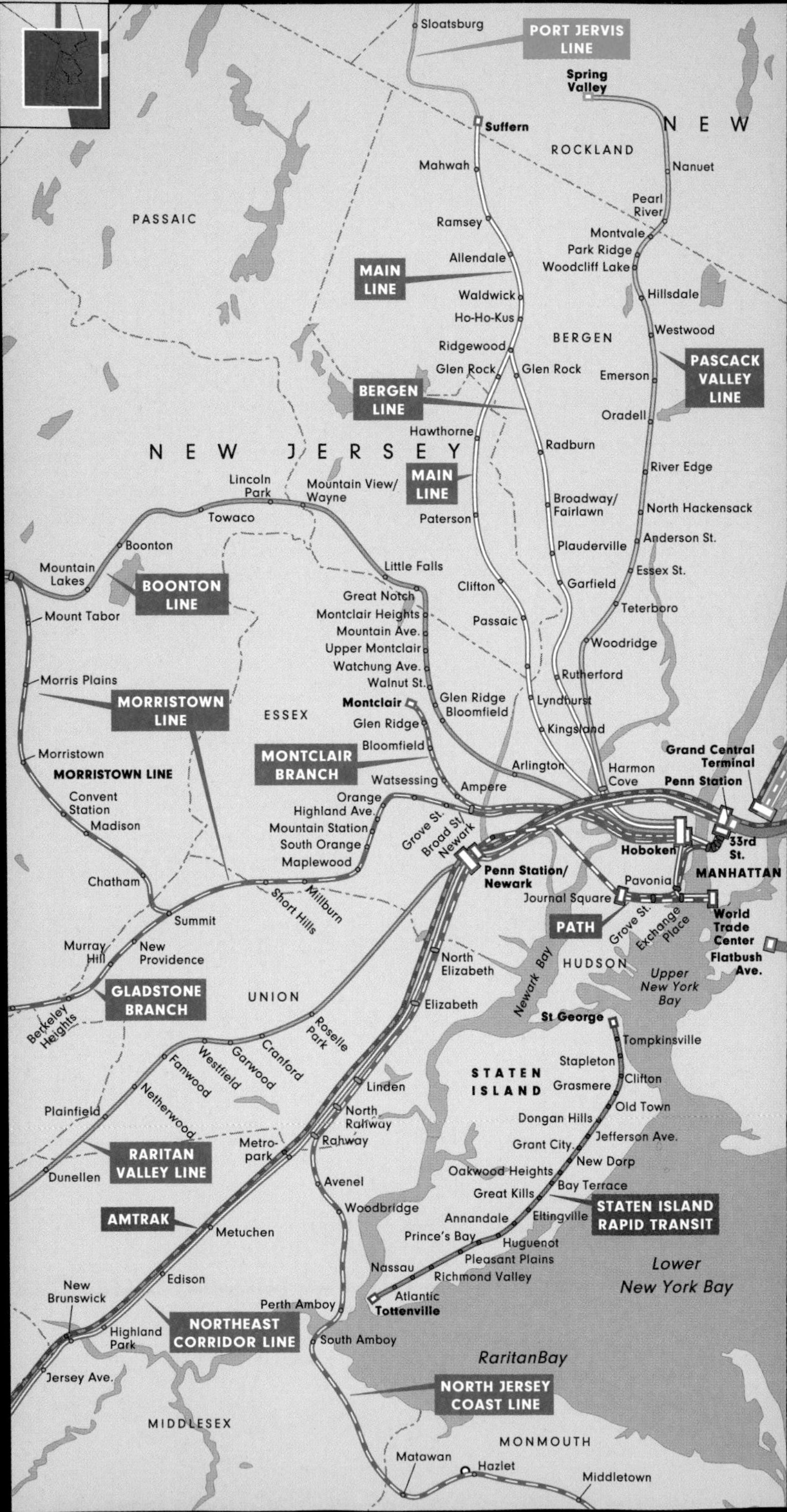

PORT JERVIS LINE
Sloatsburg
Spring Valley
Suffern
NEW
ROCKLAND
Mahwah
Nanuet
Pearl River
PASSAIC
Ramsey
Montvale
Park Ridge
Woodcliff Lake
Allendale
MAIN LINE
Waldwick
Hillsdale
Ho-Ho-Kus
Westwood
Ridgewood
BERGEN
Glen Rock
Glen Rock
Emerson
PASCACK VALLEY LINE
BERGEN LINE
Oradell
Hawthorne
Radburn
NEW JERSEY
MAIN LINE
River Edge
Lincoln Park
Mountain View/ Wayne
Broadway/ Fairlawn
North Hackensack
Towaco
Paterson
Anderson St.
Boonton
Plauderville
Mountain Lakes
Little Falls
Essex St.
BOONTON LINE
Clifton
Garfield
Great Notch
Teterboro
Mount Tabor
Montclair Heights
Passaic
Mountain Ave.
Woodridge
Upper Montclair
Watchung Ave.
Rutherford
Walnut St.
Morris Plains
Glen Ridge Bloomfield
Montclair
MORRISTOWN LINE
Lyndhurst
ESSEX
Glen Ridge
Kingsland
Bloomfield
Morristown
MONTCLAIR BRANCH
Grand Central Terminal
MORRISTOWN LINE
Arlington
Harmon Cove
Penn Station
Convent Station
Watsessing
Ampere
Orange
Highland Ave.
Madison
Mountain Station
Grove St.
Broad St. Newark
33rd St.
South Orange
Hoboken
MANHATTAN
Maplewood
Penn Station/ Newark
Chatham
Pavonia
Journal Square
Millburn
Short Hills
World Trade Center
Summit
PATH
Grove St.
Exchange Place
Flatbush Ave.
Murray Hill
New Providence
North Elizabeth
Newark Bay
HUDSON
Upper New York Bay
GLADSTONE BRANCH
UNION
Elizabeth
Berkeley Heights
Roselle Park
St George
Tompkinsville
Cranford
Westfield
Garwood
Stapleton
Fanwood
Linden
STATEN ISLAND
Clifton
Grasmere
Netherwood
Old Town
Plainfield
North Rahway
Dongan Hills
Rahway
Jefferson Ave.
Metropark
Grant City
RARITAN VALLEY LINE
New Dorp
Dunellen
Oakwood Heights
Avenel
Bay Terrace
Great Kills
Woodbridge
STATEN ISLAND RAPID TRANSIT
Eltingville
AMTRAK
Annandale
Metuchen
Prince's Bay
Huguenot
Pleasant Plains
Lower New York Bay
Nassau
Edison
Richmond Valley
New Brunswick
Atlantic
Perth Amboy
Tottenville
NORTHEAST CORRIDOR LINE
Highland Park
South Amboy
Raritan Bay
Jersey Ave.
NORTH JERSEY COAST LINE
MIDDLESEX
MONMOUTH
Matawan
Hazlet
Middletown

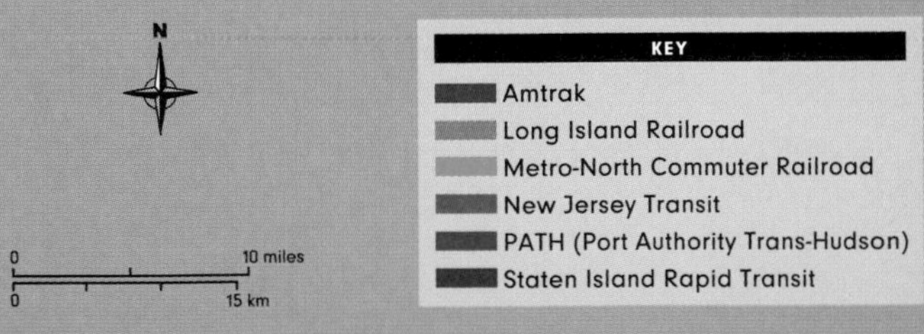

KEY
Amtrak
Long Island Railroad
Metro-North Commuter Railroad
New Jersey Transit
PATH (Port Authority Trans-Hudson)
Staten Island Rapid Transit
0
10 miles
0
15 km
N
ATLANTIC OCEAN
YORK
CONNECTICUT
WESTCHESTER
BRONX
QUEENS
BROOKLYN
NASSAU
Hudson River
Long Island Sound
East River
AMTRAK
HUDSON LINE
HARLEM LINE
NEW HAVEN LINE
OYSTER BAY BRANCH
PORT WASHINGTON BRANCH
PORT JEFFERSON BRANCH
RONKONKOMA BRANCH
BABYLON BRANCH/ MONTAUK BRANCH
Ossining
Scarborough
Philipse Manor
Tarrytown
Irvington
Ardsley
Dobbs Ferry
Hastings-on-Hudson
Greystone
Glenwood
Yonkers
Ludlow
Riverdale
Spuyten Duyvil
Marble Hill
University Heights
Morris Heights
Chappaqua
Pleasantville
Hawthorne
Mount Pleasant
Valhalla
North White Plains
White Plains
Hartsdale
Scarsdale
Crestwood
Tuckahoe
Bronxville
Fleetwood
Mt. Vernon W.
Mount Vernon
Pelham
Wakefield
Woodlawn
Williams Bridge
Botanical Gardens
Fordham
125th St.
New Canaan
Springdale
Springdale
Glenbrook
Stamford
Darien
Noroton Heights
Old Greenwich
Riverside
Cos Cob
Greenwich
Port Chester
Rye
Harrison
Mamaroneck
Larchmont
New Rochelle
La Guardia Airport
Hunterspoint Ave.
Woodside
Penny Bridge
Haberman
Long Island City
Fresh Pond
Glendale
Nostrand Ave.
East New York
Richmond Hill
Kennedy International Airport
Shea Stadium
Flushing
Murray Hill
Broadway
Auburndale
Bayside
Douglaston
Little Neck
Great Neck
Plandome
Manhasset
Port Washington
Forest Hills
Kew Gdns.
Jamaica
Hollis
St. Albans
Queens Village
Bellerose
Floral Park
Stewart Manor
Nassau Blvd.
Garden City
New Hyde Park
Merrilon Ave.
Mineola
Hempstead
West Hempstead
Hempstead Gdns
Lakeview
Malverne
Westwood
Locust Manor
Laurelton
Rosedale
Valley Stream
Lynbrook
Hewlett
Woodmere
Cedarhurst
Lawrence
Inwood
Far Rockaway
Island Park
Long Beach
East Rockaway
Ocean Side
Rockville Center
Baldwin
Freeport
Merrick
Bellmore
Wantagh
Seaford
Massapequa
Bethpage
Hicksville
Westbury
Carle Place
East Williston
Albertson
Roslyn
Greenvale
Muttontown
Glen Head
Sea Cliff
Glen Cove
Locust Valley
Mill Neck
Oyster Bay
Cold Spring Harbor
Syosset

Piers & Terminals

George Washington Bridge Bus Terminal (178th St.)
125th St. Station
107th St. Recreation Pier
Hudson Harbor/ 79th St. Boat Basin
E. 63rd St. Ferry Landing
Passenger Ship Terminal
The Intrepid Sea-Air-Space Museum
Pier 83
Pier 78
Grand Central Terminal
Port Authority Bus Terminal
E. 34th St. Pier
NYC Heliport
Javits Center
West 30th St. Heliport
Pennsylvania Station
Pier 62
Hoboken Terminal
New York Cove Yacht Harbor
South Street Seaport
Pier 11
Downtown Manhattan Heliport
Staten Island Ferry Terminal
Slip 5
Pier A
Battery Park Ferry Landing (Ferries to Statue of Liberty and Ellis Island)
MIDTOWN
DOWNTOWN
Hudson River
East River
NEW JERSEY
QUEENS
BROOKLYN
0 1500 feet
0 500 meters

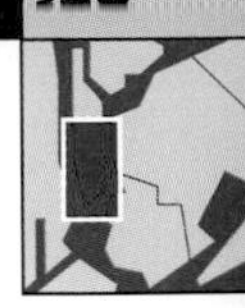

Listed Alphabetically

BOAT TOURS

Circle Line, Pier 83 ☎ 563-3200

Seaport Liberty Cruise, Pier 16 ☎ 748-8618

Spirit of New York, Pier 62 ☎ 727-2789

TNT Hydrolines, Pier 11 ☎ 800/262-8743

World Yacht Cruises, Pier 81 ☎ 630-8100

FERRY SERVICE

Ellis Island, Battery Park ☎ 269-5755

Hoboken (New Jersey), North Cove Harbor ☎ 201/420-4422

Delta Water Shuttle (to LaGuardia Airport), Pier 11 ☎ 800/543-3779

Port Imperial (to New Jersey), Pier 78 ☎ 201/902-8735

Staten Island, Battery Park ☎ 718/815-2658

Statue of Liberty, Battery Park ☎ 269-5755

HELICOPTER SERVICE

Island Helicopter, E 34th St Heliport ☎ 564-9290 (scheduled tours)

Liberty Helicopter, W 30th St Heliport ☎ 465-8905

National Helicopter, E 34th St Heliport ☎ 800/645-3494 (service to JFK)

Port Authority of NY and NJ, Downtown Manhattan Heliport ☎ 248-7240

Wall Street Helicopters, Downtown Manhattan Heliport ☎ 943-5959

TRAIN SERVICE

Amtrak, Grand Central Terminal, Park Ave & 42nd St ☎ 582-6875

Amtrak, Pennsylvania Station, Eighth Ave & 34th St ☎ 800/523-8720

Long Island Railroad (LIRR), Pennsylvania Station, Eighth Ave & 34th St ☎ 718/217-5477

Metro North, Grand Central Terminal, Park Ave & 42nd St ☎ 532-4900

New Jersey Transit, Pennsylvania Station, Eighth Ave & 34th St ☎ 800/626-7433 (NJ), 201/762-5100

PATH, Pennsylvania Station, Eighth Ave & 34th St ☎ 800/234-7284

BUS TERMINALS

George Washington Bridge Bus Station, Broadway & 178th St ☎ 564-1114

Port Authority Bus Terminal, Eighth Ave & 42nd St ☎ 564-8484

CRUISE TERMINALS

Passenger Ship Terminal, Piers 88-94 ☎ 246-5450

Subways/Manhattan below 42nd St

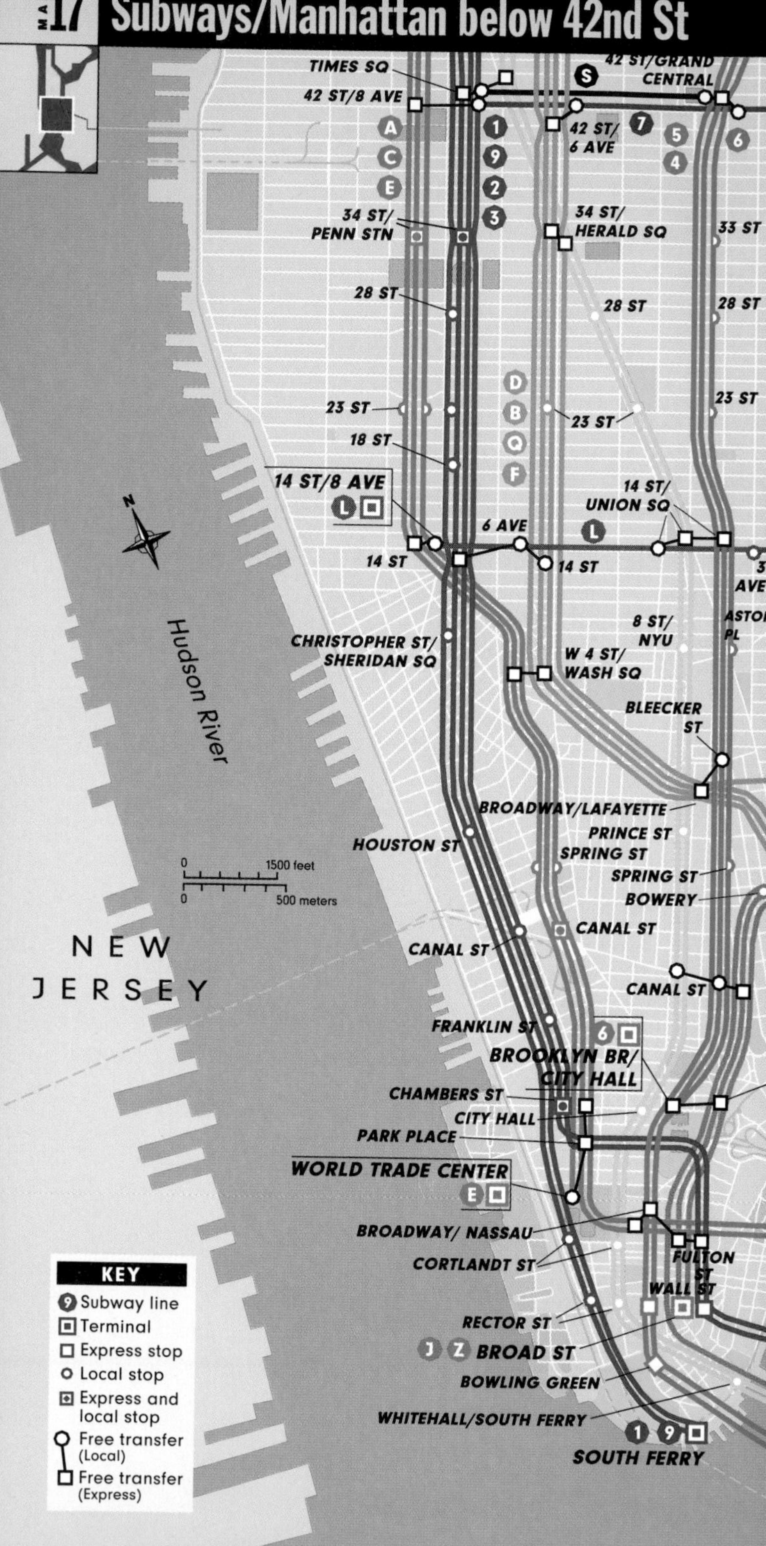

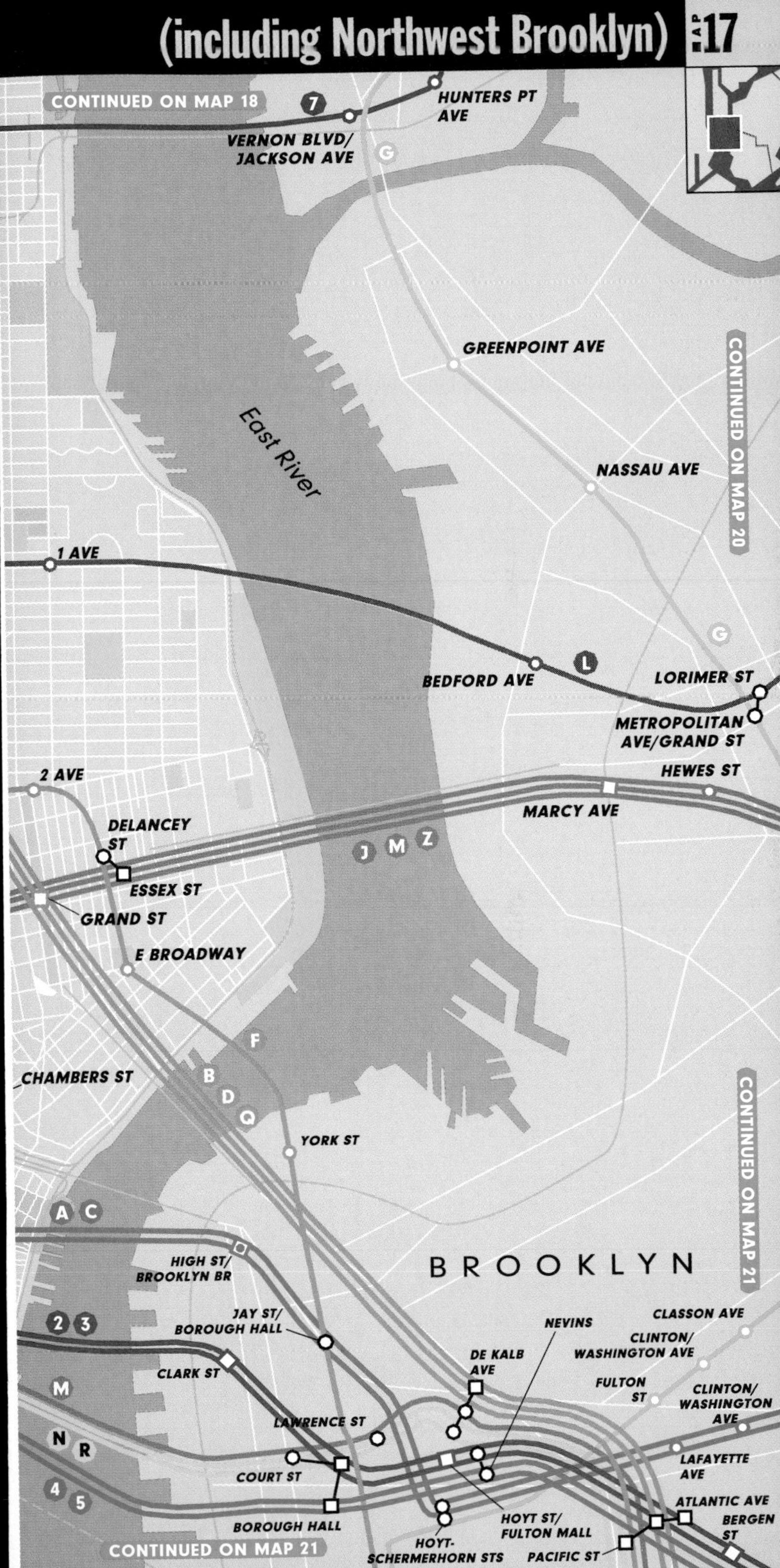
(including Northwest Brooklyn)
MAP 17
CONTINUED ON MAP 18
7
HUNTERS PT AVE
VERNON BLVD/ JACKSON AVE
G
GREENPOINT AVE
CONTINUED ON MAP 20
East River
NASSAU AVE
1 AVE
G
L
BEDFORD AVE
LORIMER ST
METROPOLITAN AVE/GRAND ST
HEWES ST
2 AVE
MARCY AVE
DELANCEY ST
J
M
Z
ESSEX ST
GRAND ST
E BROADWAY
F
CHAMBERS ST
B
D
Q
YORK ST
CONTINUED ON MAP 21
A
C
HIGH ST/ BROOKLYN BR
BROOKLYN
JAY ST/ BOROUGH HALL
NEVINS
CLASSON AVE
2
3
CLARK ST
DE KALB AVE
CLINTON/ WASHINGTON AVE
FULTON ST
M
CLINTON/ WASHINGTON AVE
LAWRENCE ST
N
R
COURT ST
LAFAYETTE AVE
4
5
ATLANTIC AVE
HOYT ST/ FULTON MALL
BERGEN ST
BOROUGH HALL
HOYT- SCHERMERHORN STS
PACIFIC ST
CONTINUED ON MAP 21

125 ST
1 9
A C B D
125 ST
2 3
125 ST
4 5 6
125 ST/
METRO NORTH
116 ST/
COLUMBIA
UNIV
116 ST
116 ST
116 ST
CATHEDRAL
PKWY
(110 ST)
CATHEDRAL
PKWY
(110 ST)
110th ST/
CENTRAL
PARK N
110 ST
103 ST
103 ST
103 ST
96 ST
96 ST
96 ST
Hudson River
86 ST
86 ST
A C B D
86 ST
81 ST
Central
Park
79 ST
77 ST
2 3
1 9
72 ST
72 ST
68 ST/
HUNTER
COLLEGE
66 ST/
LINCOLN
CENTER
LEXINGTON
AVE
LEXINGTON
AVE
59 ST/
COLUMBUS
CIRCLE
57 ST
5 AVE
59 ST
N
R
57 ST
7 AVE
LEXINGTON
AVE
5 AVE
50 ST
47-50 ST/
ROCKEFELLER
CENTER
51 ST
49 ST
5
4
42 ST/GRAND
CENTRAL
6
42 ST/TIMES SQ
42 ST/8 AVE
S 7
42 ST/
6 AVE

CONTINUED ON MAP 17

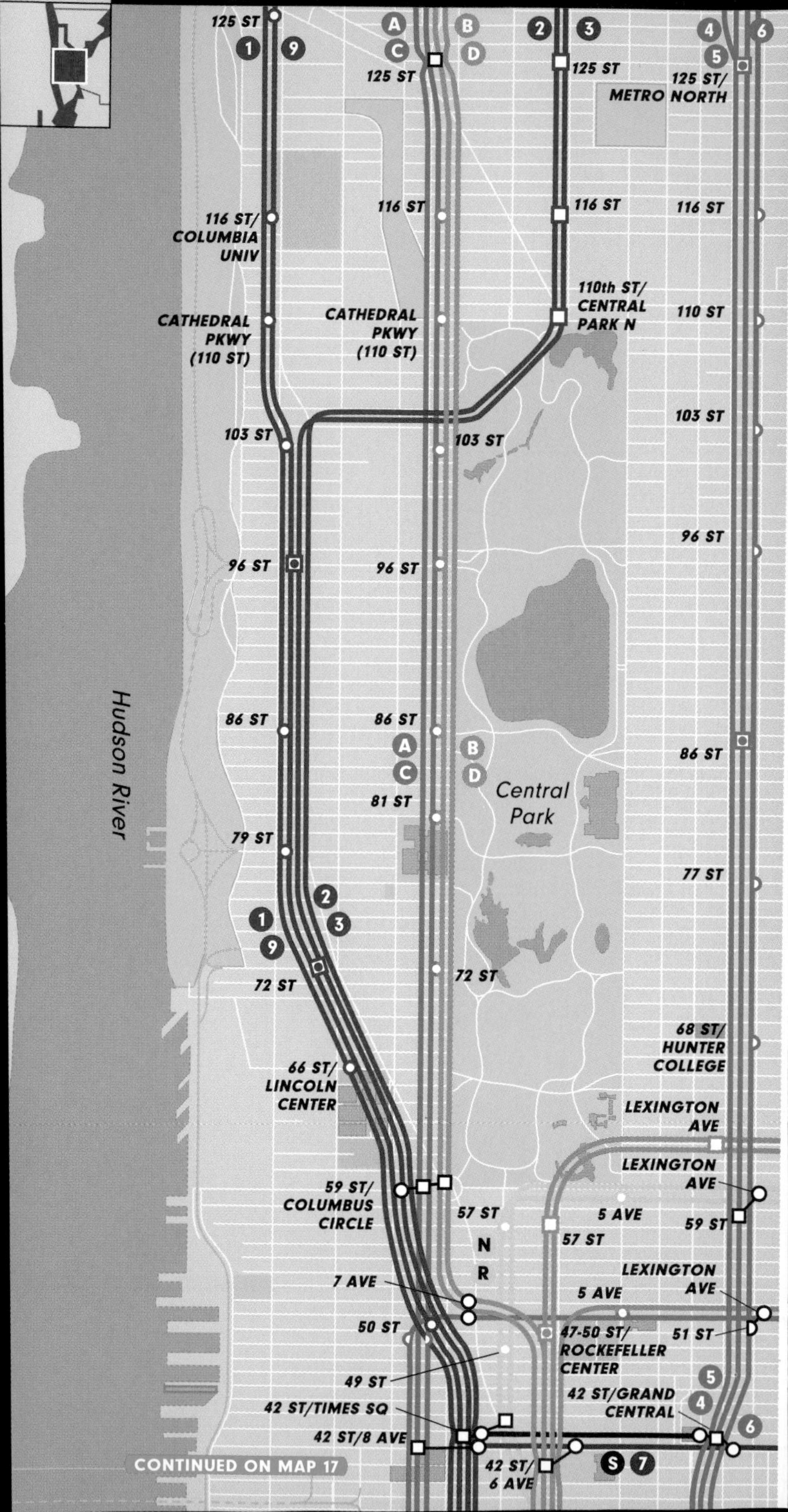

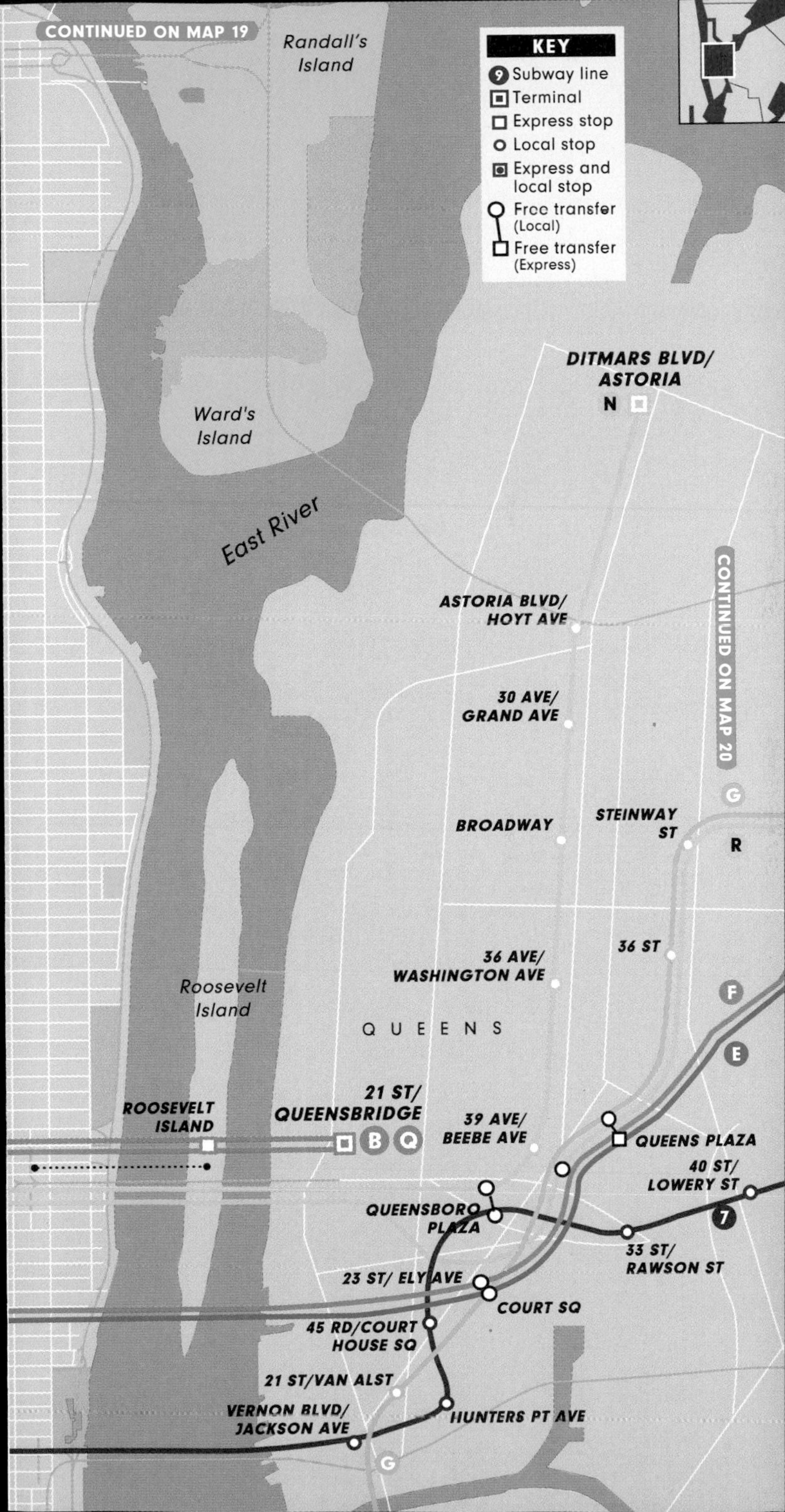

CONTINUED ON MAP 19

Randall's Island

KEY
9 Subway line
Terminal
Express stop
Local stop
Express and local stop
Free transfer (Local)
Free transfer (Express)

Ward's Island

East River

DITMARS BLVD/ ASTORIA
N

ASTORIA BLVD/ HOYT AVE

30 AVE/ GRAND AVE

CONTINUED ON MAP 20

BROADWAY

STEINWAY ST

G

R

36 ST

36 AVE/ WASHINGTON AVE

Roosevelt Island

QUEENS

F

E

21 ST/ QUEENSBRIDGE B Q

ROOSEVELT ISLAND

39 AVE/ BEEBE AVE

QUEENS PLAZA

40 ST/ LOWERY ST

QUEENSBORO PLAZA

7

33 ST/ RAWSON ST

23 ST/ ELY AVE

COURT SQ

45 RD/COURT HOUSE SQ

21 ST/VAN ALST

VERNON BLVD/ JACKSON AVE

HUNTERS PT AVE

G

Subways/Bronx & Northern Manhattan

WESTCHESTER
Van Cortlandt Park
Hudson River
Harlem River
NEW JERSEY
WOODLAWN
242 ST/ VAN CORTLANDT PARK
MOSHOLU PKWY
BEDFORD PARK BLVD/ LEHMAN COLLEGE
238 ST
231 ST
BEDFORD PARK BLVD
225 ST/ METRO NORTH (MARBLE HILL)
KINGSBRIDGE RD
KINGSBRIDGE RD
215 ST
207 ST/ INWOOD
FORDHAM RD
FORDHAM RD
207 ST
183 ST
182-183 ST
200 ST/ DYCKMAN ST
DYCKMAN ST
BURNSIDE AVE
TREMONT AVE
190 ST
191 ST
176 ST
181 ST
181 ST
174-175 ST
MT EDEN AVE
175 ST
170 ST
170 ST
168 ST/ BROADWAY
163 ST/ AMSTERDAM AVE
167 ST
167 ST
157 ST
161 ST/YANKEE STADIUM
155 ST
155 ST
148 ST/ LENOX TERMINAL
149 ST/ GRAND CONCOURSE
145 ST
145 ST
145 ST
138 ST/ GRAND CONCOURSE
138 ST/ 3 AVE
137 ST/ CITY COLLEGE
135 ST
135 ST
125 ST
125 ST
125 ST
125 ST/ METRO NORTH
KEY
Subway line
Terminal
Express stop
Local stop
Express and local stop
Free transfer (Local)
Free transfer (Express)
N
0 1 mile
0 1 km

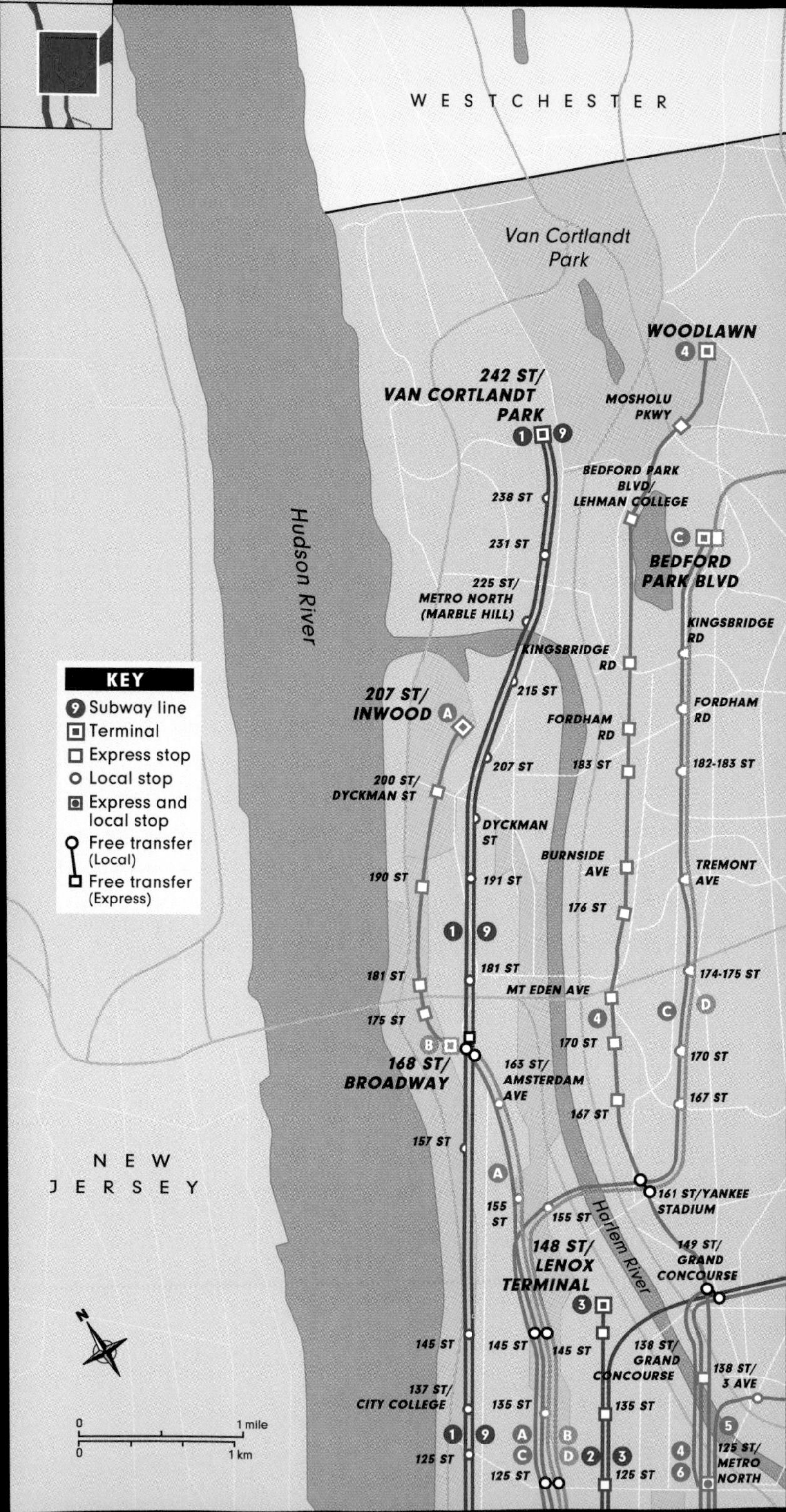

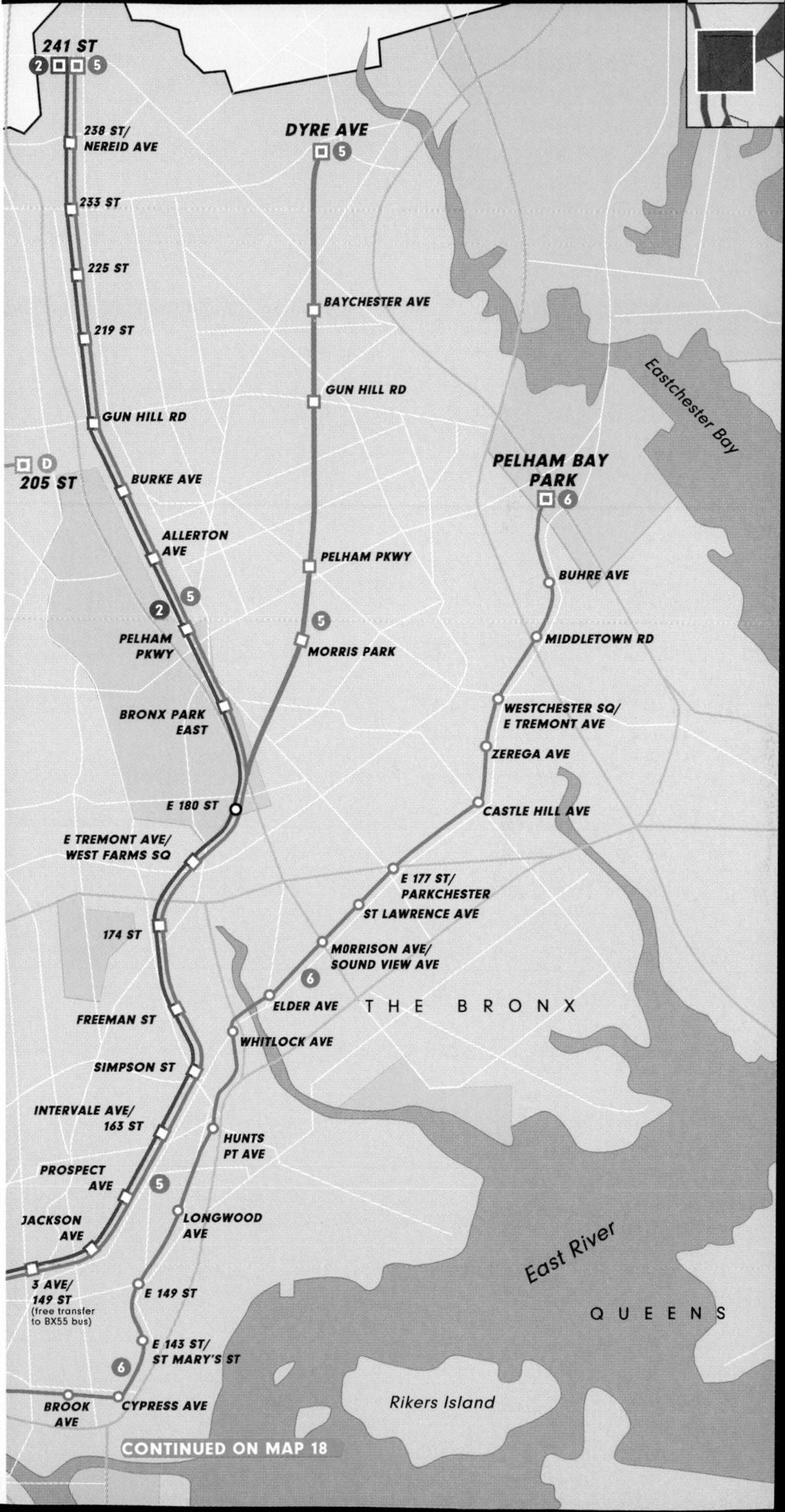

241 ST
2 5
238 ST/ NEREID AVE
233 ST
225 ST
219 ST
GUN HILL RD
205 ST
D
BURKE AVE
ALLERTON AVE
2 5
PELHAM PKWY
BRONX PARK EAST
E 180 ST
E TREMONT AVE/ WEST FARMS SQ
174 ST
FREEMAN ST
SIMPSON ST
INTERVALE AVE/ 163 ST
PROSPECT AVE
5
JACKSON AVE
3 AVE/ 149 ST
(free transfer to BX55 bus)
DYRE AVE
5
BAYCHESTER AVE
GUN HILL RD
PELHAM PKWY
5
MORRIS PARK
Eastchester Bay
PELHAM BAY PARK
6
BUHRE AVE
MIDDLETOWN RD
WESTCHESTER SQ/ E TREMONT AVE
ZEREGA AVE
CASTLE HILL AVE
E 177 ST/ PARKCHESTER
ST LAWRENCE AVE
MORRISON AVE/ SOUND VIEW AVE
6
ELDER AVE
THE BRONX
WHITLOCK AVE
HUNTS PT AVE
LONGWOOD AVE
E 149 ST
E 143 ST/ ST MARY'S ST
6
BROOK AVE
CYPRESS AVE
East River
QUEENS
Rikers Island

CONTINUED ON MAP 18

MAP 20 Subways/Queens & Northeast Brooklyn

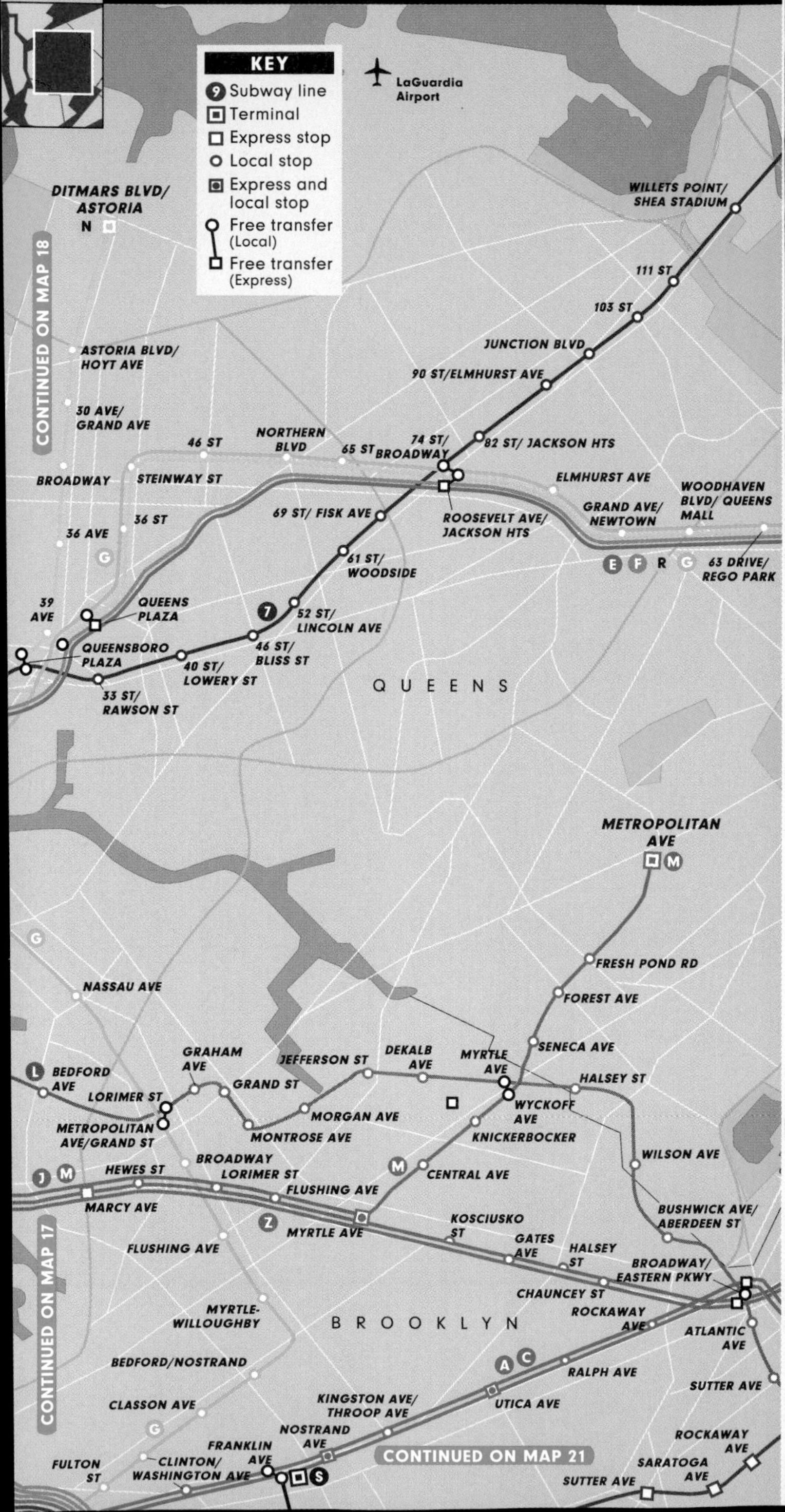

KEY

- 9 Subway line
- Terminal
- Express stop
- Local stop
- Express and local stop
- Free transfer (Local)
- Free transfer (Express)

LaGuardia Airport

DITMARS BLVD/ ASTORIA
N
ASTORIA BLVD/ HOYT AVE
30 AVE/ GRAND AVE
BROADWAY
36 AVE
G
39 AVE
46 ST
STEINWAY ST
36 ST
NORTHERN BLVD
65 ST
74 ST/ BROADWAY
82 ST/ JACKSON HTS
90 ST/ELMHURST AVE
JUNCTION BLVD
103 ST
111 ST
WILLETS POINT/ SHEA STADIUM
ELMHURST AVE
ROOSEVELT AVE/ JACKSON HTS
GRAND AVE/ NEWTOWN
WOODHAVEN BLVD/ QUEENS MALL
63 DRIVE/ REGO PARK
E F R G
69 ST/ FISK AVE
61 ST/ WOODSIDE
52 ST/ LINCOLN AVE
7
46 ST/ BLISS ST
40 ST/ LOWERY ST
33 ST/ RAWSON ST
QUEENS PLAZA
QUEENSBORO PLAZA

QUEENS

METROPOLITAN AVE
M
FRESH POND RD
FOREST AVE
SENECA AVE
G
NASSAU AVE
L
BEDFORD AVE
LORIMER ST
METROPOLITAN AVE/GRAND ST
GRAHAM AVE
GRAND ST
JEFFERSON ST
DEKALB AVE
MYRTLE AVE
MORGAN AVE
MONTROSE AVE
WYCKOFF AVE
HALSEY ST
KNICKERBOCKER
M
CENTRAL AVE
WILSON AVE
J M
HEWES ST
BROADWAY
LORIMER ST
FLUSHING AVE
MARCY AVE
Z
MYRTLE AVE
KOSCIUSKO ST
GATES AVE
HALSEY ST
BUSHWICK AVE/ ABERDEEN ST
BROADWAY/ EASTERN PKWY
CHAUNCEY ST
FLUSHING AVE
MYRTLE-WILLOUGHBY

BROOKLYN

ROCKAWAY AVE
ATLANTIC AVE
A C
RALPH AVE
SUTTER AVE
BEDFORD/NOSTRAND
CLASSON AVE
KINGSTON AVE/ THROOP AVE
UTICA AVE
G
NOSTRAND AVE
FRANKLIN AVE
S
CLINTON/ WASHINGTON AVE
FULTON ST
ROCKAWAY AVE
SARATOGA AVE
SUTTER AVE

CONTINUED ON MAP 18

CONTINUED ON MAP 17

CONTINUED ON MAP 21

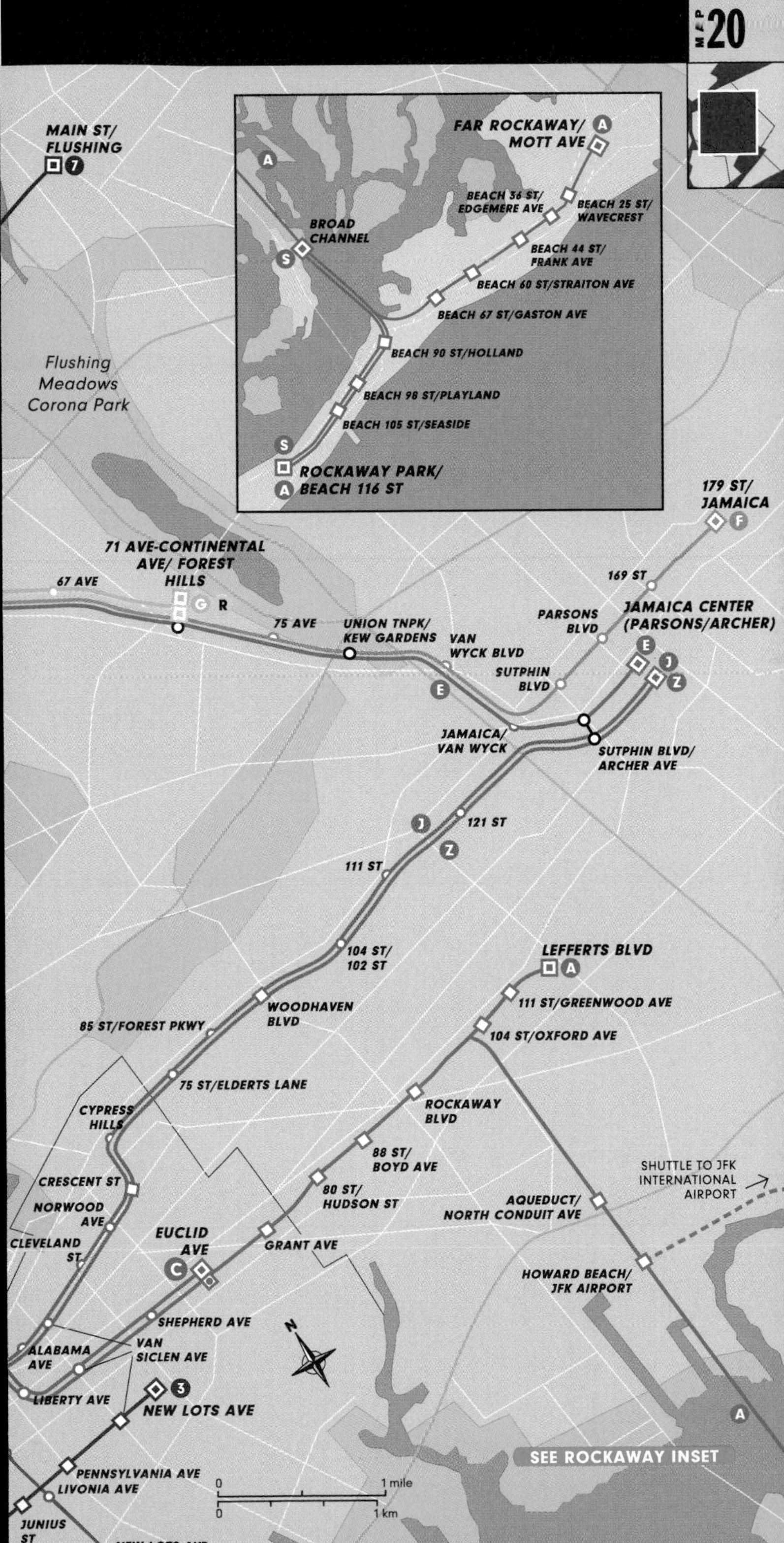
FAR ROCKAWAY/ MOTT AVE
BEACH 36 ST/ EDGEMERE AVE
BEACH 25 ST/ WAVECREST
BROAD CHANNEL
BEACH 44 ST/ FRANK AVE
BEACH 60 ST/STRAITON AVE
BEACH 67 ST/GASTON AVE
BEACH 90 ST/HOLLAND
BEACH 98 ST/PLAYLAND
BEACH 105 ST/SEASIDE
ROCKAWAY PARK/ BEACH 116 ST
MAIN ST/ FLUSHING
Flushing Meadows Corona Park
179 ST/ JAMAICA
71 AVE-CONTINENTAL AVE/ FOREST HILLS
67 AVE
169 ST
PARSONS BLVD
JAMAICA CENTER (PARSONS/ARCHER)
75 AVE
UNION TNPK/ KEW GARDENS
VAN WYCK BLVD
SUTPHIN BLVD
JAMAICA/ VAN WYCK
SUTPHIN BLVD/ ARCHER AVE
121 ST
111 ST
104 ST/ 102 ST
LEFFERTS BLVD
111 ST/GREENWOOD AVE
WOODHAVEN BLVD
85 ST/FOREST PKWY
104 ST/OXFORD AVE
75 ST/ELDERTS LANE
ROCKAWAY BLVD
CYPRESS HILLS
88 ST/ BOYD AVE
CRESCENT ST
80 ST/ HUDSON ST
SHUTTLE TO JFK INTERNATIONAL AIRPORT
AQUEDUCT/ NORTH CONDUIT AVE
NORWOOD AVE
EUCLID AVE
CLEVELAND ST
GRANT AVE
HOWARD BEACH/ JFK AIRPORT
SHEPHERD AVE
ALABAMA AVE
VAN SICLEN AVE
LIBERTY AVE
NEW LOTS AVE
SEE ROCKAWAY INSET
PENNSYLVANIA AVE
LIVONIA AVE
JUNIUS ST
NEW LOTS AVE
0 1 mile
0 1 km

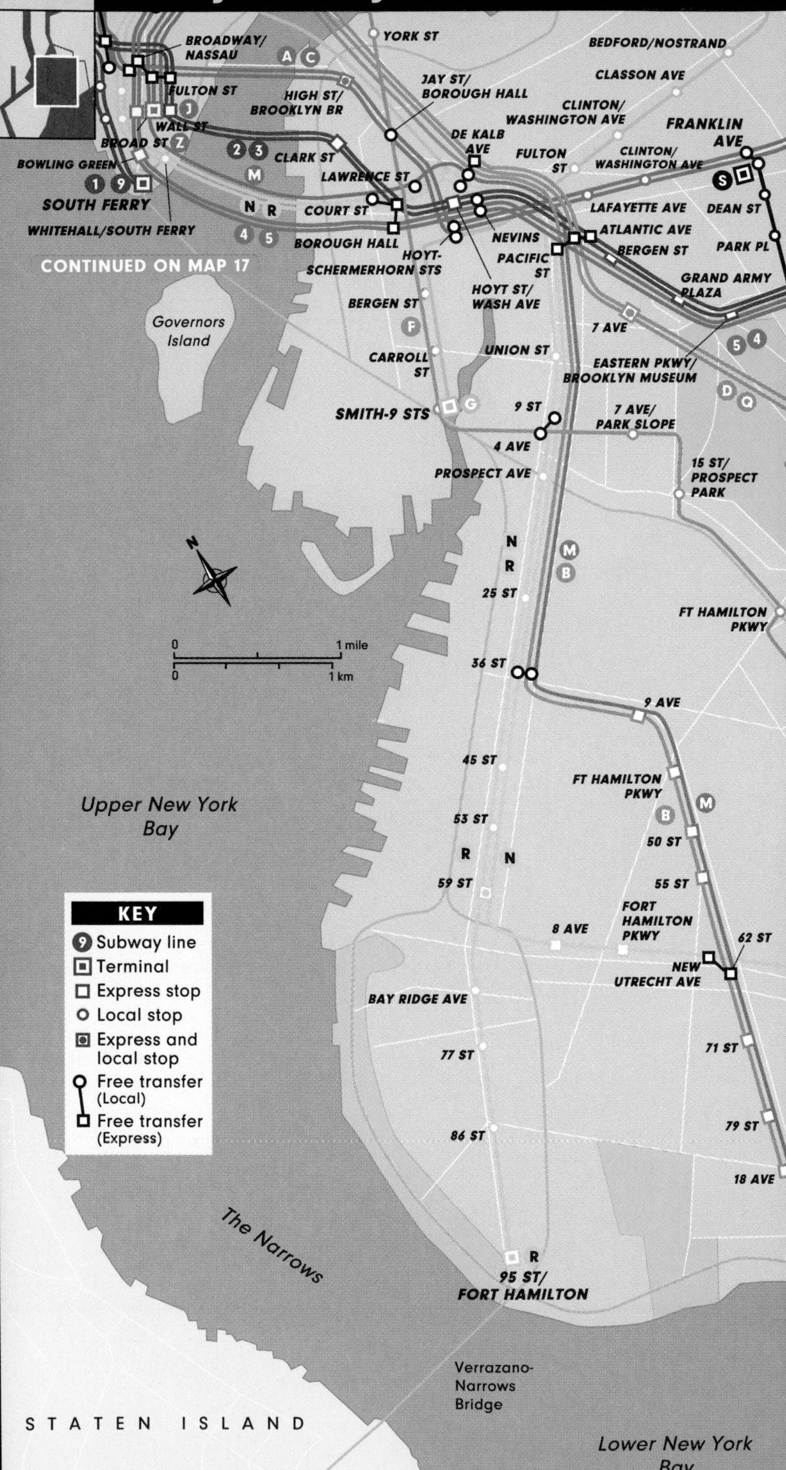
BROADWAY/ NASSAU
FULTON ST
WALL ST
BROAD ST
BOWLING GREEN
SOUTH FERRY
WHITEHALL/SOUTH FERRY
CONTINUED ON MAP 17
YORK ST
HIGH ST/ BROOKLYN BR
JAY ST/ BOROUGH HALL
CLARK ST
LAWRENCE ST
COURT ST
BOROUGH HALL
DE KALB AVE
HOYT-SCHERMERHORN STS
HOYT ST/ WASH AVE
NEVINS
PACIFIC ST
ATLANTIC AVE
BERGEN ST
FULTON ST
LAFAYETTE AVE
CLINTON/ WASHINGTON AVE
BEDFORD/NOSTRAND
CLASSON AVE
FRANKLIN AVE
DEAN ST
PARK PL
GRAND ARMY PLAZA
7 AVE
EASTERN PKWY/ BROOKLYN MUSEUM
UNION ST
BERGEN ST
CARROLL ST
SMITH-9 STS
9 ST
4 AVE
7 AVE/ PARK SLOPE
PROSPECT AVE
15 ST/ PROSPECT PARK
Governors Island
25 ST
FT HAMILTON PKWY
0 1 mile
0 1 km
36 ST
9 AVE
45 ST
FT HAMILTON PKWY
50 ST
53 ST
55 ST
59 ST
Upper New York Bay
8 AVE
FORT HAMILTON PKWY
62 ST
NEW UTRECHT AVE
BAY RIDGE AVE
71 ST
77 ST
79 ST
86 ST
18 AVE
95 ST/ FORT HAMILTON
The Narrows
Verrazano-Narrows Bridge
STATEN ISLAND
Lower New York Bay
KEY
Subway line
Terminal
Express stop
Local stop
Express and local stop
Free transfer (Local)
Free transfer (Express)

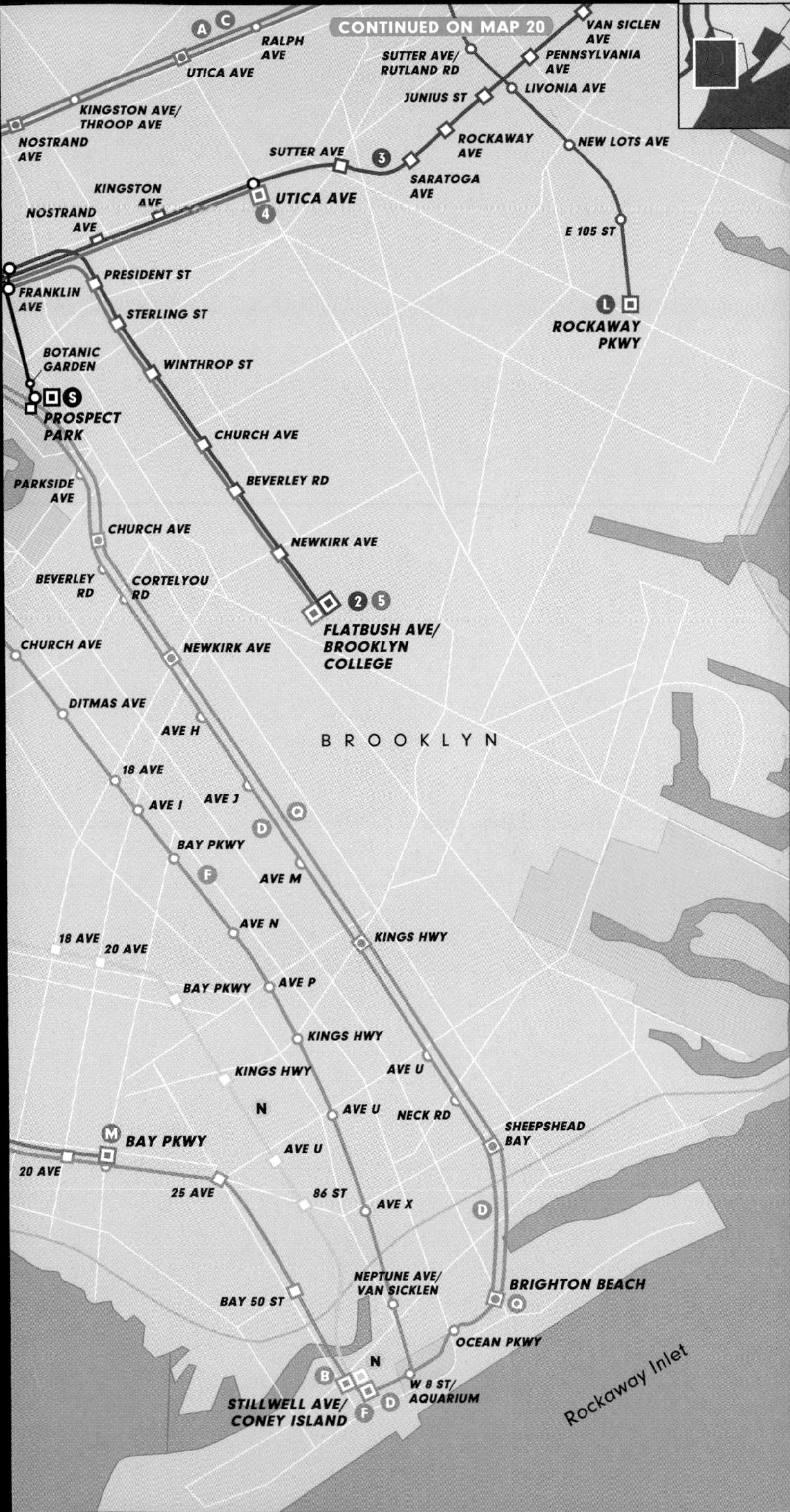

CONTINUED ON MAP 20

A C
RALPH AVE
UTICA AVE
KINGSTON AVE/ THROOP AVE
NOSTRAND AVE
SUTTER AVE/ RUTLAND RD
VAN SICLEN AVE
PENNSYLVANIA AVE
LIVONIA AVE
JUNIUS ST
ROCKAWAY AVE
NEW LOTS AVE
SUTTER AVE
3
SARATOGA AVE
KINGSTON AVE
UTICA AVE
4
NOSTRAND AVE
E 105 ST
PRESIDENT ST
FRANKLIN AVE
L
ROCKAWAY PKWY
STERLING ST
BOTANIC GARDEN
WINTHROP ST
S
PROSPECT PARK
CHURCH AVE
PARKSIDE AVE
BEVERLEY RD
CHURCH AVE
NEWKIRK AVE
BEVERLEY RD
CORTELYOU RD
2 5
FLATBUSH AVE/ BROOKLYN COLLEGE
CHURCH AVE
NEWKIRK AVE
DITMAS AVE
AVE H
BROOKLYN
18 AVE
AVE I
AVE J
Q
D
BAY PKWY
F
AVE M
AVE N
KINGS HWY
18 AVE
20 AVE
BAY PKWY
AVE P
KINGS HWY
AVE U
KINGS HWY
N
AVE U
NECK RD
SHEEPSHEAD BAY
M
BAY PKWY
AVE U
20 AVE
25 AVE
86 ST
AVE X
D
NEPTUNE AVE/ VAN SICKLEN
BRIGHTON BEACH
BAY 50 ST
Q
OCEAN PKWY
N
B
W 8 ST/ AQUARIUM
STILLWELL AVE/ CONEY ISLAND
F D
Rockaway Inlet

Driving/Uptown Entrances & Exits

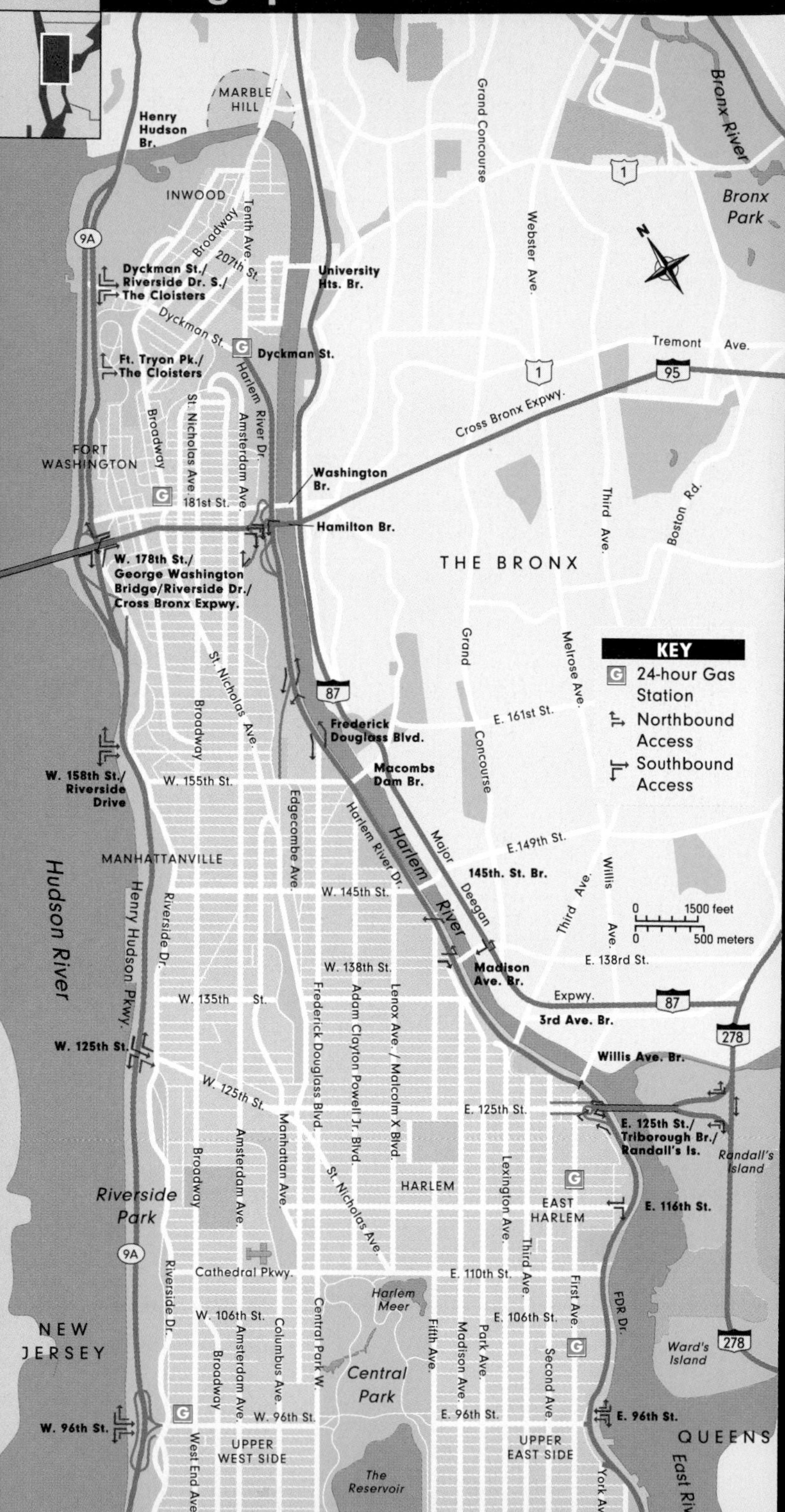

KEY
24-hour Gas Station
Northbound Access
Southbound Access
NOTE: West Side south of Chambers St. access on every street
1500 feet
500 meters
MIDTOWN
DOWNTOWN
UPPER WEST SIDE
UPPER EAST SIDE
Central Park
The Reservoir
The Lake
The Pond
THEATER DISTRICT
TURTLE BAY
MURRAY HILL
CHELSEA
GRAMERCY
WEST VILLAGE
GREENWICH VILLAGE
EAST VILLAGE
NOHO
LOWER EAST SIDE
SOHO
LITTLE ITALY
TRIBECA
CHINATOWN
Civic Center
FINANCIAL DISTRICT
SOUTH STREET SEAPORT
BATTERY PARK CITY
Battery Park
Hudson River
East River
NEW JERSEY
HOBOKEN
JERSEY CITY
Roosevelt Island
LONG ISLAND CITY
QUEENS
GREENPOINT
BROOKLYN
BROOKLYN HEIGHTS
Queensboro Bridge
Queens-Midtown Tunnel
Lincoln Tunnel
Holland Tunnel
Williamsburg Bridge
Manhattan Bridge
Brooklyn Bridge
Brooklyn-Battery Tunnel
Brooklyn-Queens Expwy.
Flatbush Ave.
Vernon Blvd.
W. 79th St. Boat Basin
W. 72nd St.
W. 57th St.
W. 56th St.
W. 55th St.
W. 54th St.
W. 52nd St.
W. 51st St.
W. 50th St.
W. 49th St.
W. 48th St.
W. 47th St.
W. 46th St.
W. 45th St.
W. 44th St.
W. 43rd St.
W.42nd St.
W. 41st St.
W. 39 St./Javits Center
W.34th St.
W. 30th St.
W.29th St.
W. 26th St.
W. 23rd St.
W. 18th St.
W. 14th St.
W. 12th St.
W.12th St.
W.11th St.
Christopher St.
Clarkson St.
W. Houston St.
Canal St.
Laight St.
Chambers St.
Barclay St.
Vesey St.
Liberty St.
Morris St.
Whitehall
State St.
E. 92nd St.
E. 79th St.
E. 73rd St.
E. 72nd St.
E. 71st St.
E. 63rd St.
E. 61st St.
E. 53rd St.
E. 48th St.
E. 47th St.
E. 42nd St.
E. 37th St.
E. 34th St.
E. 25th St.
E. 23rd St.
E. 20th St.
E. 14th St.
Ave. C
E. Houston St.
Delancey St.
Grand St.
Cherry St.
Montgomery St.
W. 96th St.
W. 92nd St.
W. 86th St.
W. 79th St.
W. 72nd St.
W. 57th St.
W.50th St.
W. 34th St.
W. 23rd St.
W. 14th St.
E. 96th St.
E. 92nd St.
E. 86th St.
E. 79th St.
E. 65th St.
Central Park S.
E. 59th St.
E. 57th St.
E. 34th St.
E. 14th St.
Houston St.
Canal St.
Riverside Dr.
West End Ave.
Amsterdam Ave.
Broadway
Columbus Ave.
Central Park W.
Fifth Ave.
Madison Ave.
Park Ave.
Lexington Ave.
Third Ave.
Second Ave.
First Ave.
York Ave.
FDR Dr.
West Side Hwy.
Tenth Ave.
Ninth Ave.
Eighth Ave.
Eleventh Ave.
Seventh Ave.
Ave. of the Americas (Sixth Ave.)
Park Ave. S.
Greenwich Ave.
Fourth Ave.
Ave. A
Ave. B
Ave. D
Bowery
Varick St.
9A
495
278

Driving/Midtown Manhattan

E. 65th St.
E. 64th St.
E. 63rd St.
E. 62nd St.
E. 61st St.
E. 60th St.
E. 59th St.
E. 58th St.
E. 57th St.
E. 56th St.
E. 55th St.
E. 54th St.
E. 53rd St.
E. 52nd St.
E. 51st St.
E. 50th St.
E. 49th St.
E. 48th St.
E. 47th St.
E. 46th St.
E. 45th St.
E. 44th St.
E. 43rd St.
E. 42nd St.
E. 41st St.
E. 40th St.
E. 39th St.
E. 38th St.
E. 37th St.
E. 36th St.
E. 35th St.
E. 34th St.
E. 33rd St.
E. 32nd St.
E. 31st St.
E. 30th St.
E. 29th St.
E. 28th St.
E. 27th St.
E. 26th St.
E. 25th St.
E. 24th St.
E . 23rd St.
E. 22nd St.
Lexington Ave.
Third Ave.
Fifth Ave.
Madison Ave.
Park Ave.
Second Ave.
First Ave.
Sutton Place South
Ave. of the Americas
(Sixth Ave.)
Vanderbilt Ave.
Park Ave. South
Broadway
Rockefeller Plaza
Beekman Pl.
Mitchell Pl.
Macarthur Plaza
United Nations Plaza
Tudor City Pl.
Tunnel Exit
Tunnel Entrance
FDR Drive
East River
Wollman Rink
The Pond
Central Park Wildlife Conservation Center
Grand Army Plaza
Plaza Hotel
TRAMWAY TO ROOSEVELT ISLAND
Queensboro Bridge
Sutton Square
Radio City Music Hall
St. Patrick's Cathedral
Rockefeller Center
United Nations Headquarters
Grand Central Terminal
Chrysler Building
Queens-Midtown Tunnel
Bryant Park
N.Y. Public Library (Main)
Pierpont Morgan Library
Herald Square
Empire State Building
Kips Bay Plaza
NYU Medical Center
Bellevue Hospital
Madison Square Park
Flatiron Building
B,Q
N,R
4,5,6, N,R
E,F
6
B,D,F, Q
B,D, F,Q
S
4,5,6,7
B,D,F, N,Q,R
F,Q

Buses/Manhattan below 14th Street

CONTINUED ON MAP 26

W.16th St.
W.15th St.
W.14th St.
Eighth Ave.
Seventh Ave. South
Ave. of the Americas
Greenwich St.
West Side Hwy.
GREENWICH VILLAGE
W. 10th St.
Christopher St.
(Sixth Ave.)
W. Houston St.
Varick St.
Hudson St.
West St.
Canal St.
TRIBECA
Holland Tunnel
Hudson River
N. Moore St.
Harrison St.
Chambers St.
W.Broadway
Vesey St.
W. Thames
NEW JERSEY

KEY
Northbound
Southbound
Eastbound
Westbound
101 Route number
20 Terminal

CONTINUED ON MAP 26

Union Square
E. 14th St.
EAST VILLAGE
5th Ave.
University Pl.
Fourth Ave.
Third Ave.
E. 10th St.
E. 9th St.
St. Mark's Pl.
Tompkins Square
E. 8th St.
East 8th St.
Washington Square
Lafayette St.
Second Ave.
First Ave.
E. 4th St.
Ave. A
Ave. B
Ave. C
Ave. D
FDR Dr.
E. Houston St.
W. Houston St.
LOWER EAST SIDE
SOHO
Spring St.
Broome St.
Grand St.
Bowery
Allen St.
Essex St.
Clinton St.
Delancey St.
Williamsburg Bridge
Grand St.
LITTLE ITALY
Jackson St.
Cherry St.
E. Broadway
Madison St.
Canal St.
CHINA-TOWN
Broadway
Church St.
Worth St.
Pearl St.
FDR Dr.
Manhattan Bridge
East River
South St.
Barclay St.
Frankfort St.
Brooklyn Bridge
Pearl St.
Broadway
Water St.
BROOKLYN
FINANCIAL DISTRICT
Whitehall St.
Battery Pl.
Brooklyn-Battery Tunnel
N
0 1500 feet
0 500 meters

Buses/Manhattan 14th St–72nd St

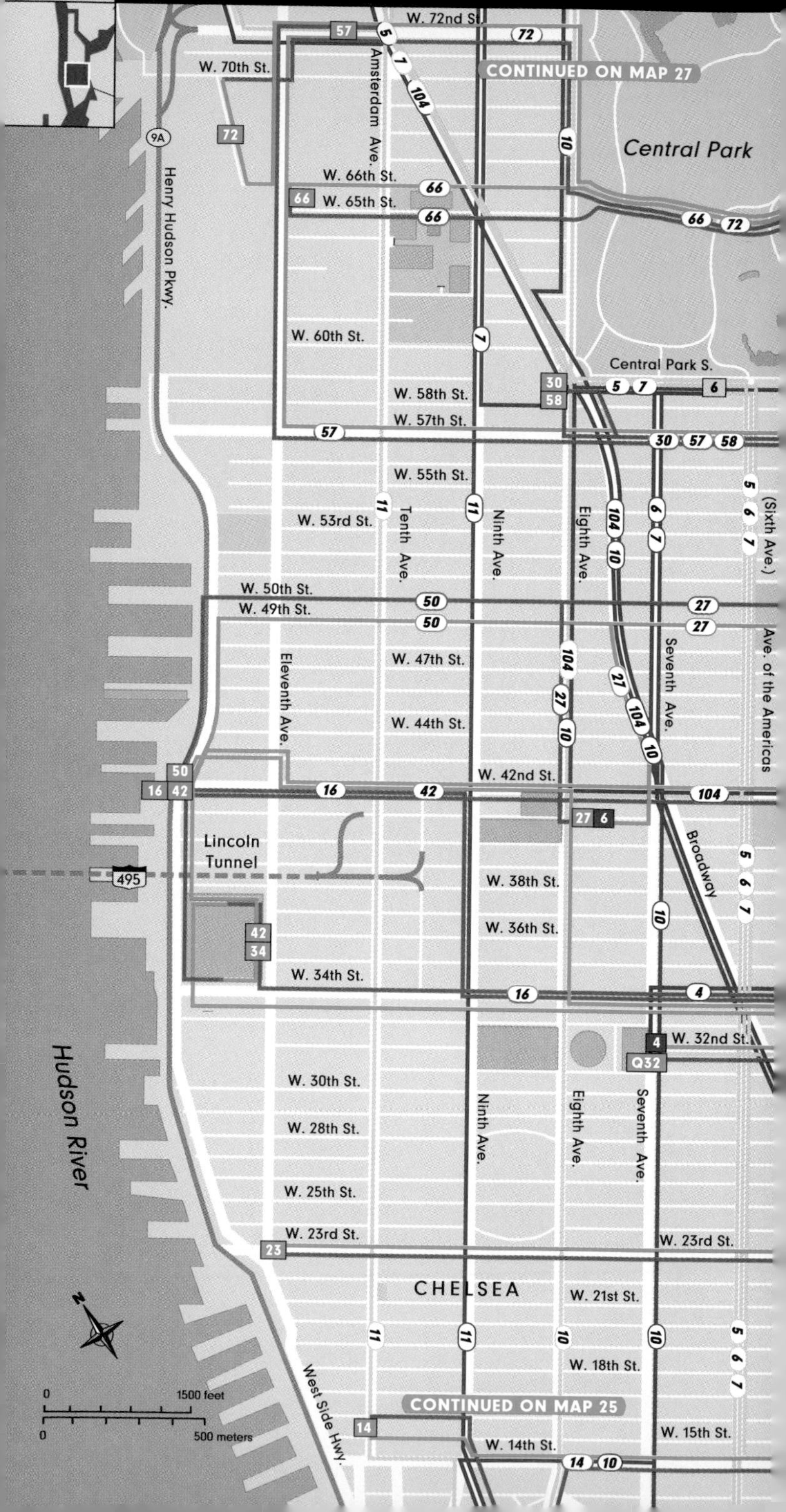

W. 72nd St.
57
5
7
104
72
W. 70th St.
CONTINUED ON MAP 27
Amsterdam Ave.
9A
72
10
Central Park
Henry Hudson Pkwy.
W. 66th St.
66
W. 65th St.
66
66
66
72
W. 60th St.
7
Central Park S.
30
58
5
7
6
W. 58th St.
W. 57th St.
57
30
57
58
W. 55th St.
11
11
104
10
6
7
5
6
7
(Sixth Ave.)
W. 53rd St.
Tenth Ave.
Ninth Ave.
Eighth Ave.
W. 50th St.
W. 49th St.
50
50
27
27
Eleventh Ave.
W. 47th St.
104
27
10
27
104
10
Seventh Ave.
Ave. of the Americas
W. 44th St.
W. 42nd St.
50
16
42
16
42
104
27
6
Lincoln Tunnel
495
Broadway
5
6
7
W. 38th St.
W. 36th St.
10
42
34
W. 34th St.
16
4
4
W. 32nd St.
Q32
Hudson River
W. 30th St.
W. 28th St.
Ninth Ave.
Eighth Ave.
Seventh Ave.
W. 25th St.
W. 23rd St.
23
W. 23rd St.
CHELSEA
W. 21st St.
11
11
10
10
5
6
7
W. 18th St.
West Side Hwy.
0
1500 feet
0
500 meters
CONTINUED ON MAP 25
14
W. 15th St.
W. 14th St.
14
10

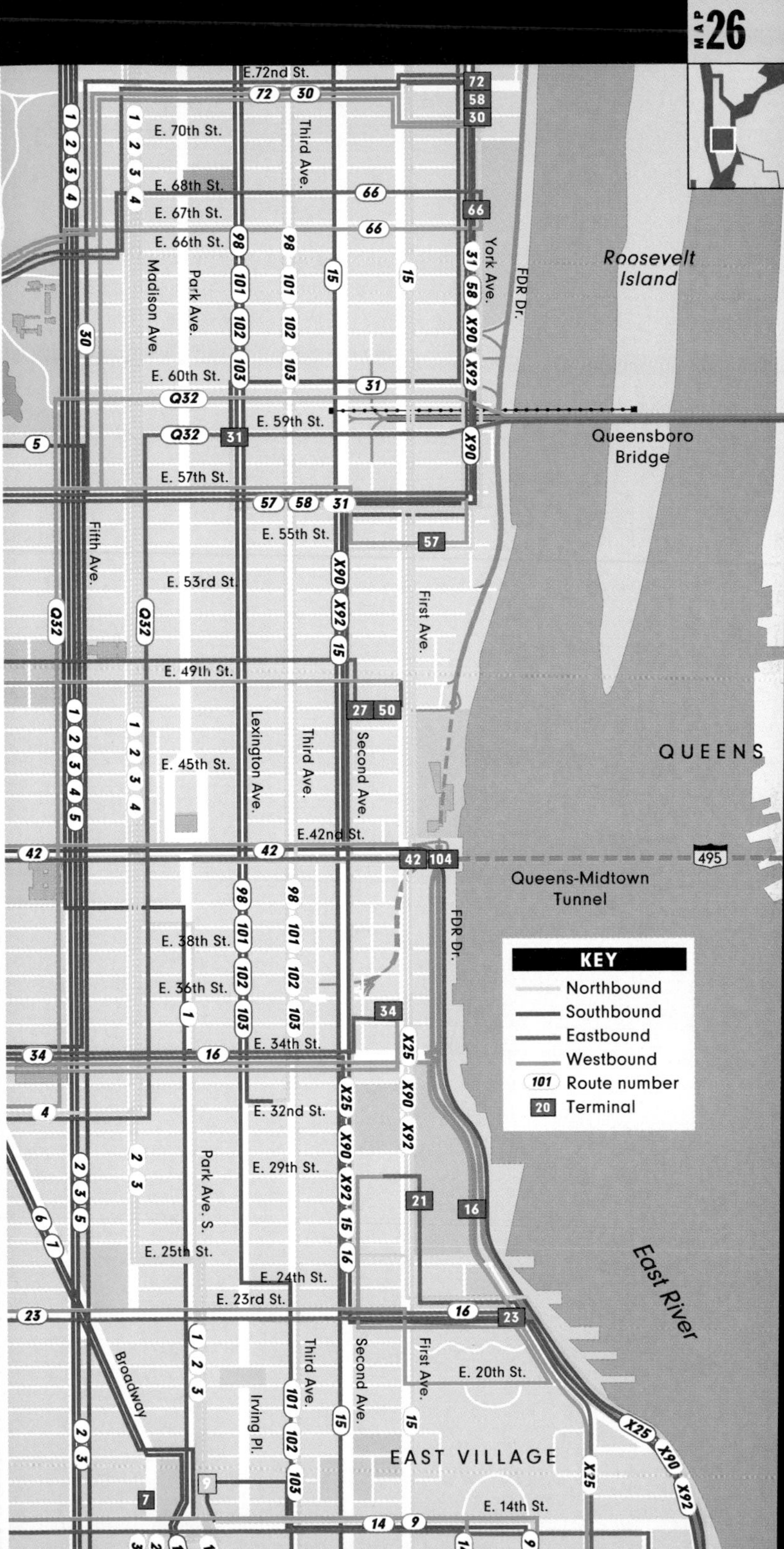
E.72nd St.
E. 70th St.
E. 68th St.
E. 67th St.
E. 66th St.
E. 60th St.
E. 59th St.
E. 57th St.
E. 55th St.
E. 53rd St.
E. 49th St.
E. 45th St.
E.42nd St.
E. 38th St.
E. 36th St.
E. 34th St.
E. 32nd St.
E. 29th St.
E. 25th St.
E. 24th St.
E. 23rd St.
E. 20th St.
E. 14th St.
Third Ave.
Madison Ave.
Park Ave.
York Ave.
FDR Dr.
Fifth Ave.
First Ave.
Lexington Ave.
Second Ave.
Park Ave. S.
Broadway
Irving Pl.
Roosevelt Island
Queensboro Bridge
QUEENS
Queens-Midtown Tunnel
495
East River
EAST VILLAGE
KEY
Northbound
Southbound
Eastbound
Westbound
101 Route number
20 Terminal

Buses/Manhattan 72nd St–125th St

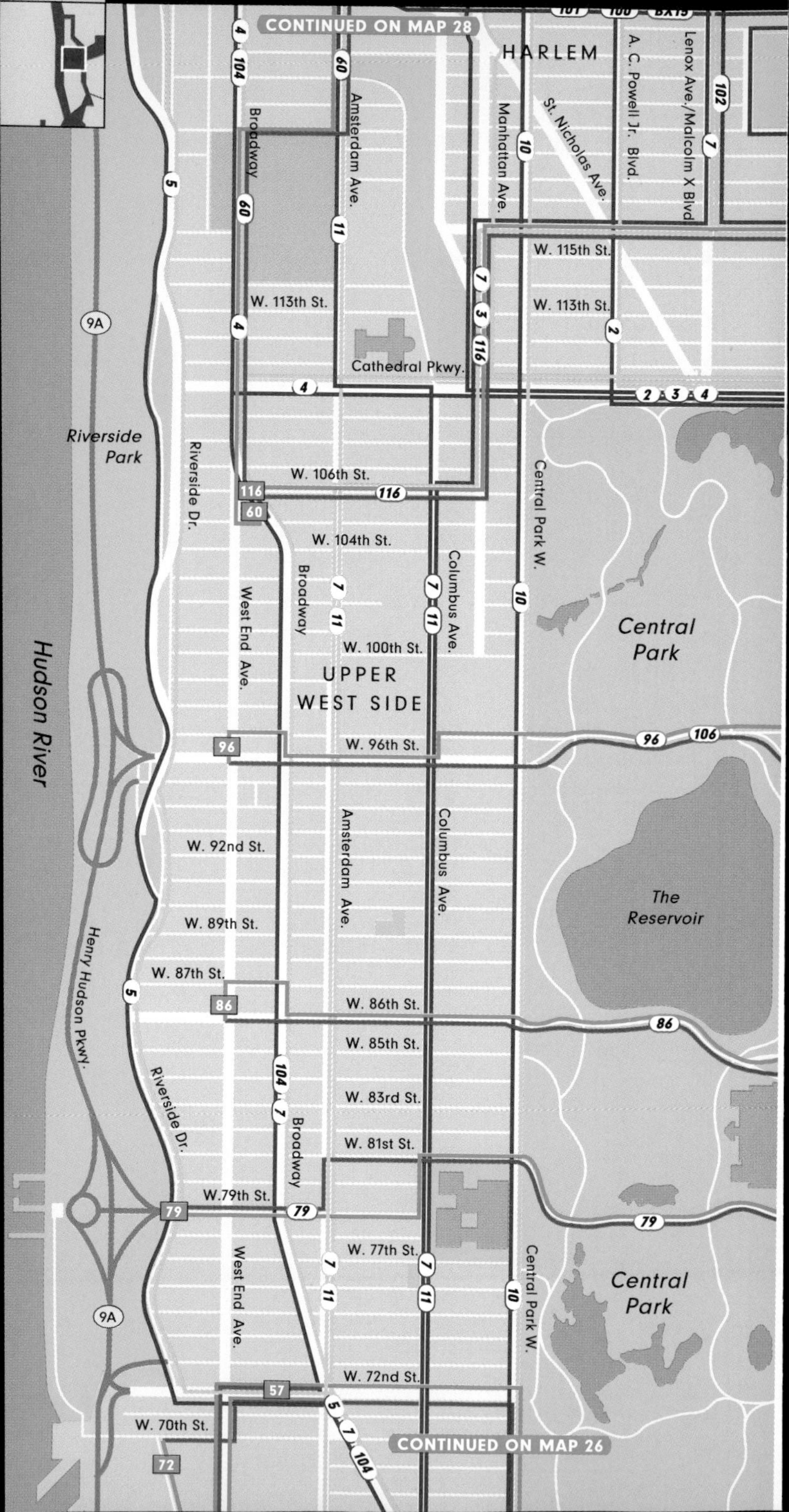

CONTINUED ON MAP 26

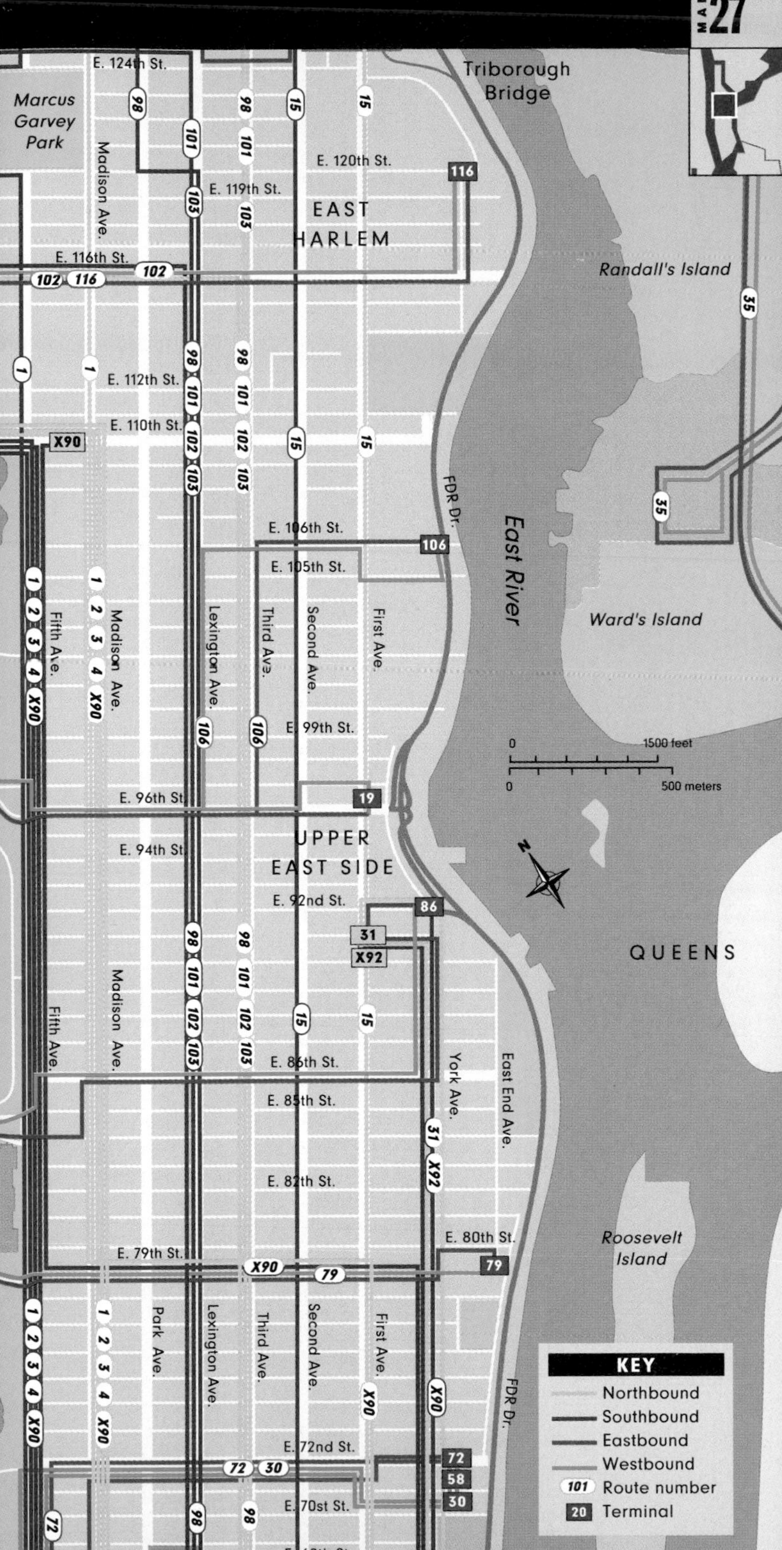

Triborough Bridge
Marcus Garvey Park
EAST HARLEM
Randall's Island
East River
Ward's Island
UPPER EAST SIDE
QUEENS
Roosevelt Island
E. 124th St.
E. 120th St.
E. 119th St.
E. 116th St.
E. 112th St.
E. 110th St.
E. 106th St.
E. 105th St.
E. 99th St.
E. 96th St.
E. 94th St.
E. 92nd St.
E. 86th St.
E. 85th St.
E. 82th St.
E. 80th St.
E. 79th St.
E. 72nd St.
E. 70st St.
E. 68th St.
Madison Ave.
Fifth Ave.
Park Ave.
Lexington Ave.
Third Ave.
Second Ave.
First Ave.
York Ave.
East End Ave.
FDR Dr.
0 1500 feet
0 500 meters
KEY
Northbound
Southbound
Eastbound
Westbound
101 Route number
20 Terminal

MAP 28 Buses/Manhattan above 125th Street

CONTINUED ON MAP 27

Listed by Site Number

1 The Cloisters
2 Grant's Tomb
3 Columbia Univ
4 St John the Divine
5 Guggenheim
6 Metropolitan Museum of Art
7 Hayden Planetarium
8 American Museum of Natural History
9 Whitney Museum
10 The Frick Collection
11 Bethesda Terrace
12 The Dakota
13 Lincoln Center
14 Central Park Wildlife Conservation Center
15 Grand Army Plaza
16 Trump Tower
17 Carnegie Hall
18 Museum of Modern Art (MOMA)
19 Radio City
20 Rockefeller Center
21 St Patrick's
22 Times Square
23 Grand Central
24 Chrysler Bldg
25 NY Public Library
26 United Nations
27 Madison Sq Garden
28 Empire State Bldg
29 Flatiron Bldg
30 Gramercy Park
31 Union Square
32 Grace Church
33 Washington Square
34 St Mark's Place
35 SoHo Art Galleries
36 Chinatown
37 City Hall
38 Woolworth Bldg
39 World Trade Center
40 St Paul's Chapel
41 Battery Park City
42 Trinity Church
43 Staten Island Ferry
44 Statue of Liberty
45 Ellis Island
46 South Street Seaport
47 NY Stock Exchange
48 Fraunces Tavern
49 Brooklyn Bridge

MAP 30 Architecture

Listed by Site Number

1 Bartow-Pell Mansion
2 Van Cortlandt House
3 The Cloisters
4 Morris Jumel Mansion
5 St John the Divine
6 Guggenheim
7 Henderson Place Historic District
8 Metropolitan Museum of Art
9 Whitney Museum
10 Belvedere Castle
11 The Dakota
12 Lincoln Center
13 The Plaza Hotel
14 Carnegie Hall
15 Daily News Building
16 Lever House
17 Seagram Building
18 Rockefeller Center
19 International Building
20 Villard Houses
21 MetLife Building
22 Grand Central
23 Chrysler Building
24 UN Headquarters
25 NY Public Library
26 Morgan Library
27 Javits Center
28 Empire State Building
29 NY Life Ins Bldg
30 Flatiron Building
31 Nat'l Arts Club
32 Washington Mews
33 Colonnade Row
34 Old Merchant's House
35 Haughwout Building
36 Bayard Building
37 Singer Building
38 Municipal Building
39 Brooklyn Bridge
40 City Hall
41 Woolworth Building
42 World Trade Center
43 Fed Hall Nat'l Mem
44 Citibank Building
45 NY Stock Exchange
46 Fraunces Tavern

Listed Alphabetically

Bartow-Pell Mansion, 1. 895 Shore Rd N, Pelham Bay Park, Bronx

Bayard Building, 36. 65-69 Bleecker St

Belvedere Castle, 10. Vista Rock, at the base of Central Park's Great Lawn

Brooklyn Bridge, 39. City Hall Park to Parkes Cadman Plaza, over East River

Carnegie Hall, 14. 881 Seventh Ave

Chrysler Building, 23. Lexington Ave & 42nd St

City Hall/City Hall Park, 40. Broadway, south of Chambers St

Citibank Building, 44. 55 Wall St

The Cloisters, 3. Fort Tryon Park

Colonnade Row, 33. Lafayette St, between E 4th St & Astor Pl

Daily News Building, 15. 220 E 42nd St

The Dakota, 11. W 72nd St & Central Park West

Empire State Building, 28. Fifth Ave & 34th St

Federal Hall National Memorial, 43. 28 Wall St

Flatiron Building, 30. Fifth Ave & 23rd St

Fraunces Tavern, 46. Broad & Pearl Sts

Grand Central Terminal, 22. Park Ave, between 42nd & 44th Sts

Guggenheim Museum, 6. 1071 Fifth Ave

Haughwout Building, 35. 488 Broadway

Henderson Place Historic District, 7. York Ave & 86th St

International Building, 19. 5th Ave between 50th & 51st Sts

Jacob K Javits Convention Center, 27. 11th Ave & 35th St

Lever House, 16. 390 Park Ave

Lincoln Center, 12. Broadway between 62nd & 66th Sts

Met Life Building, 21. 200 Park Ave

Metropolitan Museum of Art, 8. Fifth Ave & 82nd St

Morris Jumel Mansion, 4. 160th St & Jumel Ter

Municipal Building, 38. Centre & Chambers Sts

National Arts Club, 31. 15 Gramercy Park S

New York Life Insurance Building, 29. Madison Ave & 26th St

New York Public Library, 25. Fifth Ave, between 40th & 42nd Sts

New York Stock Exchange, 45. 20 Broad St

Old Merchant's House, 34. 29 E 4th St

Pierpont Morgan Library, 26. 29 E 36th St

The Plaza Hotel, 13. Fifth Ave & 59th St

Rockefeller Center, 18. Fifth Ave & 50th St

St. John the Divine, 5. Amsterdam Ave & 112th St

Seagram Building, 17. 375 Park Ave

Singer Building, 37. 561 Broadway

UN Headquarters, 24. First Ave, between 42nd & 48th Sts

Van Cortlandt House, 2. Broadway & 246th St, Bronx

Villard Houses, 20. Madison Ave & 50th St

Washington Mews, 32. between Fifth Ave & Univ Pl

Whitney Museum, 9. 945 Madison Ave

Woolworth Building, 41. Park Pl & Broadway

World Trade Ctr, 42. West & Vesey Sts

MAP 31 Churches & Temples

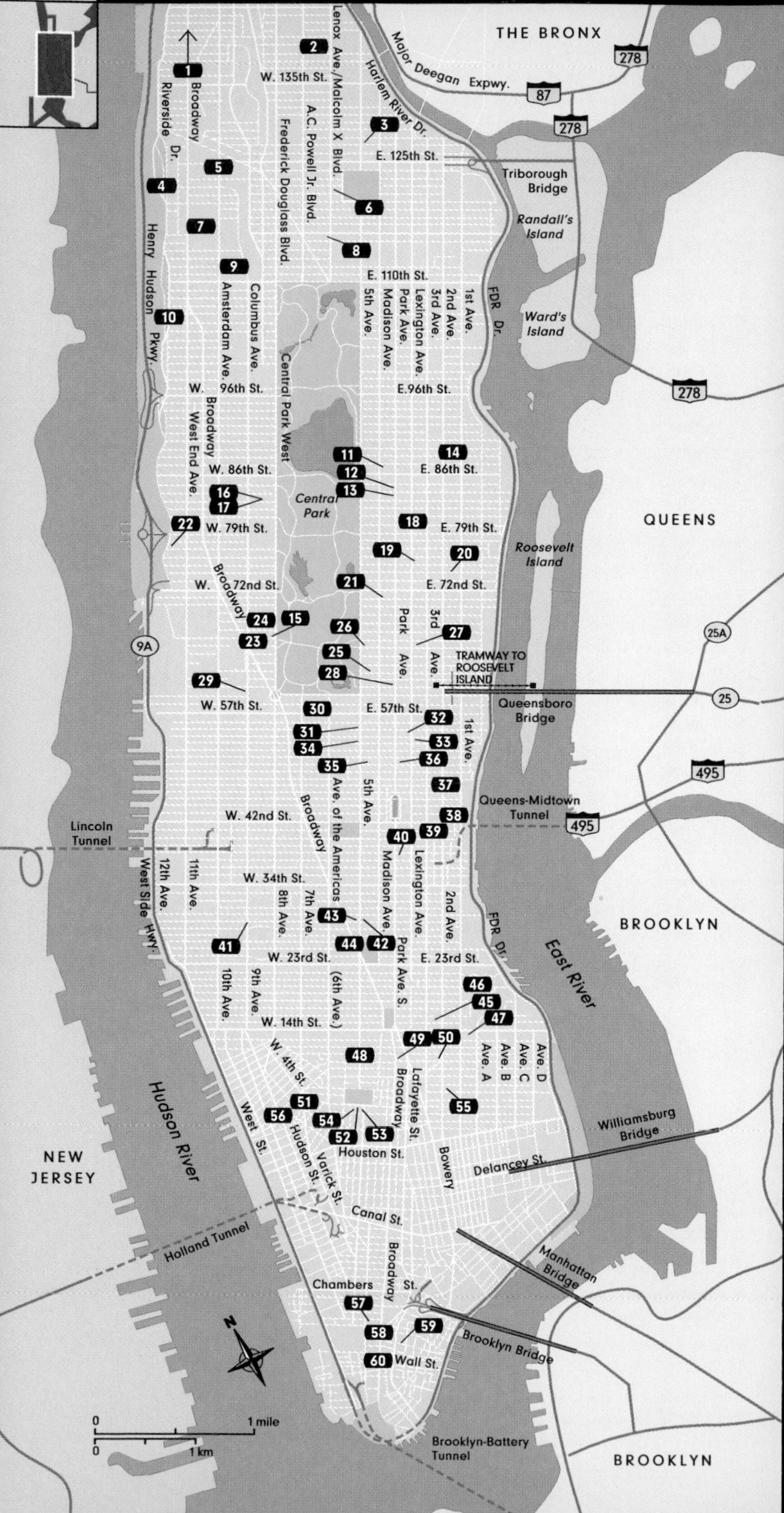

Listed by Site Number

1 Church of the Intercessions
2 Abyssinian Baptist
3 St Andrew's
4 Riverside
5 James Chapel
6 St Martin's Episcopal
7 St Paul's Chapel
8 Masjid Malcolm Shabazz
9 Cathedral of St John the Divine
10 NY Buddhist Church
11 Park Ave Synagogue
12 Park Ave Christian
13 St Ignatius Loyola
14 Church of the Holy Trinity
15 Holy Trinity
16 St Matthew & St Timothy
17 Congregation Rodeph Sholom
18 All Souls Unitarian
19 Church of St Jean Baptiste
20 Holy Trinity Cathedral
21 St James
22 West End Collegiate
23 Church of Latter Day Saints
24 Stephen Wise Free Synagogue
25 Fifth Ave Synagogue
26 Temple Emanu-El
27 St Vincent Ferrer
28 Christ Church
29 St Paul the Apostle
30 Calvary Baptist
31 Fifth Ave Presbyterian
32 Central Synagogue
33 St Peter's
34 St Thomas
35 St Patrick's Cathedral
36 St Bartholomew's
37 Holy Family
38 Church of the UN
39 Church of the Covenant
40 Church of Our Savior
41 Holy Apostles
42 Little Church Around the Corner
43 Marble Collegiate
44 Cathedral of St Sava
45 Friends Meeting House
46 Calvary/St George
47 Immaculate Conception
48 Church of the Ascension
49 Grace Church
50 St Mark's in the Bowery
51 St John's Evangelical Lutheran
52 Washington Square Church
53 Holy Trinity Chapel
54 Judson Memorial
55 Middle Collegiate
56 Church of St Luke's
57 St Peter's
58 St Paul's Chapel
59 John Street United Methodist
60 Trinity

Listed Alphabetically

Abyssinian Baptist, 2. 132 W 138th St ☎ 862-7474

All Souls Unitarian, 18. 1157 Lexington Ave ☎ 535-5530

Calvary Baptist, 30. 123 W 57th St ☎ 975-0170

Calvary/St George, 46. 209 E 16th St ☎ 475-0830. Episcopal

Cathedral of St John the Divine, 9. Amsterdam Ave & 112th St ☎ 316-7400. Episcopal

Cathedral of St Sava, 44. 15 W 25th St ☎ 242-9417. Serbian Orthodox

Central Synagogue, 32. 652 Lexington Ave ☎ 838-5122. Jewish

Christ Church, 28. 520 Park Ave ☎ 838-3036. Methodist

Church of the Ascension, 48. 12 W 11th St ☎ 254-8620. Episcopal

Church of the Covenant, 39. 310 E 42nd St ☎ 697-3185. Presbyterian

Church of the Holy Trinity, 14. 316 E 88th St ☎ 289-4100. Episcopal

Church of the Intercessions, 1. B'way & 155th St ☎ 283-6200. Episcopal

Church of Latter Day Saints, 23. 125 Columbus Ave ☎ 580-1919. Mormon

Church of Our Savior, 40. 59 Park Ave ☎ 679-8166. Roman Catholic

Church of St Jean Baptiste, 19. 184 E 76th St ☎ 288-5082. Roman Catholic

Church of St Luke's, 56. 487 Hudson St ☎ 924-0562. Episcopal

Church of the UN, 38. 777 UN Plaza ☎ 661-1762. Inter-Denominational

Congregation Rodeph Sholom, 17. 7 W 83rd ☎ 362-8800. Jewish

Churches & Temples

Listed Alphabetically (cont.)

Fifth Ave Presbyterian, 31. Fifth Ave & 55th St ☎ 247-0490

Fifth Ave Synagogue, 25. 5 E 62nd St ☎ 838-2122. Jewish

Friends Meeting House, 45. 15 Rutherford Pl ☎ 777-8866. Quaker

Grace Church, 49. 802 Broadway ☎ 254-2000. Episcopal

Holy Apostles, 41. 296 Ninth Ave ☎ 807-6799. Episcopal

Holy Family, 37. 315 E 47th St ☎ 753-3401. Roman Catholic

Holy Trinity, 15. Central Park W & 65th St ☎ 877-6815. Lutheran

Holy Trinity Cathedral, 20. 319 E 74th St ☎ 288-3215. Greek Orthodox

Holy Trinity Chapel, 53. 58 Washington Sq S ☎ 674-7236. Roman Catholic

Immaculate Conception, 47. 414 E 14th St ☎ 254-0200. Roman Catholic

James Chapel, 5. 3041 Broadway ☎ 280-1522. Inter-Denominational

John Street United Methodist, 59. 44 John St ☎ 269-0014

Judson Memorial, 54. 55 Washington Sq ☎ 477-0351. Baptist

Little Church Around the Corner, 42. 1 E 29th St ☎ 684-6770. Episcopal

Marble Collegiate, 43. Fifth Ave & 29th St ☎ 686-2770. Dutch Protestant

Masjid Malcolm Shabazz, 8. 102 W 116 St ☎ 662-2200. Muslim

Middle Collegiate, 55. Second Ave & 7th St ☎ 477-0666. Lutheran

NY Buddhist Temple, 10. 332 Riverside Dr ☎ 678-0305

Park Ave Christian, 12. 1010 Park Ave ☎ 288-3246

Park Ave Synagogue, 11. 50 E 87th St ☎ 369-2600. Jewish

Riverside, 4. Riverside Dr & 122nd ☎ 870-6700. Inter-Denominational

St Andrew's, 3. Fifth Ave & 127th St ☎ 534-0896. Episcopal

St Bartholomew's, 36. 109 E 50th St ☎ 751-1616. Episcopal

St Ignatius Loyola, 13. 980 Park Ave ☎ 288-3588. Roman Catholic

St James, 21. 865 Madison Ave ☎ 288-4100. Episcopal

St John's Evangelical Lutheran, 51. 81 Christopher St ☎ 242-5737

St Mark's-in-the-Bowery, 50. Second Ave & 10th St ☎ 674-6377. Episcopal

St Martin's Episcopal, 6. 230 Lenox Ave ☎ 534-4531

St Matthew & St Timothy, 16. 26 W 84th St ☎ 362-6750. Episcopal

St Patrick's Cathedral, 35. Fifth Ave & 50th St ☎ 753-2261. Roman Catholic

St Paul the Apostle, 29. 415 W 59th St ☎ 265-3209. Roman Catholic

St Paul's Chapel, 58. Broadway & Fulton St ☎ 602-0874. Episcopal

St Paul's Chapel, 7. Columbia Univ, Broadway & 117th St ☎ 854-6625. Roman Catholic

St Peter's, 57. 16 Barclay St ☎ 233-8355. Roman Catholic

St Peter's, 33. 619 Lexington Ave ☎ 935-2200. Lutheran

St Thomas, 34. 1 W 53rd St ☎ 757-7013. Episcopal

St Vincent Ferrer, 27. Lexington Ave & 66th St ☎ 744-2080. Roman Catholic

Stephen Wise Free Synagogue, 24. 30 W 68th St ☎ 877-4050. Jewish

Temple Emanu-El, 26. 1 E 65th St ☎ 744-1400. Jewish

Trinity, 60. 74 Trinity Pl ☎ 602-0800. Episcopal

Washington Square Church, 52. 135 W 4th St ☎ 777-2528. Roman Catholic

West End Collegiate, 22. 368 West End Ave ☎ 787-1566. Reformed Church in America

Listed by Site Number

1. International Center of Photography
2. Jewish Museum
3. Cooper-Hewitt/The Smithsonian
4. National Academy of Design
5. Guggenheim
6. Children's Museum of Manhattan
7. Metropolitan Museum of Art
8. American Museum of Natural History
9. NY Historical Society
10. Whitney Museum of American Art
11. Frick Collection
12. Asia Society Gallery
13. The Americas Society
14. Museum of American Folk Art
15. China Institute Gallery
16. Abigail Adams Smith Museum
17. Sony Wonder Technology Lab
18. Museum of Modern Art (MOMA)
19. American Craft Museum
20. Museum of Television & Radio
21. Japan Society
22. International Center of Photography/ Midtown
23. Whitney Museum at Philip Morris
24. Pierpont Morgan Library

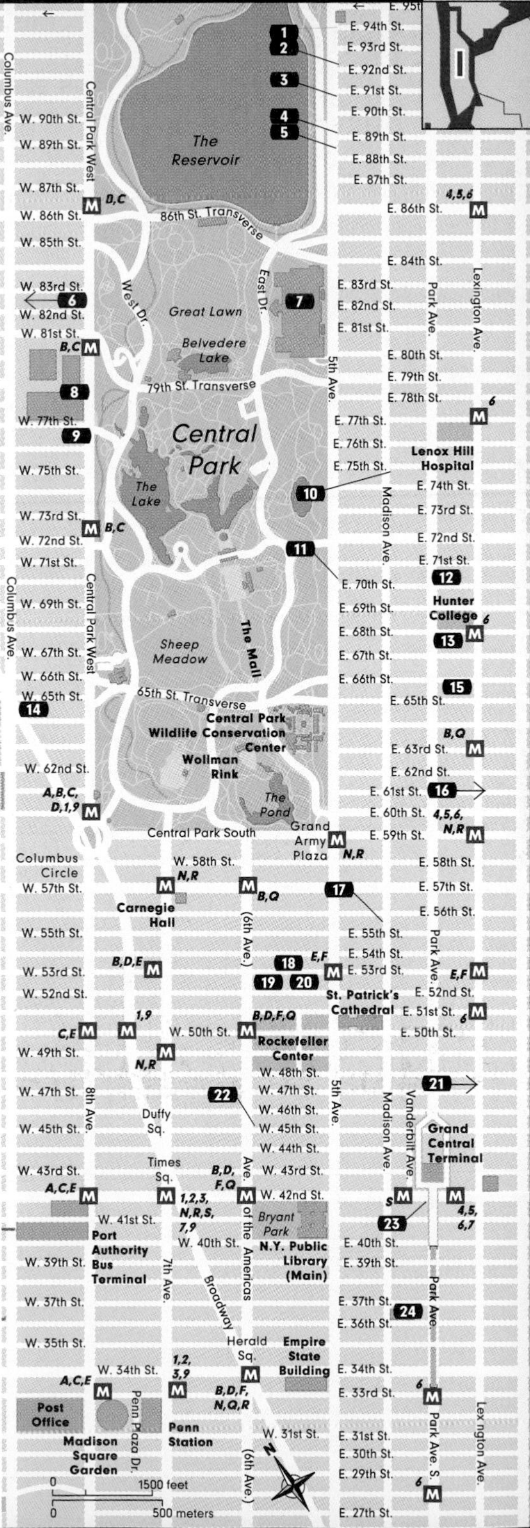

MAP 32 Museums/Elsewhere in Manhattan

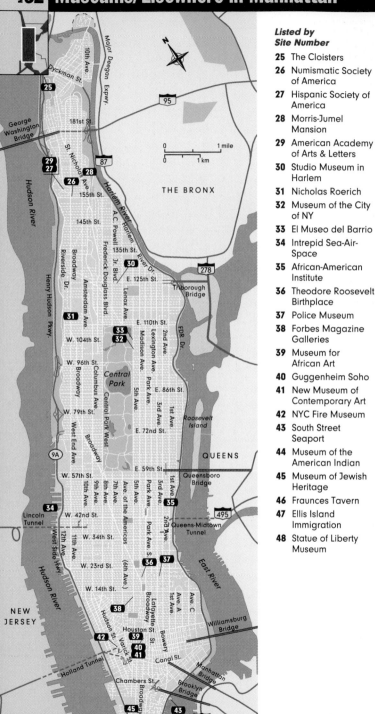

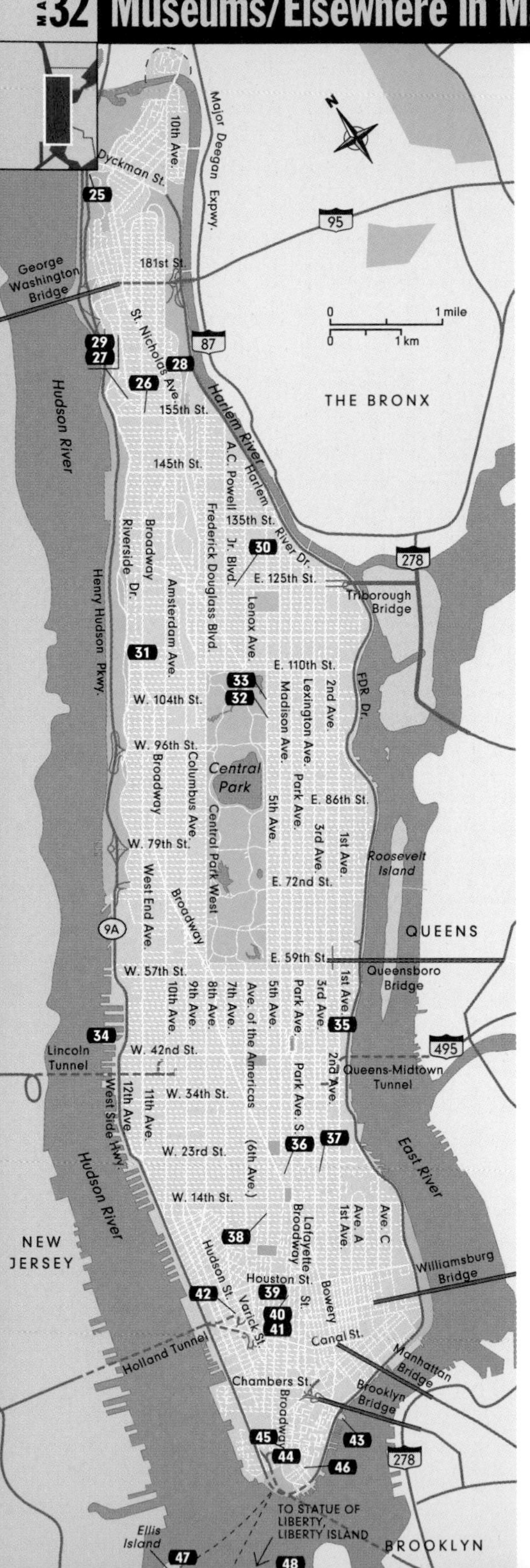

Listed by Site Number

25 The Cloisters

26 Numismatic Society of America

27 Hispanic Society of America

28 Morris-Jumel Mansion

29 American Academy of Arts & Letters

30 Studio Museum in Harlem

31 Nicholas Roerich

32 Museum of the City of NY

33 El Museo del Barrio

34 Intrepid Sea-Air-Space

35 African-American Institute

36 Theodore Roosevelt Birthplace

37 Police Museum

38 Forbes Magazine Galleries

39 Museum for African Art

40 Guggenheim Soho

41 New Museum of Contemporary Art

42 NYC Fire Museum

43 South Street Seaport

44 Museum of the American Indian

45 Museum of Jewish Heritage

46 Fraunces Tavern

47 Ellis Island Immigration

48 Statue of Liberty Museum

Listed Alphabetically

Abigail Adams Smith, 16. 421 E 61st St ☎ 838–6878

African-American Institute, 35. 833 UN Plaza ☎ 949–5666

American Academy of Arts & Letters, 29. 633 W 155th St ☎ 368–5900

American Craft, 19. 40 W 53rd St ☎ 956–6047

American Museum of Natural History, 8. Central Park W & 79th St ☎ 769–5100

The Americas Society, 13. 680 Park Ave ☎ 249–8950

Asia Society Gallery, 12. 725 Park Ave ☎ 288–6400

Children's Museum of Manhattan, 6. 212 W 83rd St ☎ 721–1234

China Institute Gallery, 15. 125 E 65th St ☎ 744–8181

The Cloisters, 25. Fort Tryon Park ☎ 923–3700

Cooper-Hewitt/The Smithsonian, 3. 2 E 91st St ☎ 860–6898

Ellis Island Immigration, 47. Ellis Island ☎ 363–7620

Forbes Magazine Galleries, 38. 62 Fifth Ave ☎ 206–5548

Fraunces Tavern, 46. 54 Pearl St ☎ 425–1778

Frick Collection, 11. 1 E 70th St ☎ 288–0700

Guggenheim, 5. 1071 Fifth Ave ☎ 423-3600

Guggenheim Soho, 40. 575 Broadway ☎ 423-3800

Hispanic Society of America, 27. 613 W 155th St ☎ 926–2234

Intrepid Sea-Air-Space, 34. Pier 86, Twelfth Ave & W 46th St ☎ 245–0072

International Center of Photography, 1. 1130 Fifth Ave ☎ 860–1777

International Center of Photography/Midtown, 22. 1133 Sixth Ave ☎ 768–4680

Japan Society, 21. 333 E 47th St ☎ 832–1155

Jewish, 2. 1109 Fifth Ave ☎ 423–3200

Metropolitan Museum of Art, 7. 1000 Fifth Ave ☎ 535–7710

Morris Jumel Mansion, 28. 1765 Jumel Ter ☎ 923–8008

El Museo Barrio, 33. 1230 Fifth Avenue ☎ 831–7272

Museum for African Art, 39. 593 Broadway ☎ 966-1313

Museum of American Folk Art, 14. 2 Lincoln Sq ☎ 595-9533

Museum of the American Indian, 44. 1 Bowling Green ☎ 668-6624

Museum of the City of NY, 32. 1220 Fifth Ave ☎ 534–1672

Museum of Jewish Heritage, 45. 18 First Place ☎ 968–1800

Museum of Modern Art (MOMA), 18. 11 W 53rd St ☎ 708–9480

Museum of Television & Radio, 20. 25 W 52nd St ☎ 621–6600

National Academy of Design, 4. 1083 Fifth Ave ☎ 369–4880

New Museum of Contemporary Art, 41. 583 Broadway ☎ 219–1222

NY Historical Society, 9. 170 Central Park W ☎ 873–3400

NYC Fire Museum, 42. 278 Spring St ☎ 691–1303

Nicholas Roerich, 31. 319 W 107th St ☎ 864–7752

Numismatic Society of America, 26. Broadway & 155th St ☎ 234–3130

Pierpont Morgan Library, 24. 29 E 36th St ☎ 685–0008

Police Museum, 37. 235 E 20th St ☎ 477–9753

Sony Wonder Technology Lab, 17. 550 Madison Ave ☎ 833-8100

South Street Seaport, 43. Pier 17, Fulton & South Sts ☎ 748-8600

Statue of Liberty Museum, 48. Liberty Island ☎ 363–3200

Studio Museum in Harlem, 30. 144 W 125th St ☎ 864–4500

Theodore Roosevelt Birthplace, 36. 28 E 20th St ☎ 260–1616

Whitney Museum at Philip Morris, 23. 120 Park Ave ☎ 878–2453

Whitney Museum of American Art, 10. 945 Madison Ave ☎ 570–3676

Art Galleries/Uptown

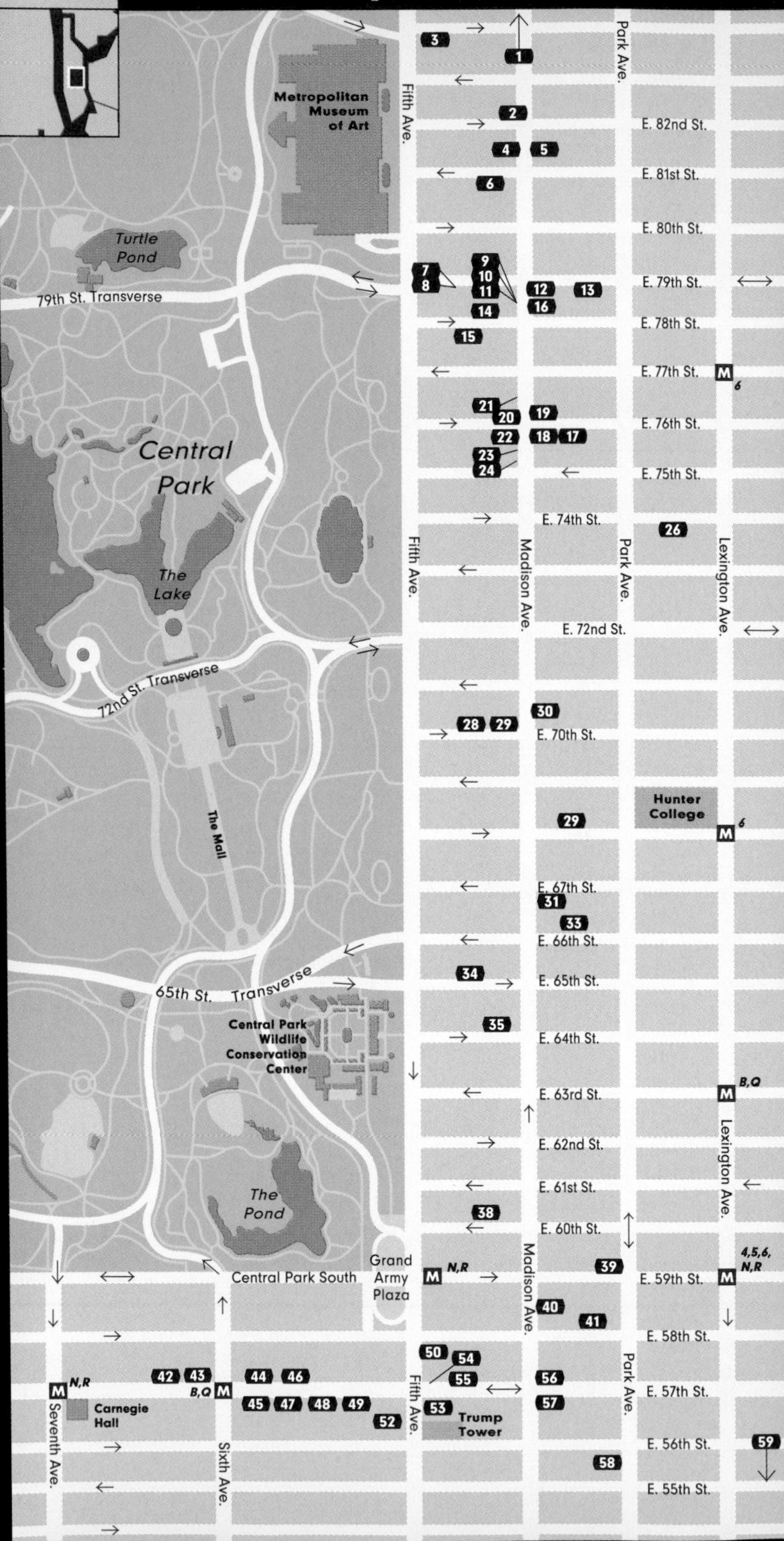

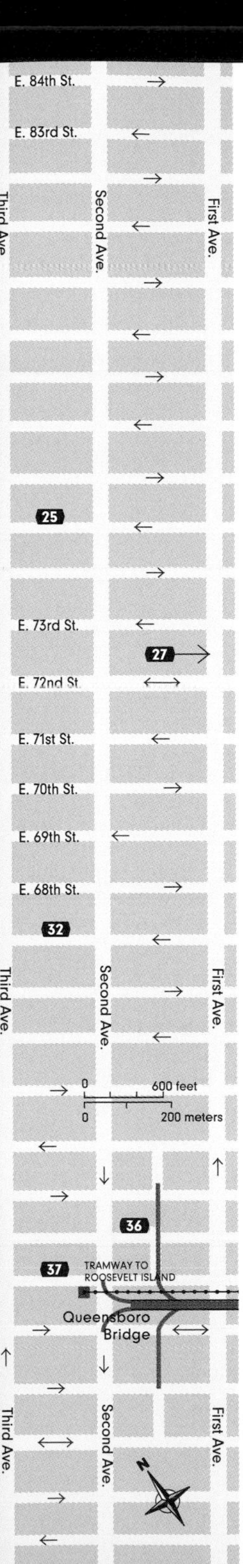

Listed by Site Number

1 The Uptown
2 Frank J. Miele
3 Schweitzer
4 Leloup
5 Raydon
6 Elkon
7 Acquavella
8 Salander-O'Reilly
9 Graham
10 Perls
11 Saidenberg
12 Terry Dintenfass
13 Soufer
14 Isselbacher
15 Ubu
16 Cordier & Ekstrom
17 Robert Mann
18 Solomon & Co
19 Davlyn
20 Safani
21 David Findlay
22 Weintraub
23 Jordan-Volpe
24 Sindin
25 Hirschl & Adler
26 Sotheby's
27 CDS
28 Knoedler
29 Richard L. Feigen
30 De Rempich
30 Kenneth Lux
31 Weinstein
32 Christie's East
33 Widing & Peck
34 Richard York
35 Wildenstein
36 Sid Deutsch
37 Davis & Langdale Co
38 Wally Findlay
39 Christie's
40 Ronin
41 Spanierman
42 Sidney Janis
43 Sylvan Cole
44 Brewster
44 Tibor de Nagy
45 Martin Sumers
45 Tatistcheff & Co
46 Hammer
47 Marlborough
48 Fischbach
48 Galerie St Etienne
48 Marion Goodman
48 Multiples
48 Reece
48 Viridian
49 Associated American Artists
49 Blum Helman
49 Franklin Parrasch
49 Washburn
50 Mary Boone
50 McKee
51 Kennedy
52 DC Moore
52 Kraushaar
53 Arras
54 Fitch & Febvrel
55 Paul Drey
56 Aberbach
56 ACA
56 André Emmerich
56 Barbara Mathes
56 David Findlay Jr
56 James Goodman
56 Jan Krugier
56 Littlejohn-Contemporary
56 Marisa Del Re
56 McCoy
56 Peter Findlay
56 Robert Miller
56 Zabriskie
57 Pace Wildenstein
57 Rosenberg & Steibel
58 Studio 53

Art Galleries/Uptown

Listed Alphabetically

Aberbach, 56. 41 E 57th St ☎ 988–1100

ACA, 56. 41 E 57th St ☎ 644–8300

Acquavella, 7. 18 E 79th St ☎ 734–6300

André Emmerich, 56. 41 E 57th St ☎ 752–0124

Arras, 53. 725 Fifth Ave ☎ 751–0080

Associated American Artists, 49. 20 W 57th St ☎ 399–5510

Barbara Mathes, 56. 41 E 57th St ☎ 752–5135

Blum Helman, 49. 20 W 57th St ☎ 245–2888

Brewster, 44. 41 W 57th St ☎ 980–1975

CDS, 27. 215 E 68th St ☎ 734-3210

Christie's, 39. 502 Park Ave ☎ 546–1000

Christie's East, 32. 219 E 67th St ☎ 606–0400

Cordier & Ekstrom, 16. 417 E 75th St ☎ 988–8857

DC Moore, 52. 724 Fifth Ave ☎ 247-2111

David Findlay, 21. 984 Madison Ave ☎ 249–2909

David Findlay Jr, 56. 41 E 57th St ☎ 486-7660

Davis & Langdale Co, 37. 231 E 60th St ☎ 838–0333

Davlyn, 19. 975 Madison Ave ☎ 879–2075

De Rempich, 30. 851 Madison Ave ☎ 772–6855

Elkon, 6. 18 E 81st St ☎ 535–3940

Fischbach, 48. 24 W 57th St ☎ 759–2345

Fitch & Febvrel, 54. 5 E 57th St ☎ 688–8522

Forum, 50. 745 Fifth Ave ☎ 355–4545

Frank J. Miele, 2. 1086 Madison Ave ☎ 249–7250

Franklin Parrasch, 49. 20 W 57th St ☎ 246-5360

Galerie St Etienne, 48. 24 W 57th St ☎ 245–6734

Graham, 9. 1014 Madison Ave ☎ 535–5767

Hammer, 46. 33 W 57th St ☎ 644–4400

Hirschl & Adler, 25. 21 E 70th St ☎ 535–8810

Isselbacher, 14. 41 E 78th St ☎ 472–1766

James Goodman, 56. 41 E 57th St ☎ 593–3737

Jan Krugier, 56. 41 E 57th St ☎ 755–7288

Jordan-Volpe, 23. 958 Madison Ave ☎ 570–9500

Kennedy, 51. 730 Fifth Ave ☎ 541–9600

Kenneth Lux, 30. 851 Madison Ave ☎ 861–6839

Knoedler, 28. 19 E 70th St ☎ 794–0550

Kraushaar, 52. 724 Fifth Ave ☎ 307–5730

Leloup, 4. 1080 Madison Ave ☎ 772–3410

Littlejohn-Contemporary, 56. 41 E 57th St ☎ 980–2323

Marion Goodman, 48. 24 W 57th St ☎ 977–7160

Marisa Del Re, 56. 41 E 57th St ☎ 688–1843

Marlborough, 47. 40 W 57th St ☎ 541–4900

Martin Sumers, 45. 50 W 57th St ☎ 541–8334

Mary Boone, 45. 745 Fifth Ave ☎ 752-2929

McCoy, 56. 41 E 57th St ☎ 319–1996

McKee, 50. 745 Fifth Ave ☎ 688–5951

Multiples, 48. 24 W 57th St ☎ 977–7160

Pace Wildenstein, 57. 32 E 57th St ☎ 421–3292

Paul Drey, 55. 11 E 57th St ☎ 753–2551

Perls, 10. 1016 Madison Ave ☎ 472–3200

Peter Findlay, 56. 41 E 57th St ☎ 644-4433

Raydon, 5. 1091 Madison Ave ☎ 288–3555

Reece, 48. 24 W 57th St ☎ 333–5830

Richard L. Feigen, 29. 49 E 68th St ☎ 628–0700

Richard York, 34. 21 E 65th St ☎ 772–9155

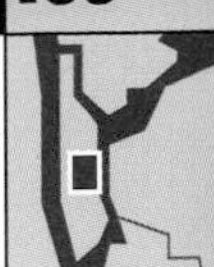

Listed Alphabetically (cont.)

Robert Mann, 17. 42 E 76th St
☎ 570–1223

Robert Miller, 56. 41 E 57th St
☎ 980–5454

Ronin, 40. 605 Madison Ave
☎ 688–0188

Rosenberg & Steibel, 57. 32 E 57th St
☎ 753–4368

Safani, 20. 980 Madison Ave
☎ 570–6360

Saidenberg, 11. 1018 Madison Ave
☎ 288–3387

Salander-O'Reilly, 8. 20 E 79th St
☎ 879–6606

Schweitzer, 3. 18 E 84th St
☎ 535–5430

Sid Deutsch, 36. 305 E 61st St
☎ 754–6660

Sidney Janis, 42. 110 W 57th St
☎ 586–0110

Sindin, 24. 956 Madison Ave
☎ 288–7902

Solomon & Co, 18. 959 Madison Ave
☎ 737–8200

Sotheby's, 26. 1334 York Ave
☎ 606–7000

Soufer, 13. 1015 Madison Ave
☎ 628–3225

Spanierman, 41. 45 E 58th St
☎ 832-0208

Sylvan Cole, 43. 101 W 57th St
☎ 333–7760

Tatistcheff & Co, 45. 50 W 57th St
☎ 664–0907

Terry Dintenfass, 12. 20 E 79th St
☎ 581–2268

Tibor de Nagy, 44. 41 W 57th St
☎ 421–3780

Ubu, 15. 16 E 78th St
☎ 794-4444

The Uptown, 1. 1194 Madison Ave
☎ 722–3677

Viridian, 48. 24 W 57th St
☎ 245–2882

Wally Findlay, 38. 14 E 60th St
☎ 421–5390

Washburn, 49. 20 W 57th St
☎ 397–6780

Weinstein, 31. 793 Madison
☎ 717-6333

Weintraub, 22. 965 Madison
☎ 879–1132

Widing & Peck, 33. 47 E 66th St
☎ 472-1455

Wildenstein, 35. 19 E 64th St
☎ 879–0500

Zabriskie, 56. 41 E 57th St
☎ 752-1223

Art Galleries/Chelsea

Art Galleries/SoHo

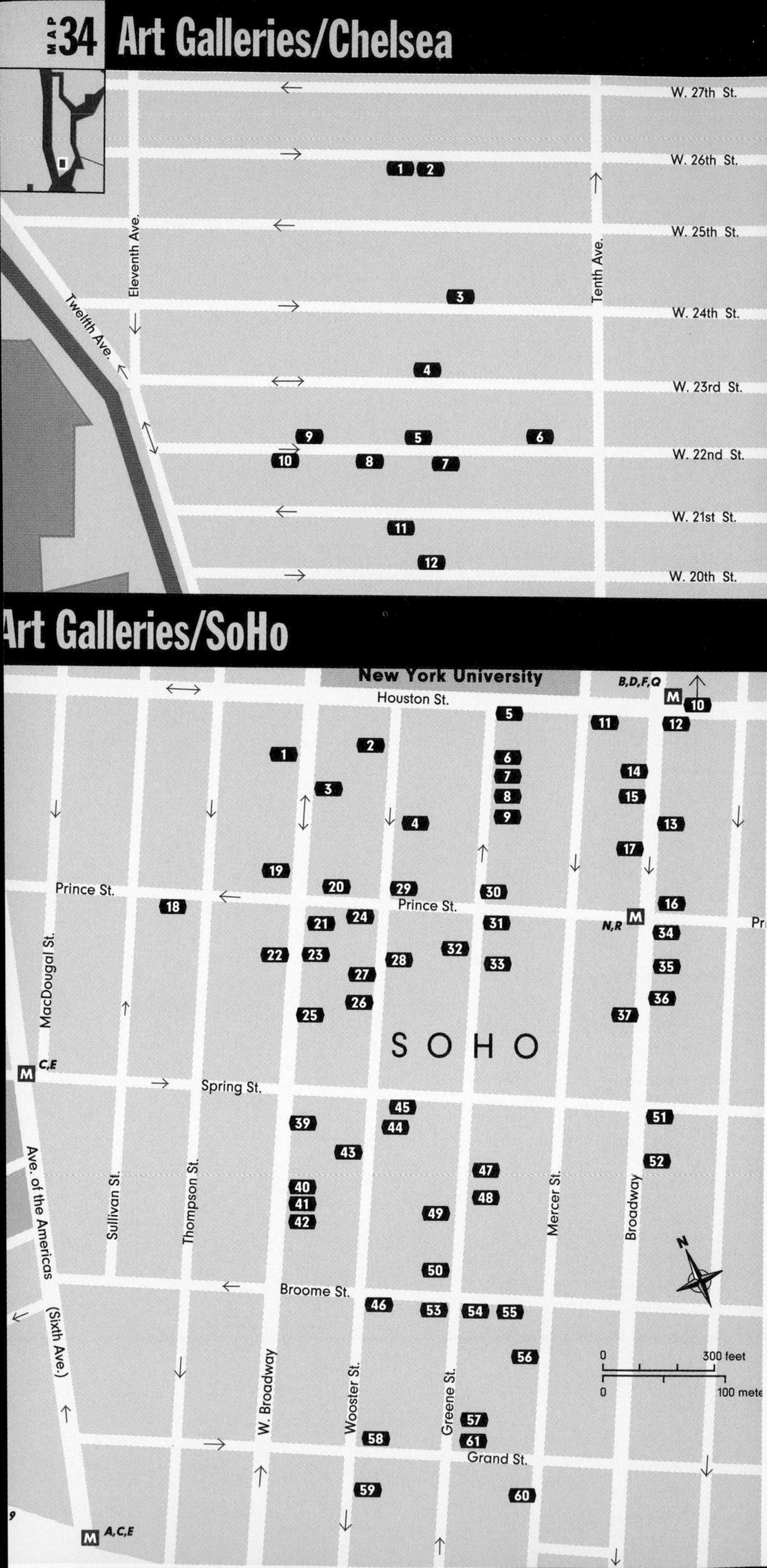

th St.
th St.
th St.
4th St.
3rd St.
2nd St.
1st St.
0th St.

Chelsea Galleries Listed by Site Number

1 Team
2 Greene Naftali
2 Clementine
3 Metro Pictures
4 Cheim & Reid
5 D'Amelio Terras
5 303
6 Linda Kirkland
6 XL
6 Jessica Fredericks
7 Marks
8 Morris Healy
8 Pat Hearn
9 Dia Center for the Arts
10 Dia Center for the Arts
11 Cooper
12 Maynes
12 Kreps

6
M
Puck Building
Mulberry St.
Lafayette St.
e St.
Cleveland Pl.
38
6
M
Spring St.
Kenmare St.
Broome St.
Lafayette St.
Grand St.

Soho Galleries Listed by Site Number

1 Dyansen of Soho
2 Paula Cooper
3 Vorpal
4 Gagosian
5 Metro Pictures
6 Pace
7 Sperone Westwater
8 Phyllis Kind
9 Steinbaum Krauss
10 Leica
11 Holly Solomon
12 American Primitive
12 Amos Eno
13 Curt Marcus
13 Leo Castelli
14 June Kelly
15 New Museum of Contemporary Art
16 John Gibson
16 Phoenix
16 Susan Teller
17 Tenri
18 Ward-Nasse
19 Sally Hawkins
20 Meisel
21 Bruce R. Lewin
22 Charles Cowles
22 DCA
22 Leo Castelli
22 Sonnabend
23 Nancy Hoffman
24 Luhring Augustine
25 Witkin
26 Peter Blum
27 Tony Shafrazi
28 Gallery 292
30 Edward Thorpe
31 Nosei
32 Barbara Gladstone
33 Jay Gorney
34 Fatouhi Cramer
34 Max Protetch
34 EM Donahue
34 First St
34 Stark
34 Stephen Haller
35 Pamela Auchincloss
36 Exit Art
37 Emily Harvey
38 Sragow
39 Dia Center for the Arts
40 OK Harris
40 Sigma
41 Nahan Contemporary
42 Bess Cutler
43 Brooke Alexander
44 Gallery Henoch
45 Reusch
46 Sandra Gering
46 PPOW
47 Blum Helman Warehouse
47 Postmasters
48 Feature
49 Heller
50 Klarfeld Perry
51 Condeso/Lawler
52 Solo Impression
53 Atlantic
54 SoHo 20
55 Penine Hart
56 55 Mercer
57 Zarre
58 Paul Kasmin
59 American Fine Arts
60 Ronald Feldman
61 Artists Space

Chelsea Galleries
Listed Alphabetically

Cheim & Reid, 4. 521 W 23rd St ☎ 242-7727

Clementine, 2. 526 W 26th St ☎ 243-5937

Cooper, 11. 534 W 21st St ☎ 255-1105

D'Amelio Terras, 5. 525 W 22nd St ☎ 226-5342

Dia Center for the Arts, 9. 545 W 22nd St ☎ 989-5566

Dia Center for the Arts, 10. 548 W 22nd St ☎ 989-5566

Greene Naftali, 2. 526 W 26th St ☎ 463-7770

Jessica Fredericks, 6. 504 W 22nd St ☎ 633-6555.

Kreps, 12. 529 W 20th St ☎ 741-8849

Linda Kirkland, 6. 504 W 22nd St ☎ 627-3930

Marks, 7. 522 w 22nd St ☎ 243-0020

Maynes, 12. 529 W 20th St ☎ 205-7100.

Metro Pictures, 3. 519 W 24th St ☎ 206-7100

Morris Healy, 8. 530 W 22nd St ☎ 243-3753

Pat Hearn, 8. 530 W 22nd St ☎ 727-7366.

Team, 1. 527 W 26th St ☎ 279-9219

303, 5. 52 W 22nd St ☎ 255-1121

XL, 6. 504 W 22nd St ☎ 462-4111.

Soho Galleries
Listed Alphabetically

American Fine Arts, 59. 22 Wooster St ☎ 941-0401

American Primitive, 12. 594 Broadway ☎ 966-1530

Amos Eno, 12. 594 Broadway ☎ 226-5342

Artists Space, 61. 38 Greene St ☎ 226-3970

Atlantic, 53. 475 Broome St ☎ 219-3183.

Barbara Gladstone, 32. 99 Greene St ☎ 431-3334

Bess Cutler, 42. 379 W Broadway ☎ 800/894-4548

Blum Helman Warehouse, 47. 80 Greene St ☎ 226-8770

Brooke Alexander, 43. 59 Wooster St ☎ 925-4338

Bruce R Lewin, 21. 136 Prince St ☎ 431-4750

Charles Cowles, 22. 420 W Broadway ☎ 925-3500

Condeso/Lawler, 51. 524 Broadway ☎ 219-1283

Curt Marcus, 13. 578 Broadway ☎ 226-3200

DCA, 22. 420 W Broadway ☎ 334-3331

Dia Center for the Arts, 39. 393 W Broadway ☎ 989-5566

Dia Center for the Arts, 29. 141 Wooster St ☎ 989-5566

Dyansen of Soho, 1. 462 W Broadway ☎ 982-3668

Edward Thorp, 30. 103 Prince St ☎ 431-6880

EM Donahue, 34. 560 Broadway ☎ 226-1111

Emily Harvey, 37. 537 Broadway ☎ 925-7651

Exit Art, 36. 548 Broadway ☎ 966-7745

Fatouhi Cramer, 34. 560 Broadway ☎ 431-1304

Feature, 48. 76 Greene St ☎ 941-7077

55 Mercer, 56. 55 Mercer St ☎ 226-8513

First St, 34. 560 Broadway ☎ 226-9127

Gagosian, 4. 136 Wooster St ☎ 228-2828

Gallery 292, 28. 120 Wooster St ☎ 431-0902

Henoch Gallery, 44. 80 Wooster St ☎ 966-0303

Heller, 49. 71 Greene St ☎ 966-5948

Holly Solomon, 11. 172 Mercer ☎ 941-5777

Jay Gorney, 33. 100 Greene St ☎ 966-4480

John Gibson, 16. 568 Broadway ☎ 925-1192

June Kelly, 14. 591 Broadway ☎ 226-1660

Klarfeld Perry, 50. 472 Broome St ☎ 941-0303

Leica, 10. 670 Broadway ☎ 777-3051

Listed Alphabetically (cont.)

Leo Castelli, 22. 420 W Broadway ☎ 431-5160

Leo Castelli (2), 13. 578 Broadway ☎ 431-6279

Luhring Augustine, 24. 130 Prince St ☎ 219-9600

Max Protetch, 34. 560 Broadway ☎ 966-5454

Meisel, 20. 141 Prince St ☎ 677-1340

Metro Pictures, 5. 150 Greene St ☎ 925-8335

Nahan Contemporary, 41. 381 W Broadway ☎ 966-9313

Nancy Hoffman, 23. 429 W Broadway ☎ 966-6676

New Museum of Contemporary Art, 15. 583 Broadway ☎ 219-1355

Nosei, 31. 100 Prince St ☎ 431-9253

OK Harris, 40. 383 W Broadway ☎ 431-3600

Pace Wildenstein, 6. 142 Greene St ☎ 431-9224

Pamela Auchincloss, 35. 558 Broadway ☎ 966-7753

Paul Kasmin, 58. 74 Grand St ☎ 219-3219

Paula Cooper, 2. 155 Wooster St ☎ 674-0766

Penine Hart, 55. 457 Broome St ☎ 226-2761

Peter Blum, 26. 99 Wooster St ☎ 343-0441

Phoenix, 16. 568 Broadway ☎ 226-8711

Phyllis Kind, 8. 136 Greene St ☎ 925-1200

Postmasters, 47. 80 Greene St ☎ 941-5711

PPOW, 46. 476 Broome St ☎ 941-8642

Ronald Feldman, 60. 31 Mercer St ☎ 226-3232

Reusch, 45. 134 Spring St ☎ 925-1137

Ronald Feldman, 60. 31 Mercer St ☎ 226-3232

Sally Hawkins, 19. 448 W Broadway ☎ 477-5699

Sandra Gering, 46. 476 Broome St ☎ 228-2828

Sigma, 40. 379 W Broadway ☎ 941-0014

SoHo 20, 54. 469 Broome St ☎ 226-4167

Solo Impression, 52. 520 Broadway ☎ 925-3599

Sonnabend, 22. 420 W Broadway ☎ 966-6160

Sperone Westwater, 7. 142 Greene St ☎ 431-3685

Sragow, 38. 73 Spring St ☎ 219-1793

Stark, 34. 560 Broadway ☎ 925-4484

Steinbaum Krauss, 9. 132 Greene St ☎ 431-4224

Stephen Haller, 34. 560 Broadway ☎ 219-2500

Susan Teller, 16. 568 Broadway ☎ 941-7335

Tenri, 17. 575 Broadway ☎ 925-8500

Tony Shafrazi, 27. 119 Wooster St ☎ 274-9300

Vorpal, 3. 459 W Broadway ☎ 800/586-3809

Ward-Nasse, 18. 178 Prince St ☎ 925-6951

Witkin, 25. 415 W Broadway ☎ 925-5510

Zarre, 57. 48 Greene St ☎ 966-2222

MAP 35 Exploring the Bronx

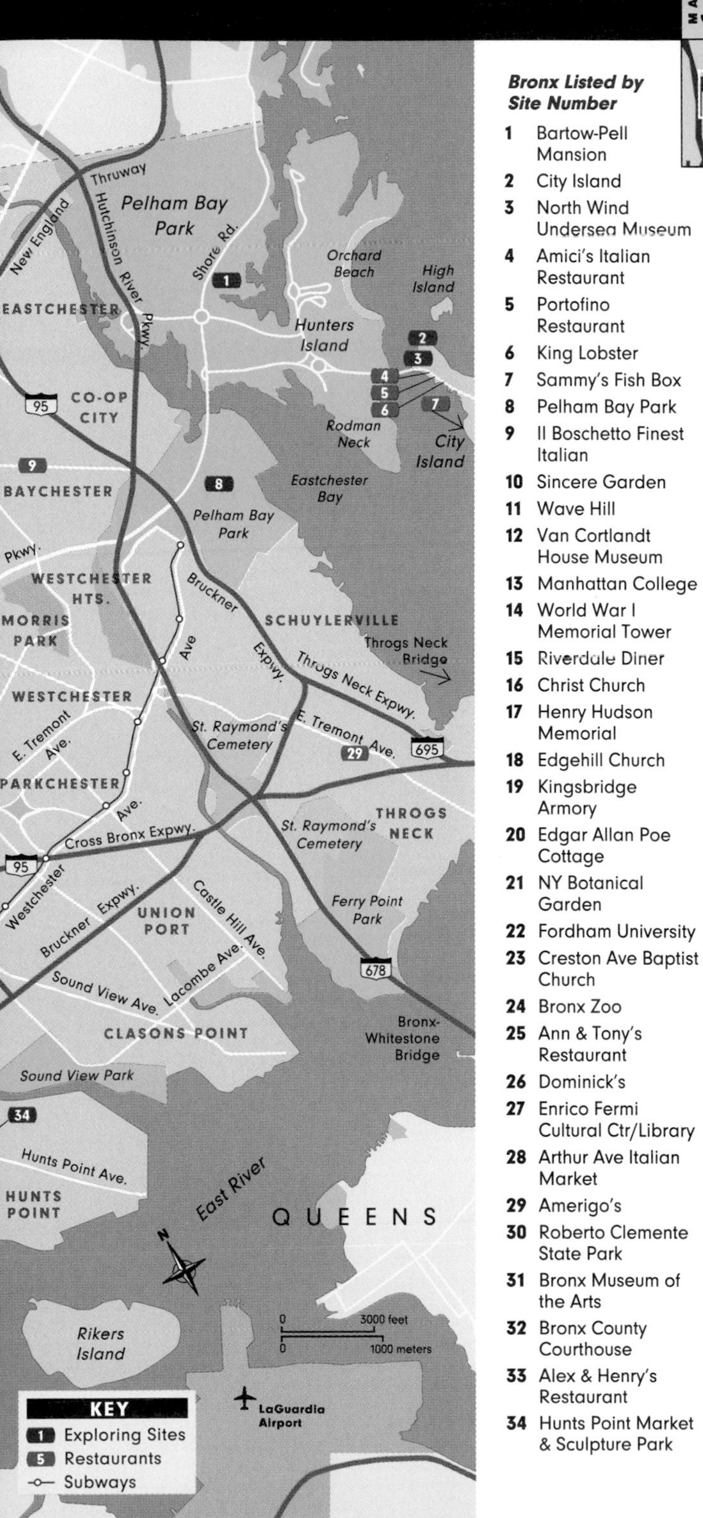

Bronx Listed by Site Number

1 Bartow-Pell Mansion
2 City Island
3 North Wind Undersea Museum
4 Amici's Italian Restaurant
5 Portofino Restaurant
6 King Lobster
7 Sammy's Fish Box
8 Pelham Bay Park
9 Il Boschetto Finest Italian
10 Sincere Garden
11 Wave Hill
12 Van Cortlandt House Museum
13 Manhattan College
14 World War I Memorial Tower
15 Riverdale Diner
16 Christ Church
17 Henry Hudson Memorial
18 Edgehill Church
19 Kingsbridge Armory
20 Edgar Allan Poe Cottage
21 NY Botanical Garden
22 Fordham University
23 Creston Ave Baptist Church
24 Bronx Zoo
25 Ann & Tony's Restaurant
26 Dominick's
27 Enrico Fermi Cultural Ctr/Library
28 Arthur Ave Italian Market
29 Amerigo's
30 Roberto Clemente State Park
31 Bronx Museum of the Arts
32 Bronx County Courthouse
33 Alex & Henry's Restaurant
34 Hunts Point Market & Sculpture Park

Exploring Brooklyn

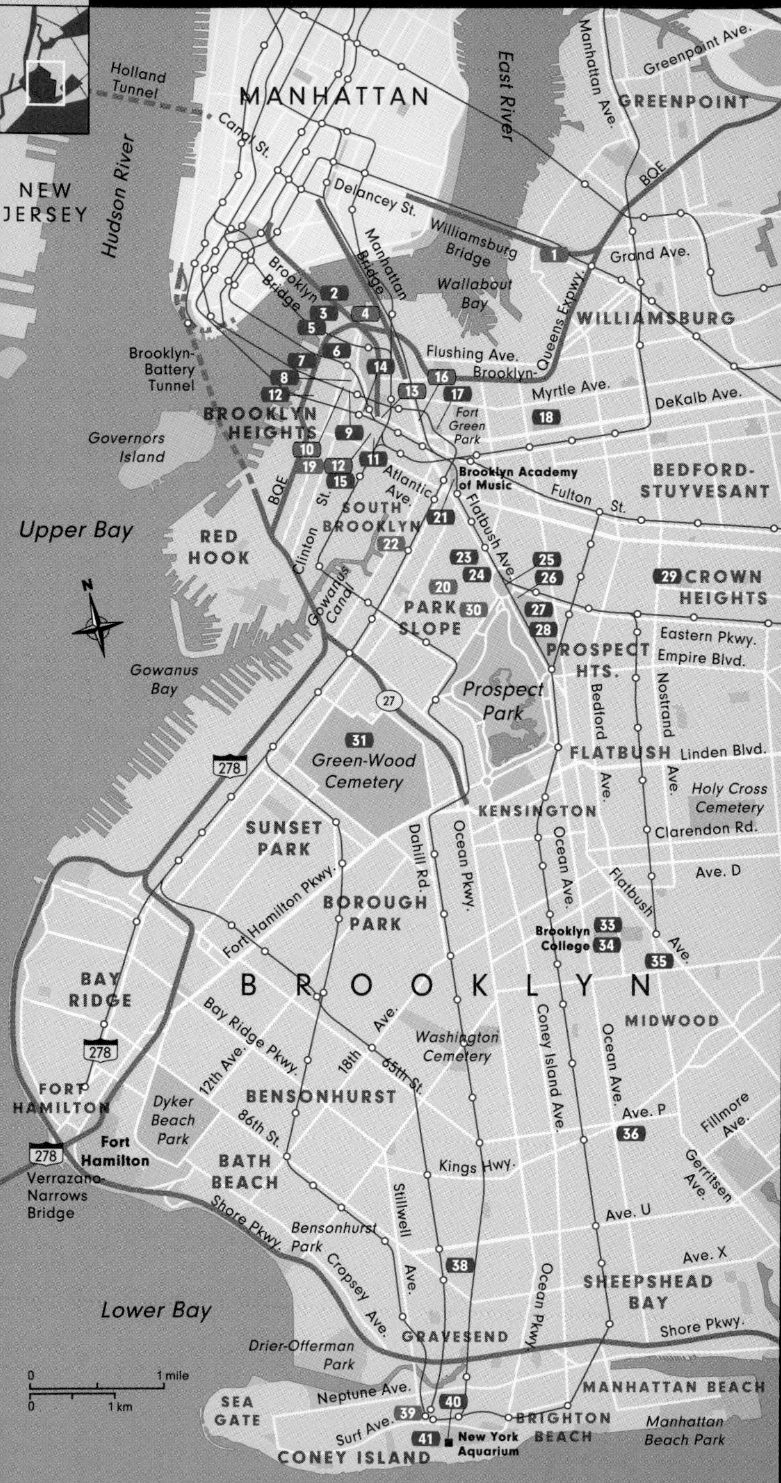

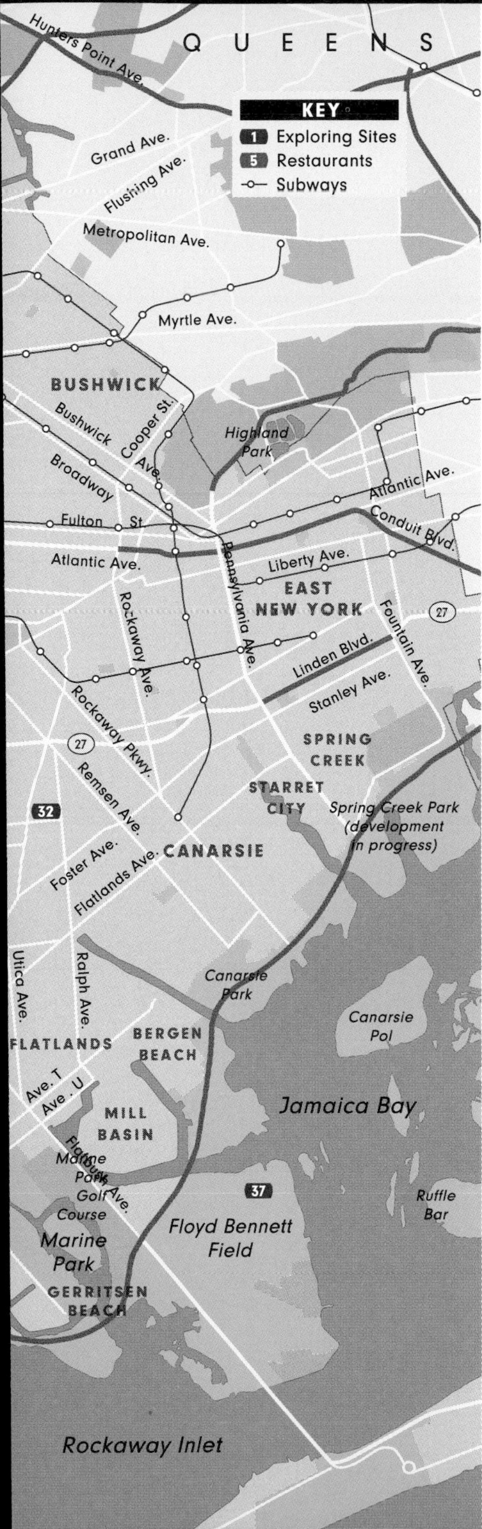

QUEENS
Hunters Point Ave.
Grand Ave.
Flushing Ave.
Metropolitan Ave.
Myrtle Ave.
KEY
1 Exploring Sites
5 Restaurants
Subways
BUSHWICK
Bushwick Ave.
Cooper St.
Highland Park
Broadway
Atlantic Ave.
Fulton St.
Conduit Blvd.
Atlantic Ave.
Liberty Ave.
EAST NEW YORK
Pennsylvania Ave.
Rockaway Ave.
Fountain Ave.
27
Linden Blvd.
Stanley Ave.
Rockaway Pkwy.
27
SPRING CREEK
Remsen Ave.
STARRET CITY
Spring Creek Park (development in progress)
32
Foster Ave.
Flatlands Ave.
CANARSIE
Utica Ave.
Ralph Ave.
Canarsie Park
Canarsie Pol
FLATLANDS
BERGEN BEACH
Ave. T
Ave. U
MILL BASIN
Jamaica Bay
Flatbush Ave.
Marine Park Golf Course
37
Ruffle Bar
Marine Park
Floyd Bennett Field
GERRITSEN BEACH
Rockaway Inlet

Brooklyn Listed by Site Number

1 Peter Luger
2 Bklyn Bridge
3 Fulton Ferry
4 River Cafe
5 Bargemusic
6 Plymouth Church
7 The Promenade
8 Bklyn Hist Society
9 Church of St Ann
10 Teresa's
10 Heights Cafe
11 State Street Houses
12 Caffe Buon Gusto
13 Gage & Tollner
14 Bklyn Borough Hall
15 NY Transit Museum
16 Junior's Restaurant
17 Long Island Univ
18 Pratt Institute
19 Cammareri Brothers Bakery
20 Cucina
21 Bklyn Academy of Music (BAM)
22 Monte's
23 Bklyn Conservatory
24 Montauk Club
25 Soldiers' & Sailors' Memorial Arch
26 Bklyn Public Library
27 Bklyn Museum
28 Bklyn Botanic Garden
29 Bklyn Children's Museum
30 Two Boots
31 Green-Wood Cemetery
32 Wyckoff House/ Pieter Claesen
33 Bklyn College CUNY
34 Bklyn Center of Performing Arts
35 Coe House
36 Wyckoff-Bennett Homestead
37 Gateway National Recreation Area
38 Old Gravesend Cemetery
39 Gargiulo's
40 NY Aquarium
41 Coney Island

MAP 37

Exploring Queens

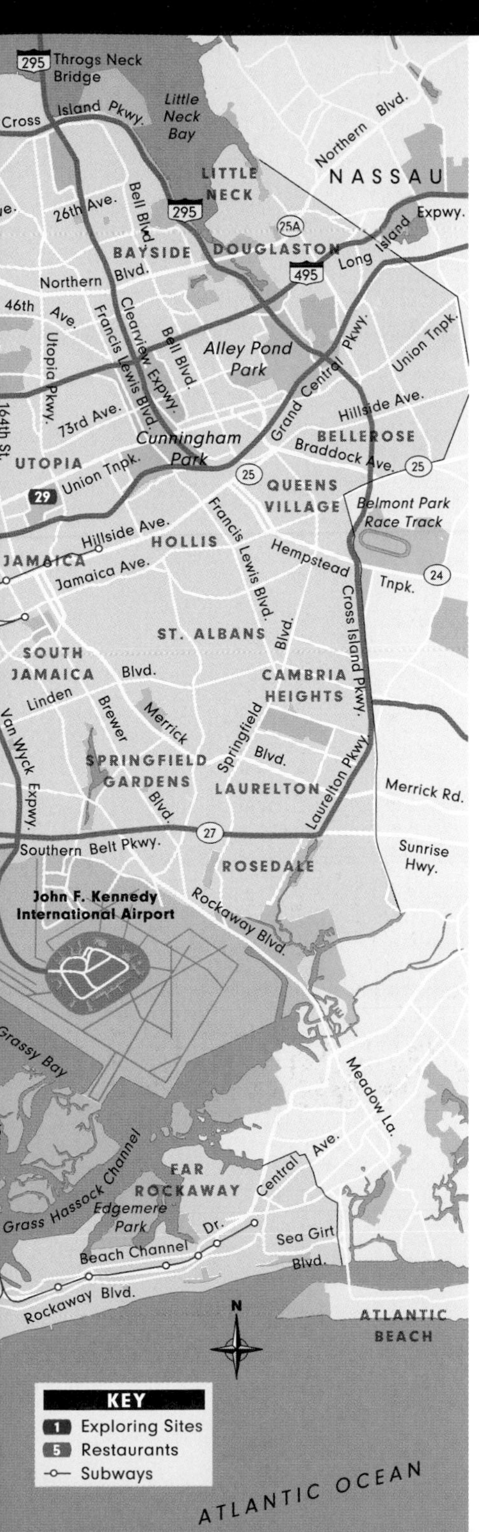

Queens Listed by Site Number

1 Water's Edge Restaurant
2 Café Vernon
3 Silvercup Studios
4 PS 1 Museum
5 Hunter's Point Historic District
6 Court House Square
7 American Museum of the Moving Image
8 Kaufman Astoria Studios
9 Karyatis
10 Isamu Noguchi Garden Museum
11 St Demitrios
12 Zenon Taverna Meze House
13 The Omonia Cafe
14 Elias Corner
15 Piccola Venezia
16 Jai Ya Thai
17 Park Side
18 NY Hall of Science
19 World's Fair Ice Skating Rink
20 Queens Museum
21 Queens Botanical Gardens
22 Flushing Meadows-Corona Park
23 Kissena Park
24 Friends Meeting House
25 Bowne House
26 Queens Historical Society
27 Weeping Beech Tree
28 West Side Tennis Club
29 St John's Univ
30 Jamaica Bay Wildlife Refuge
31 Jacob Riis Park
32 Fort Tilden

MAP 38

Exploring Staten Island

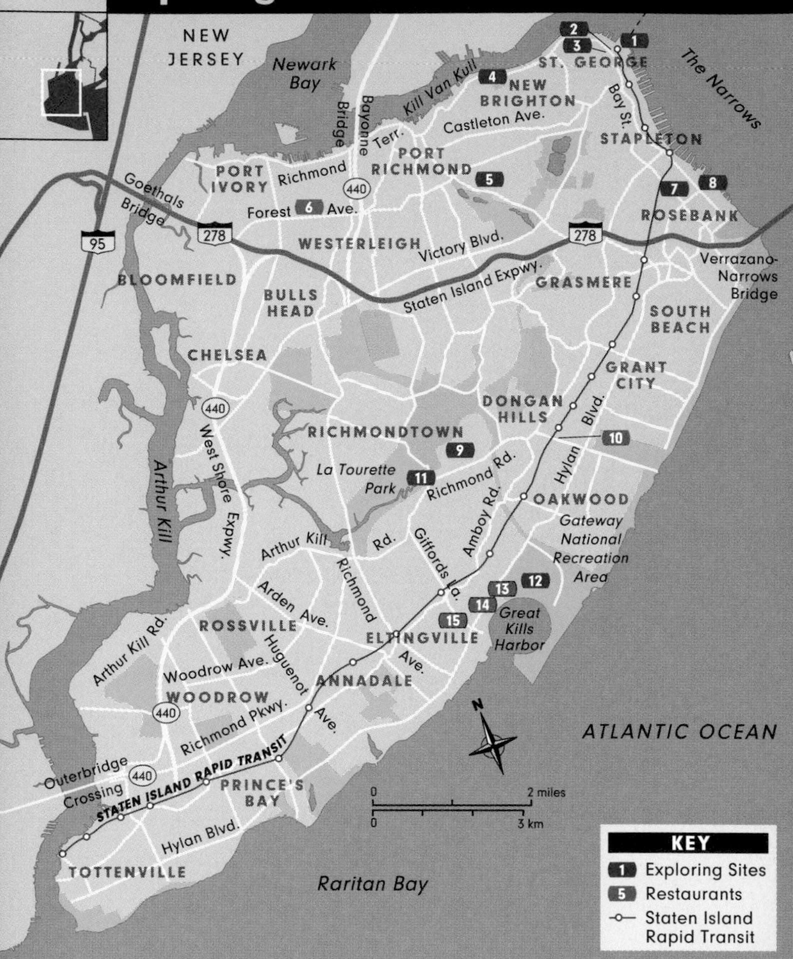

Staten Island Listed by Site Number

1 Staten Island Ferry
2 Museum of Staten Island
3 Staten Island Institute
4 Snug Harbor Cultural Center
5 Staten Island Zoo
6 Real Madrid
7 Garibaldi-Meucci Museum
8 Alice Austin House
9 Jacques Marchais Museum of Tibetan Art
10 Pennyfeathers
11 Richmondtown Restoration, Staten Island Historical Society
12 Gateway National Recreation Area
13 Casa del Mar
14 Marina Cafe
15 Arirang

Outer Boroughs Listed Alphabetically

BRONX SITES

Arthur Ave Italian Market, 28. Arthur Ave, betw E Fordham Rd & E Tremont Ave

Bartow-Pell Mansion, 1. Shore Rd & Pelham Bay Pkwy ☎ 718/885-1461

Bronx County Courthouse, 32. 851 Grand Concourse ☎ 718/590-3646

Bronx Museum of the Arts, 31. 1040 Grand Concourse ☎ 718/681-6000

Bronx Zoo (IWCP), 24. Fordham Rd & Southern Blvd ☎ 718/367-1010

Christ Church, 16. Henry Hudson Pkwy & 252nd St

City Island, 2. Long Island Sound

Creston Ave Baptist Church, 23. 114 E 188th St ☎ 718/367-1754

Edgar Allan Poe Cottage, 20. Grand Concourse & E Kingsbridge Rd ☎ 718/881-8900

Edgehill Church, 18. 2570 Independence Ave ☎ 718/549-7324

Enrico Fermi Cultural Center/Library, 27. 610 E 186th St ☎ 718/933-6410

Fordham University, 22. 441 E Fordham Rd ☎ 718/817-1000

Henry Hudson Memorial, 17. Independence Ave & W 227th St

Hunts Point Market & Sculpture Park, 34. Hunts Pt Ave & Food Ctr Dr ☎ 718/931-9500

Kingsbridge Armory, 19. Kingsbridge Rd & Jerome Ave ☎ 718/220-5671

Manhattan College, 13. Manhattan College Pkwy & W 242nd St ☎ 718/862-8000

North Wind Undersea Museum, 3. 610 City Island Ave ☎ 718/885-0701

NY Botanical Garden, 21. Southern Blvd & 200th St ☎ 718/817-8500

Pelham Bay Park, 8. Pelham Bay

Roberto Clemente State Park, 30. W Tremont Ave & Matthewson Rd ☎ 718/299-8750

Van Cortlandt House Museum, 12. B'way & W 246th St ☎ 718/543-3344

Wave Hill, 11. 249th St & Independence Ave. ☎ 718/549-3200

World War I Memorial Tower, 14. Riverdale Ave & 239th St

BRONX RESTAURANTS

Alex & Henry's Restaurant, 33. 862 Cortlandt Ave ☎ 718/585-3290. Italian. $

Amerigo's, 29. 3587 E Tremont Ave ☎ 718/792-3600. Italian. $$

Amici's Italian Restaurant, 4. 566 E 187th St ☎ 718/364-8598. Italian. $$

Ann & Tony's Restaurant, 25. 2407 Arthur Ave ☎ 718/364-8250. Italian. $$

Dominick's, 26. 2335 Arthur Ave ☎ 718/733-2807. Italian. $$

Il Boschetto Finest Italian, 9. 1660 E Gunn Hill Rd ☎ 718/379-9335. Italian. $$$

King Lobster, 6. 500 City Island Ave ☎ 718/885-1579. Seafood. $$

Portofino Restaurant, 5. 555 City Island Ave ☎ 718/885-1220. Continental. $$$

Riverdale Diner, 15. 3657 Kingsbridge Ave ☎ 718/884-6050. Diner. $

Sammy's Fish Box, 7. 41 City Island Ave ☎ 718/885-0920. Seafood. $$$

Sincere Garden, 10. 89 E Gunhill Rd ☎ 718/882-5923. Chinese. $$

BROOKLYN SITES

Bargemusic, Ltd, 5. Fulton Ferry Landing, Old Fulton St & Waterfront ☎ 718/624-4061

Bklyn Acad of Music (BAM), 21. 30 Lafayette Ave ☎ 718/636-4100

Bklyn Borough Hall, 14. 209 Joralemon St

Bklyn Botanic Garden, 28. 1000 Washington Ave ☎ 718/622-4433

Bklyn Bridge, 2. Parkes Cadman Plaza, Bklyn, to City Hall Park, Manhattan

Bklyn Center of Performing Arts, 34. Brooklyn College, Bedford & H Aves ☎ 718/951-4500

Bklyn Children's Museum, 29. 145 Brooklyn Ave ☎ 718/735-4432

Bklyn College CUNY, 33. Bedford & H Aves ☎ 718/951-5000

$$$$ = ***over $50*** $$$ = ***$30-$50*** $$ = ***$20-$30*** $ = ***under $20***

Based on cost per person, excluding drinks, service, and 8 1/4% sales tax.

Outer Boroughs Listed Alphabetically (Cont.)

BROOKLYN SITES (cont.)

Bklyn Conservatory of Music, 23. 58 7th Ave ☎ 718/622-3300

Brooklyn Historical Society, 8. 128 Pierrepont St ☎ 718/624-0890

Brooklyn Museum, 27. 200 Eastern Pkwy ☎ 718/638-5000

Brooklyn Public Library, 26. Flatbush Ave & Eastern Pkwy ☎ 718/780-7700

Church of St Ann & the Holy Trinity, 9. 157 Montague St ☎ 718/834-8794

Coe House, 35. 1128 E 34th St

Coney Island Amusement Park, 41. Surf Ave ☎ 718/372-0275

Fulton Ferry Pier, 3. foot of Old Fulton St

Gateway National Recreation Area, 37. Floyd Bennet Field, Flatbush Ave & Shore Pkwy ☎ 718/338-3338

Green-Wood Cemetery, 31. Fifth Ave & 25th St ☎ 718/768-7300

Long Island Univ, 17. Univ Plaza, DeKalb & Flatbush Aves ☎ 718/488-1000

Montauk Club, 24. 25 Eighth Ave ☎ 718/638-0800

NY Aquarium, 40. Boardwalk & W 8th St ☎ 718/265-3400

NY Transit Museum, 15. Boerum Pl & Schermerhorn St ☎ 718/243-3060

Old Gravesend Cemetery, 38. Gravesend Neck Rd & MacDonald Ave

Plymouth Church, 6. 75 Hicks St ☎ 718/624-4743

Pratt Institute, 18. 200 Willoughby Ave ☎ 718/636-3600

The Promenade, 7. between Montague & Clark Sts

Soldiers' & Sailors' Memorial Arch, 25. Flatbush Ave & Eastern Pkwy

State St Houses, 11. 290-324 State St

Wyckoff House/Pieter Claesen, 32. 5816 Clarendon Rd ☎ 718/629-5400

Wyckoff-Bennett Homestead, 36. 1669 E 22nd St

BROOKLYN RESTAURANTS

Caffe Buon Gusto, 12. 151 Montague St ☎ 718/624-3838. Italian. $$

Cammareri Brothers Bakery, 19. 502 Henry St ☎ 718/852-3606. Bakery. $

Cucina, 20. 256 Fifth Avenue ☎ 718/230-0711. Italian. $$

Gage & Tollner, 13. 372 Fulton St ☎ 718/875-5181. American. $$$

Gargiulo's Restaurant, 39. 2911 W 15th St ☎ 718/266-4891. Italian. $$

Heights Cafe, 10. 84 Montague St ☎ 718/625-5555. American. $$

Junior's Restaurant, 16. 386 Flatbush Ave ☎ 718/852-5257. American. $

Monte's, 22. 451 Carroll St ☎ 718/624-8984. Italian. $$

Peter Luger Steak House, 1. 178 B'way ☎ 718/387-7400. Steakhouse. $$$$

River Cafe, 4. 1 Water St ☎ 718/522-5200. Continental. $$$$

Teresa's, 10. 80 Montague St ☎ 718/797-3996. Polish. $

Two Boots Restaurant, 30. 514 2nd St ☎ 718/499-3253. Italian. $

QUEENS SITES

American Museum of the Moving Image, 7. 35th Ave & 36th St ☎ 718/784-0077

Bowne House, 25. 37-01 Bowne St ☎ 718/359-0528

Court House Square, 6. 45th Ave & 21st St

Flushing Meadows-Corona Park, 22. Flushing Bay & Grand Central Pkwy ☎ 718/760-6565

Fort Tilden, 32. Breezy Pt ☎ 718/318-4300

Friends Meeting House, 24. 137-16 Northern Blvd ☎ 718/358-9636

Hunter's Point Historic District, 5. 45th Ave & 23rd St

Isamu Noguchi Garden Museum, 10. 32-37 Vernon Blvd ☎ 718/204-7088

Jacob Riis Park, 31. Marine Bridge Pkwy at Rockaway Pt Blvd ☎ 718/318-4300

Jamaica Bay Wildlife Refuge, 30. Broad Channel & First Rd ☎ 718/318-4340

Kaufman Astoria Studios, 8. 34-12 36th St ☎ 718/392-5600

Kissena Park, 23. Rose Ave & Parsons Blvd ☎ 718/353-1047

NY Hall of Science, 18. 47-01 111th St ☎ 718/699-0005

Outer Boroughs Listed Alphabetically (Cont.)

QUEENS SITES (cont.)

PS 1 Museum, 4. 46-01 21st St ☎ 718/784-2084

Queens Botanical Gardens, 21. 43-50 Main St ☎ 718/886-3800

Queens Historical Society, 26. 143-35 37th Ave ☎ 718/939-0647

Queens Museum, 20. Flushing Meadows-Corona Park ☎ 718/592-5555

Silvercup Studios, 3. 42-25 21st St ☎ 718/784-3390

St Demitrios, 11. 30-11 30th Dr ☎ 718/728-1718

St John's University, 29. Grand Central & Utopia Pkwys ☎ 718/990-6161

Weeping Beech Tree, 27. 37th Ave & Parsons Blvd

West Side Tennis Club, 28. 1 Tennis Pl ☎ 718/268-2300

World's Fair Ice Skating Rink, 19. Flushing Meadows-Corona Park ☎ 718/271-1996

QUEENS RESTAURANTS

Café Vernon, 2. 46-18 Vernon Blvd ☎ 718/472-9694. Italian. $$

Elias Corner, 14. 31st St & 24th Ave ☎ 718/932-1510. Seafood. $

Jai Ya Thai, 16. 81-11 Broadway ☎ 718/651-1330. Thai. $

Karyatis, 9. 35-03 Broadway ☎ 718/204-0666. Greek. $

The Omonia Café, 13. 32-20 Broadway ☎ 718/274-6650. Greek. $

Park Side, 17. 107-01 Corona Ave ☎ 718/271-9274. Italian. $$

Piccola Venezia, 15. 42-01 28th Ave ☎ 718/721-8470. Italian. $

Water's Edge Restaurant, 1. 44th Dr at East River ☎ 718/482-0033. Continental. $$

Zenon Taverna Meze House, 12. 34-10 31st Ave ☎ 718/956-0133. Greek. $

STATEN ISLAND SITES

Alice Austin House, 8. 2 Hylan Blvd ☎ 718/816-4506

Garibaldi-Meucci Museum, 7. 420 Tompkins Ave ☎ 718/442-1608

Gateway National Recreation Area, 12. 26 Miller Field ☎ 718/338-3338

Jacques Marchais Museum of Tibetan Art, 9. 338 Lighthouse Ave ☎ 718/987-3500

Museum of Staten Island, 2. 75 Stuyvesant Pl ☎ 718/727-1135

Richmondtown Restoration, Staten Island Historical Society, 11. 441 Clarke Ave ☎ 718/351-1611

Snug Harbor Cultural Center, 4. 1000 Richmond Ter ☎ 718/448-2500

Staten Island Ferry, 1. St George Station, Richmond Terrace & Hyatt St ☎ 718/815-2628

Staten Island Institute, 3. 75 Stuyvesant Pl ☎ 718/727-1135

Staten Island Zoo, 5. 614 Broadway ☎ 718/442-3100

STATEN ISLAND RESTAURANTS

Arirang, 15. 23A Nelson Ave ☎ 718/966-9600. Japanese $$$

Casa del Mar, 13. 141 Mansion Ave ☎ 718/948-5772. Seafood. $$$

Marina Cafe, 14. 154 Mansion Ave ☎ 718/967-3077. American. $$

Pennyfeathers, 10. 187 New Dorp La ☎ 718/667-9722. Continental. $$

Real Madrid, 6. 2075 Forest Ave ☎ 718/447-7885. Spanish. $$

$$$$ = ***over $50*** $$$ = ***$30-$50*** $$ = ***$20-$30*** $ = ***under $20***

Based on cost per person, excluding drinks, service, and 8 1/4% sales tax.

Parks/Uptown

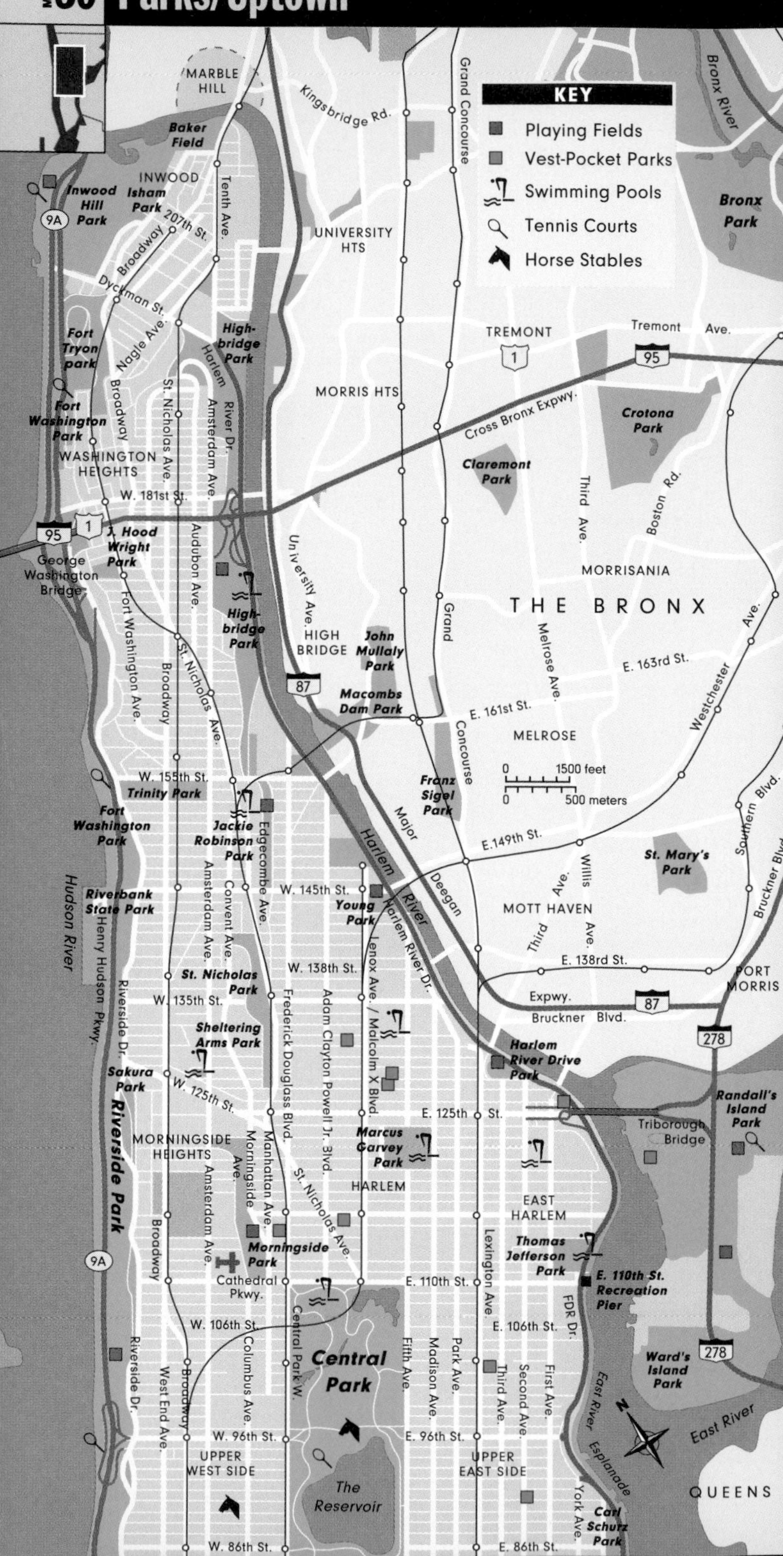

The Reservoir
Central Park
The Lake
Children's Zoo
Central Park Wildlife Conservation Center
The Pond
Riverside Park
Theodore Roosevelt Park
Damrosch Park
DeWitt Clinton Park
Carl Shurz Park
John Jay Park
UPPER WEST SIDE
UPPER EAST SIDE
Roosevelt Island
East River Esplanade
LONG ISLAND CITY
QUEENS
TRAMWAY
Queensboro Bridge
THEATER DISTRICT
Bryant Park
Lincoln Tunnel
HELL'S KITCHEN
MURRAY HILL
St. Vartan's Park
Queens-Midtown Tunnel
BROOKLYN
East River
Chelsea Park
Madison Square Park
CHELSEA
Gramercy Park
GRAMERCY
Union Square Park
Stuyvesant Square Park
Tompkins Square Park
East River Park
EAST VILLAGE
GREENWICH VILLAGE
WEST VILLAGE
Washington Square Park
Walker Park
Hudson River
SOHO
LOWER EAST SIDE
Sara D. Roosevelt Park
Williamsburg Bridge
Corlears Hook Park
LITTLE ITALY
Seward Park
HOBOKEN
Holland Tunnel
TRIBECA
CHINATOWN
Columbus Park
Gov. Smith Park
Manhattan Bridge
NEW JERSEY
North Park
City Hall Park
FINANCIAL DISTRICT
Brooklyn Bridge
BATTERY PARK CITY
Battery Park
Brooklyn-Battery Tunnel
BROOKLYN HEIGHTS
Brooklyn-Queens Expwy.
West Side Hwy.
0 1500 feet
0 500 meters
KEY
Playing Fields
Vest-Pocket Parks
Swimming Pools
Tennis Courts
Horse Stables
Marinas

MAP 41 Central Park/North

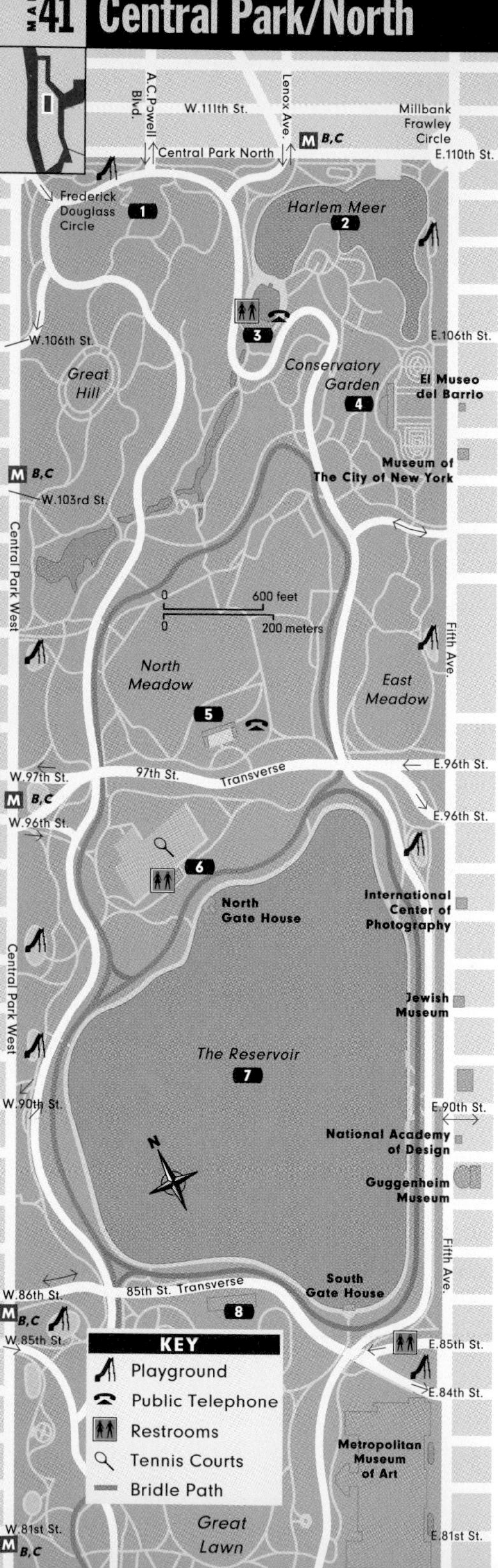

Listed by Site Number

1 Blockhouse #1 Site
2 Harlem Meer
3 Lasker Rink/Pool
4 Conservatory Garden
5 North Meadow Security
6 Tennis Courts
7 The Reservoir
8 Central Park Police Precinct

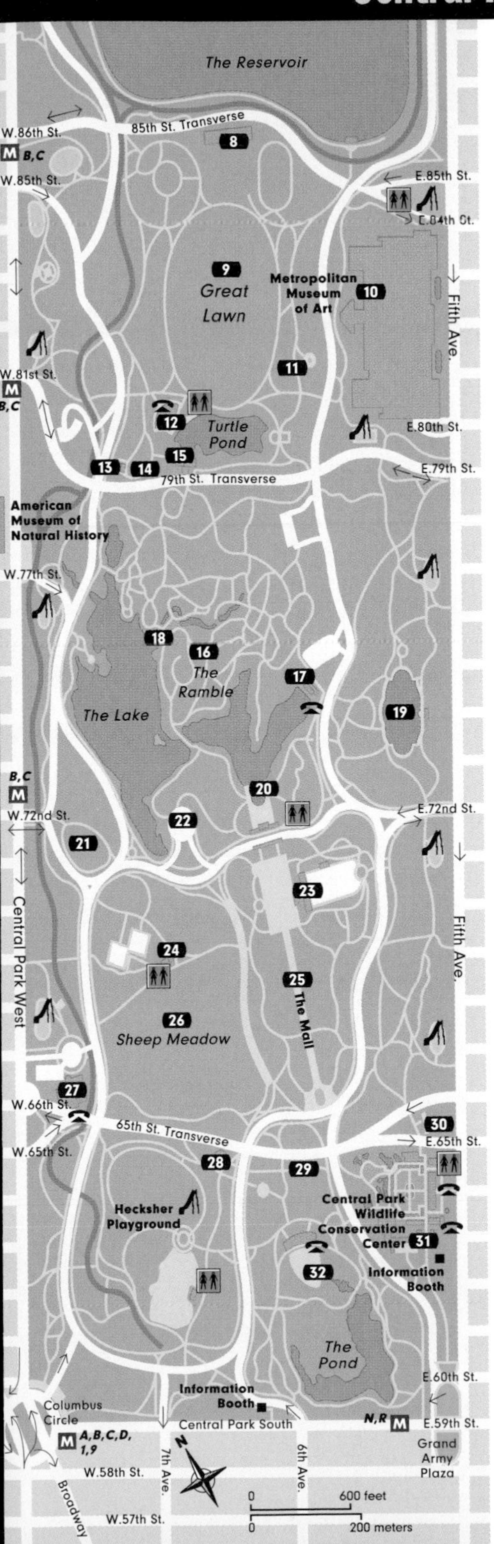

Listed by Site Number

8 Central Park Police Precinct
9 Great Lawn
10 Metropolitan Museum of Art
11 Cleopatra's Needle
12 Delacorte Theatre
13 Swedish Cottage
14 Shakespeare Garden
15 Belvedere Castle
16 The Ramble
17 Loeb Boathouse
18 Bow Bridge
19 Conservatory Water
20 Bethesda Fountain
21 Strawberry Fields
22 Cherry Hill
23 Bandshell
24 Mineral Springs Pavilion
25 The Mall
26 Sheep Meadow
27 Tavern on the Green
28 Carousel
29 Dairy (Visitor's Center)
30 Children's Zoo
31 Central Park Wildlife Conservation Center
32 Wollman Rink

Stadiums & Arenas

Flushing Bay
Whitestone Expwy.
Northern Blvd.
34th Ave.
127th St.
126th St.
Grand Central Pkwy.
Shea Stadium
Willets Point Blvd.
Van Wyck Expwy.
River
Roosevelt Ave.
Flushing
Corona Rail Road Yard
U.S. Tennis Association Arena
7
Flushing Meadows - Corona Park
0
300 feet
0
100 meters
Shea Stadium & U.S. Tennis Association Arena
Yankee Stadium
Jerome Ave.
E. 162nd St.
E. 162nd St.
Macombs Dam Park
E. 161st St.
Macombs Dam
C, D, 4
Babe Ruth Plaza
Rupert Pl.
C, D, 4
Lou Gehrig Plaza
Major Deegan Expwy.
E. 157th St.
Bronx Boro Hall
Harlem River
River Ave.
Gerard Ave.
Walton Ave.
Yankee Stadium
E. 153rd St.
Franz Sigel Park
Grand Concourse
87
0
300 feet
0
100 meters

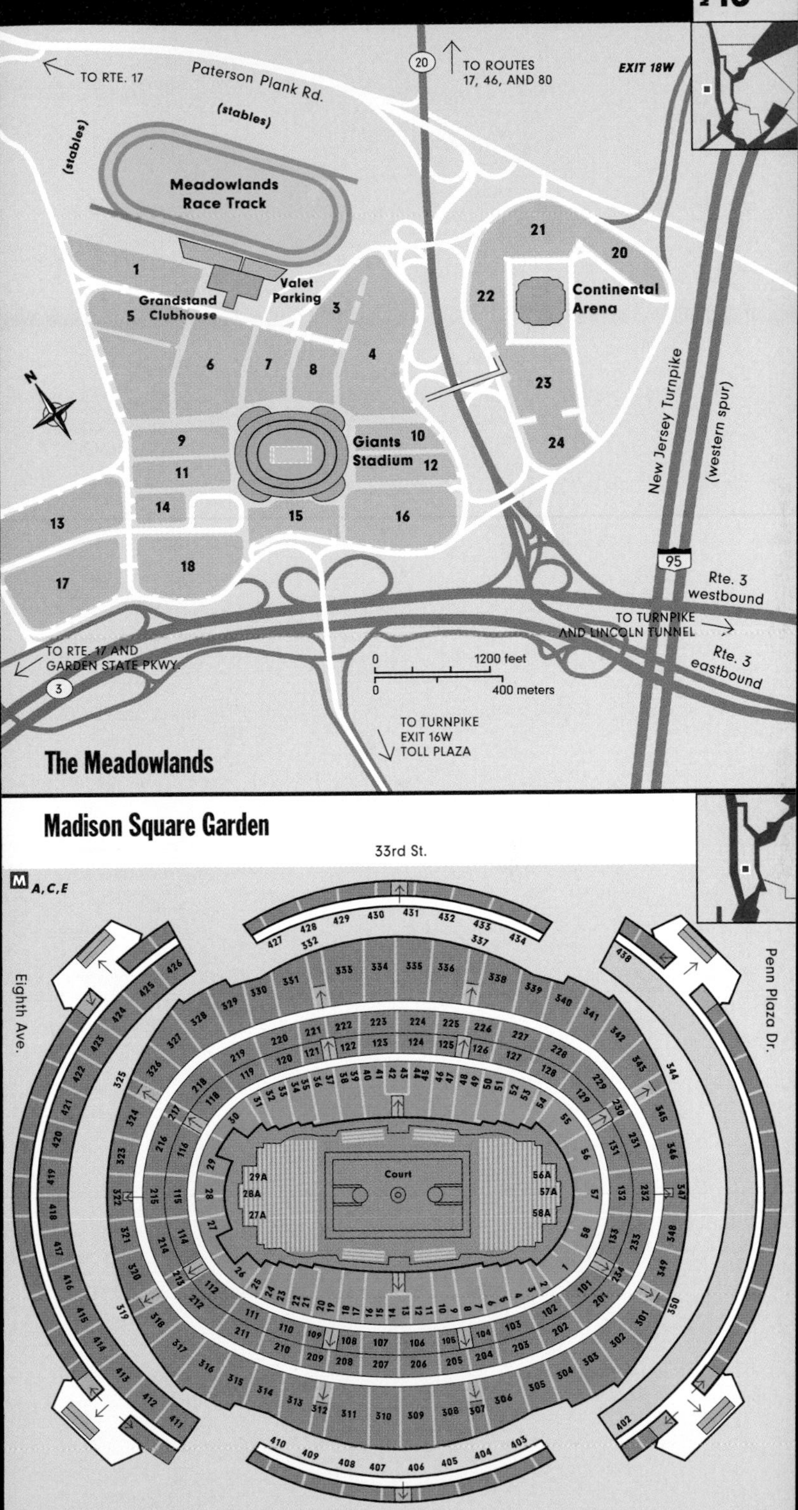
The Meadowlands
TO RTE. 17
Paterson Plank Rd.
(stables)
(stables)
20
TO ROUTES 17, 46, AND 80
EXIT 18W
Meadowlands Race Track
Grandstand Clubhouse
Valet Parking
Continental Arena
Giants Stadium
New Jersey Turnpike
(western spur)
95
Rte. 3 westbound
TO TURNPIKE AND LINCOLN TUNNEL
Rte. 3 eastbound
TO RTE. 17 AND GARDEN STATE PKWY.
3
0 1200 feet
0 400 meters
TO TURNPIKE EXIT 16W TOLL PLAZA
Madison Square Garden
33rd St.
M A,C,E
Eighth Ave.
Penn Plaza Dr.
Court
31st St.

MAP 44 Shopping Highlights

Listed by Site Number

1 Zabar's
2 IS 44 Market
3 Tower Records
4 Grace's Marketplace
5 Polo/Ralph Lauren
6 PS 183 Market
7 Barneys NY
8 F.A.O. Schwarz
9 Bergdorf Goodman
10 Petrossian
11 Bloomingdale's
12 Manhattan Art & Antiques Center
13 Tiffany & Co
14 Trump Tower
14 Tower Records
15 Henri Bendel
16 Fortunoff
17 MOMA (Shop)
18 Rockefeller Center
19 Takashimaya
20 Saks Fifth Ave
21 Brooks Brothers
22 Lord & Taylor
23 Virgin Megastore
24 Macy's
24 Stern's
25 Manhattan Mall
26 Annex Antiques Far
27 ABC Carpet & Home
28 Bed Bath & Beyond
29 Daffy's
30 Union Square Greenmarket
31 The Strand
32 Balducci's
33 PS 41 Market
34 Urban Outfitters
35 Patricia Field
36 Li-Lac Chocolates
37 Tower Market
38 Tower Records
39 Orchard St
40 Urban Outfitters
41 Dean & Deluca
42 Canal Jean
43 Canal Market
44 Pearl Paint
45 Kam Man
46 World Financial Ctr
47 World Trade Center
48 Century 21

Listed Alphabetically

ABC Carpet & Home, 27. 881 & 888 Broadway ☎ 473-3000

Balducci's, 32. 424 Sixth Ave ☎ 673-2600

Barneys NY, 7. 660 Madison Ave ☎ 826-8900

Bed, Bath & Beyond, 28. 620 Sixth Ave ☎ 255-3550

Bergdorf Goodman, 9. 754 Fifth Ave ☎ 753-7300

Bloomingdale's, 11. 1000 Third Ave ☎ 355-5900

Brooks Brothers, 21. 346 Madison Ave ☎ 682-8800

Canal Jean, 42. 504 Broadway ☎ 226-1130

Century 21, 48. 22 Cortlandt St ☎ 227-9092

Daffy's, 29. 111 Fifth Ave ☎ 529-4477

Dean & Deluca, 41. 560 Broadway ☎ 431-1691

F.A.O. Schwarz, 8. 767 Fifth Ave ☎ 644-9400

Fortunoff, 16. 681 Fifth Ave ☎ 758-6660

Grace's Marketplace, 4. 1237 Third Ave ☎ 737-0600

Henri Bendel, 15. 712 Fifth Ave ☎ 247-1100

Kam Man, 45. 200 Canal St ☎ 571-0330

Li-Lac Chocolates, 36. 120 Christopher St ☎ 242-7374

Lord & Taylor, 22. 424 Fifth Ave ☎ 391-3344

Macy's, 24. Herald Sq & 34th St ☎ 695-4400

Manhattan Art & Antiques Center, 12. 1050 Second Ave ☎ 355-4400

Manhattan Mall, 25. Sixth Ave & 33rd St ☎ 465-0500

Museum of Modern Art (Shop), 17. 11 W 53rd St ☎ 708-9700

Patricia Field, 35. 10 E Eighth St ☎ 254-1699

Pearl Paint, 44. 308 Canal St ☎ 431-7932

Petrossian, 10. 182 W 58th St ☎ 245-2217

Polo/Ralph Lauren, 5. 867 Madison Ave ☎ 606-2100 & 888 Madison Ave ☎ 434-8000

Rockefeller Center, 18. 30 Rockefeller Plaza ☎ 632-3975

Saks Fifth Ave, 20. 611 Fifth Ave ☎ 753-4000

South Street Seaport, 50. Waterfront, Fulton & South Sts ☎ 732-7678

The Strand, 31. 828 Broadway ☎ 473-1452

Syms, 49. 42 Trinity Pl ☎ 797-1199

Takashimaya, 20. 693 Fifth Ave ☎ 350-0100

Tiffany & Co, 13. 727 Fifth Ave ☎ 755-8000

Tower Records, 3. 1966 Broadway ☎ 799-2500

Tower Records, 4. 725 Fifth Ave (Trump Tower) ☎ 838-8110

Tower Records, 38. 692 Broadway ☎ 505-1500

Trump Tower, 14. 725 Fifth Ave ☎ 832-2000

Urban Outfitters, 34. 374 Sixth Ave ☎ 677-9350

Urban Outfitters, 40. 628 Broadway ☎ 475-0009

Virgin Megastore, 23. 1540 Broadway ☎ 921-1020

World Financial Center, 46. Waterfront, at West & Vesey Sts ☎ 945-0505

World Trade Center, 47. West & Vesey Sts ☎ 435-4170

Zabar's, 1. 2245 Broadway ☎ 787-2000

MARKETS

Annex Antiques Fair & Flea Market, 26. Sixth Ave, betw 25th & 26th Sts. Open Sat, Sun

Canal Market, 43. 370 Canal St. Open Sat, Sun

Orchard St, 39. Orchard St, betw Houston & Canal Sts

PS 183 Market, 6. 67th St betw York & First Aves. Open Sat

PS 41 Market, 33. Greenwich Ave & Charles St. Open Sat

IS 44 Market, 2. Columbus Ave betw 76th & 77th Sts. Open Sun

Tower Market, 37. B'way betw W 4th & Great Jones Sts. Open Sat, Sun

MAP 45 Shopping/Madison Avenue

Listed by Site Number

- **1** Wicker Garden's Baby
- **2** E.A.T.
- **3** DeLorenzo
- **4** Barnes & Noble
- **5** La Maison du Chocolat
- **6** Polo/Ralph Lauren
- **7** Pierre Deux
- **8** Yves St Laurent
- **9** Andrea Carrano
- **10** Madison Ave Bookshop
- **11** Pratesi
- **12** Gianni Versace
- **13** Missoni
- **14** Jaeger International
- **15** Joan & David
- **16** Diesel
- **17** Billy Martin's
- **18** Peter Fox
- **19** Barry Friedman
- **20** Emanuel Ungaro
- **21** Moschino
- **22** Woodard & Greenstein
- **23** Gucci
- **24** Godiva Chocolatier
- **25** Krizia
- **26** Fred Leighton
- **27** American Hurrah
- **28** Giorgio Armani
- **29** Valentino
- **30** Peress
- **31** E Braun & Co
- **31** Erica Wilson
- **32** Suzanne
- **33** Coach Store
- **34** The Limited
- **35** Christofle
- **36** Calvin Klein
- **37** Barneys NY
- **38** Julie
- **39** Georg Jensen
- **40** Sherry Lehmann Inc
- **41** Ann Taylor
- **42** Bottega Veneta
- **43** Simon Pierce
- **44** Crate & Barrel
- **45** Bally of Switzerland
- **46** Baccarat
- **47** Lederer
- **48** Paris Collections

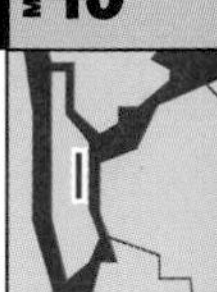

Listed Alphabetically

America Hurrah Antiques, 27. 766 Madison Ave ☎ 535-1930

Andrea Carrano, 8. 850 Madison Ave ☎ 570-1443

Ann Taylor, 41. 645 Madison Ave ☎ 832-9114

Baccarat, 6. 625 Madison Ave ☎ 826-4100

Bally of Switzerland, 45. 628 Madison Ave ☎ 751-9082

Barnes & Noble, 4. 86th & Lexington Ave. ☎ 423-9900

Barneys NY, 37. 660 Madison Ave ☎ 826-8900

Barry Friedman, 19. 32 E 67th ☎ 794-8950

Billy Martin's, 17. 810 Madison Ave ☎ 861-3100

Bottega Veneta, 42. 635 Madison Ave ☎ 371-5511

Calvin Klein, 36. 654 Madison Ave ☎ 292-9000

Christofle, 35. 680 Madison Ave ☎ 308-9390

Coach Store, 33. 710 Madison Ave ☎ 319-1772

Crate & Barrel, 44. 650 Madison Ave. ☎ 308-0011

DeLorenzo, 3. 958 Madison Ave ☎ 249-7575

Diesel, 16. 770 Lexington Ave. ☎ 308-0055

E Braun & Co, 31. 717 Madison Ave ☎ 838-0650

E.A.T., 2. 1064 Madison Ave. ☎ 772-0022

Emanuel Ungaro, 20. 792 Madison Ave ☎ 249-4090

Erica Wilson, 31. 717 Madison Ave ☎ 832-7290

Fred Leighton, 26. 773 Madison Ave ☎ 288-1872

Georg Jensen, 39. 683 Madison Ave ☎ 759-6457

Gianni Versace, 12. 817 Madison Ave ☎ 744-5572

Giorgio Armani, 28. 760 Madison Ave ☎ 988-9191

Godiva Chocolatier, 24. 793 Madison Ave ☎ 249-9444

Gucci, 23. 795 Madison Ave ☎ 535-1014

Jaeger International, 14. 818 Madison Ave ☎ 628-3350

Joan & David, 15. 816 Madison Ave ☎ 772-3970

Julie, 38. 687 Madison Ave ☎ 688-2345

Krizia, 25. 769 Madison Ave ☎ 879-1211

Lederer, 47. 613 Madison Ave ☎ 355-5515

The Limited, 34. 691 Madison Ave ☎ 838-8787

Madison Ave Bookshop, 9. 833 Madison Ave ☎ 535-6130

Missoni, 13. 836 Madison Ave ☎ 517-9339

Moschino, 21. 803 Madison Ave. ☎ 639-6900

Paris Collections, 48. 543 Madison Ave. ☎ 832-7100

Peress, 30. 739 Madison Ave. ☎ 861-6336

Peter Fox, 18. 806 Madison Ave ☎ 744-8340

Pierre Deux, 6. 870 Madison Ave ☎ 570-9343

Polo/Ralph Lauren, 5. 867 Madison Ave ☎ 606-2100 and 888 Madison Ave ☎ 434-8000

Pratesi, 10. 829 Madison Ave ☎ 288-2315

Sherry Lehmann Inc, 40. 679 Madison Ave ☎ 838-7500

Simon Pierce, 43. 500 Park Ave. ☎ 421-8801

Suzanne, 32. 700 Madison Ave. 593-3232

Valentino,29. 747 Madison Ave ☎ 772-6969

Woodard & Greenstein, 22. 799 Madison Ave ☎ 794-9404

Yves St Laurent, 7. 855 Madison Ave ☎ 472-5299

Wicker Garden's Baby, 1. 1327 Madison Ave ☎ 410-7001

MAP 46 Shopping/Fifth Avenue & 57th Street

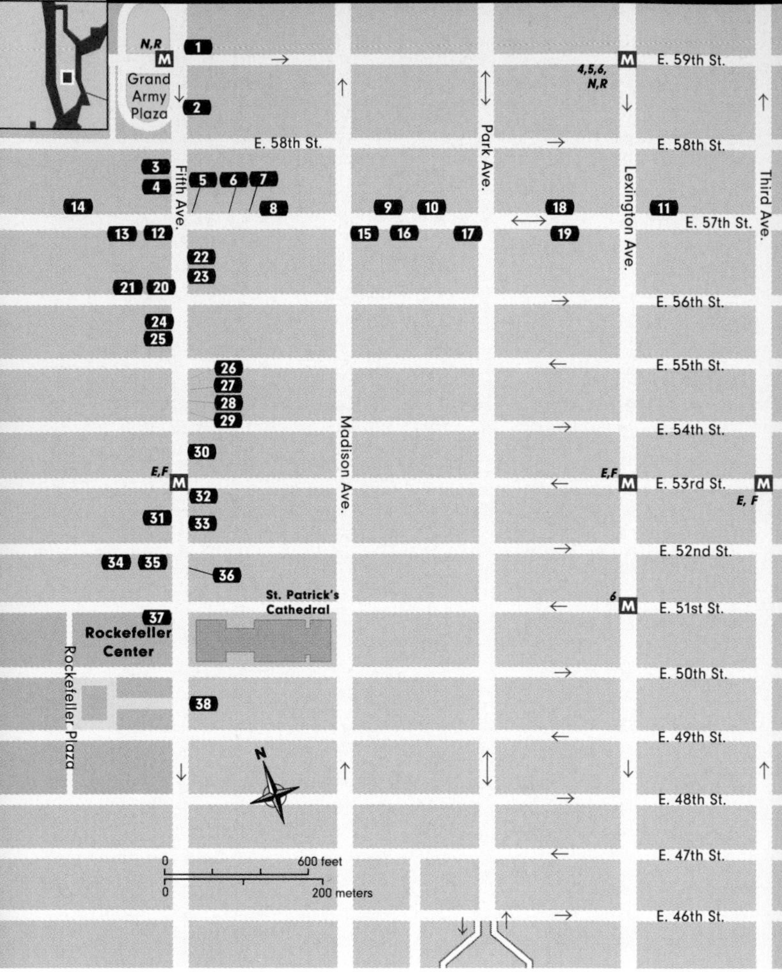

Listed by Site Number

1 A La Vielle Russie
2 F.A.O. Schwarz
3 Bergdorf Goodman
4 Van Cleef & Arpels
5 Warner Bros Studio Store
6 Chanel
7 Burberrys
8 Hermès
9 Prada
10 Louis Vuitton
11 Hammacher Schlemmer
12 Bulgari
12 Israel Sack
12 Mikimoto
13 Charivari 57
14 Rizzoli
15 Victoria's Secret
16 Buccellati
17 Dunhill
18 Gazebo
19 Dempsey & Carroll
20 Fendi
21 Norma Kamali
22 Tiffany & Co
23 Salvatore Ferragamo Men's
23 Trump Tower
24 Harry Winston
25 Henri Bendel
26 Godiva
27 Takashimaya
28 Bijan
29 Gucci
30 Fortunoff
31 Botticelli
32 Salvatore ferragamo Women's
33 Cartier
34 Traveller's Booksatore
35 Liz Claiborne
36 H Stern
37 Movado
38 Saks Fifth Ave

Listed Alphabetically

A La Vielle Russie, 1. 781 Fifth Ave ☎ 752-1727

Bergdorf Goodman, 3. 754 Fifth Ave ☎ 753-7300

Bijan, 8. 699 Fifth Ave ☎ 758-7500

Botticelli, 31. 666 Fifth Ave ☎ 582-2984

Buccellati, 16. 46 E 57th St ☎ 308-5533

Bulgari, 12. 730 Fifth Ave ☎ 315-9000

Burberrys, 7. 9 E 57th St ☎ 371-5010

Cartier, 33. 653 Fifth Ave ☎ 753-0111

Chanel, 6. 5 E 57th St ☎ 355-5050

Charivari 57, 13. 18 W 57th St ☎ 333-4040

Dempsey & Carroll, 19. 110 E 57th St ☎ 486-7526

Dunhill, 17. 450 Park Ave ☎ 753-9292

F.A.O. Schwarz, 2. 767 Fifth Ave ☎ 644-9400

Fendi, 20. 720 Fifth Ave ☎ 767-0100

Fortunoff, 30. 681 Fifth Ave ☎ 758-6660

Gazebo, 18. 114 E 57th St ☎ 832-7077

Godiva, 26. 701 Fifth Ave ☎ 593-2845

Gucci, 29. 685 Fifth Ave ☎ 826-2600

H Stern, 36. 645 Fifth Ave ☎ 688-0300

Hammacher Schlemmer, 11. 147 E 57th St ☎ 421-9000

Harry Winston, 24. 718 Fifth Ave ☎ 245-2000

Henri Bendel, 25. 712 Fifth Ave ☎ 247-1100

Hermès, 8. 11 E 57th St ☎ 751-3181

Israel Sack, 12. 730 Fifth Ave ☎ 399-6562

Liz Claiborne, 35. 650 Fifth Ave ☎ 956-6505

Louis Vuitton, 10. 49 E 57th St ☎ 371-6111

Mikimoto, 12. 730 Fifth Ave ☎ 664-1800

Movado, 37. 630 Fifth Ave ☎ 262-2059

Norma Kamali, 21. 11 W 56th St ☎ 957-9797

Prada, 9. 45 E 57th St ☎ 308-2332

Rizzoli, 17. 31 W 57th St ☎ 759-2424

Saks Fifth Ave, 8. 611 Fifth Ave ☎ 753-4000

Salvatore Ferragamo Men's, 23. 661 Fifth Ave ☎ 759-7990

Salvatore Ferragamo Women's, 32. 725 Fifth Ave ☎ 759-3822

Takashimaya, 27. 693 Fifth Ave. ☎ 350-0100

Tiffany & Co, 2. 727 Fifth Ave ☎ 755-8000

Traveller's Bookstore, 34. 22 W 52nd St ☎ 664-0995

Trump Tower, 231. 725 Fifth Ave ☎ 832-2000

Van Cleef & Arpels, 4. 744 Fifth Ave ☎ 644-9500

Victoria's Secret, 15. 34 E 57th St ☎ 758-5592

Warner Bros Studio Store, 5. 1 E 57th St ☎ 754-0300

Shopping/Upper West Side

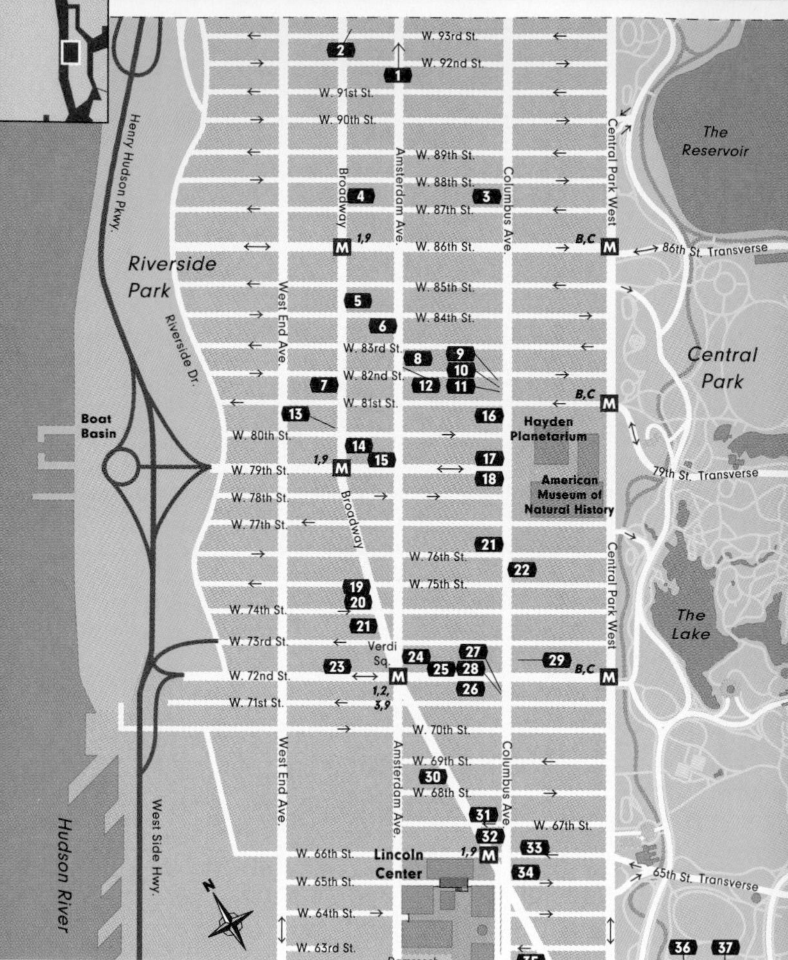

Listed by Site Number

1 Albee
2 Murder Ink
3 Welcome Home Antiques
4 Liberty House
5 Morris Brothers
6 West Side Kids
7 Barnes & Noble
8 Avventura
9 Penny Whistle Toys
10 Greenstones et Cie
11 Frank Stella Ltd
12 Bath Island
13 Zabar's
14 Filene's Basement
15 Uncle Futz
16 Maxilla and Mandible
17 Laura Ashley
18 Only Hearts
19 Citarella
20 Fairway
21 IS 44 Market
22 Kenneth Cole
23 Gryphon Record Shop
24 Star Magic
25 Acker Merrall & Condit
26 Blades, Board & Skate
27 To Boot
28 Betsey Johnson
29 Savage Jewelry
30 Ann Taylor
31 Pottery Barn
32 Tower Records
33 Barnes & Noble
34 Mus Amer Folk Art Gift Shop
35 The Ballet Shop
36 Petrossian
37 Mason's Tennis Mart

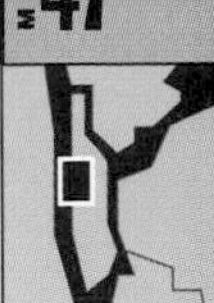

Listed Alphabetically

Acker Merrall & Condit, 25. 160 W 72nd St ☎ 787-1700

Albee, 1. 715 Amsterdam Ave ☎ 662-5740

Ann Taylor, 30. 2017 Broadway ☎ 873-7344

Avventura, 8. 463 Amsterdam Ave ☎ 769-2510

The Ballet Shop, 35. 1887 Broadway ☎ 246-6893

Barnes & Noble, 7. 2289 Broadway ☎ 362-8835

Barnes & Noble, 33. 1972 Broadway ☎ 595-6859

Bath Island, 12. 469 Amsterdam Ave ☎ 787-9415

Betsey Johnson, 28. 248 Columbus Ave ☎ 362-3364

Blades, Board & Skate, 26. 120 W 72nd St ☎ 787-3911

Citarella, 19. 2135 Broadway ☎ 874-0383

Fairway, 20. 2127 Broadway ☎ 595-1888

Filene's Basement, 14. 2220 Broadway ☎ 873-8000

Frank Stella Ltd, 11. 440 Columbus Ave ☎ 877-5566

Greenstones et Cie, 10. 442 Columbus Ave ☎ 580-4322

Gryphon Record Shop, 23. 233 W 72nd St ☎ 874-1588

IS 44 Market, 21. Columbus Ave between 76th & 77th Sts

Kenneth Cole, 22. 353 Columbus Ave ☎ 873-2061

Laura Ashley, 17. 398 Columbus Ave ☎ 496-5110

Liberty House, 4. 2389 Broadway ☎ 799-7640

Mason's Tennis Mart, 37. 911 Seventh Ave ☎ 757-5374

Maxilla and Mandible, 16. 451 Columbus Ave ☎ 724-6173

Morris Brothers, 5. 2322 Broadway ☎ 724-9000

Murder Ink, 2. 2486 Broadway ☎ 362-8905

Museum of American Folk Art Gift Shop, 34. 2 Lincoln Sq ☎ 496-2966

Only Hearts, 18. 386 Columbus Ave ☎ 724-5608

Penny Whistle Toys, 9. 448 Columbus Ave ☎ 873-9090

Petrossian, 36. 182 W 58th St ☎ 245-2217

Pottery Barn, 31. 1965 Broadway ☎ 579-8477

Savage Jewelry, 29. 267 Columbus Ave ☎ 724-4662

Star Magic, 24. 275 Amsterdam Ave ☎ 769-2020

To Boot, 27. 256 Columbus Ave ☎ 724-8249

Tower Records, 32. 1966 Broadway ☎ 799-2500

Uncle Futz, 15. 408 Amsterdam Ave ☎ 799-6723

Welcome Home Antiques, 3. 562 Columbus Ave ☎ 362-4293

West Side Kids, 6. 498 Amsterdam Ave ☎ 496-7282

Zabar's, 13. 2245 Broadway ☎ 787-2000

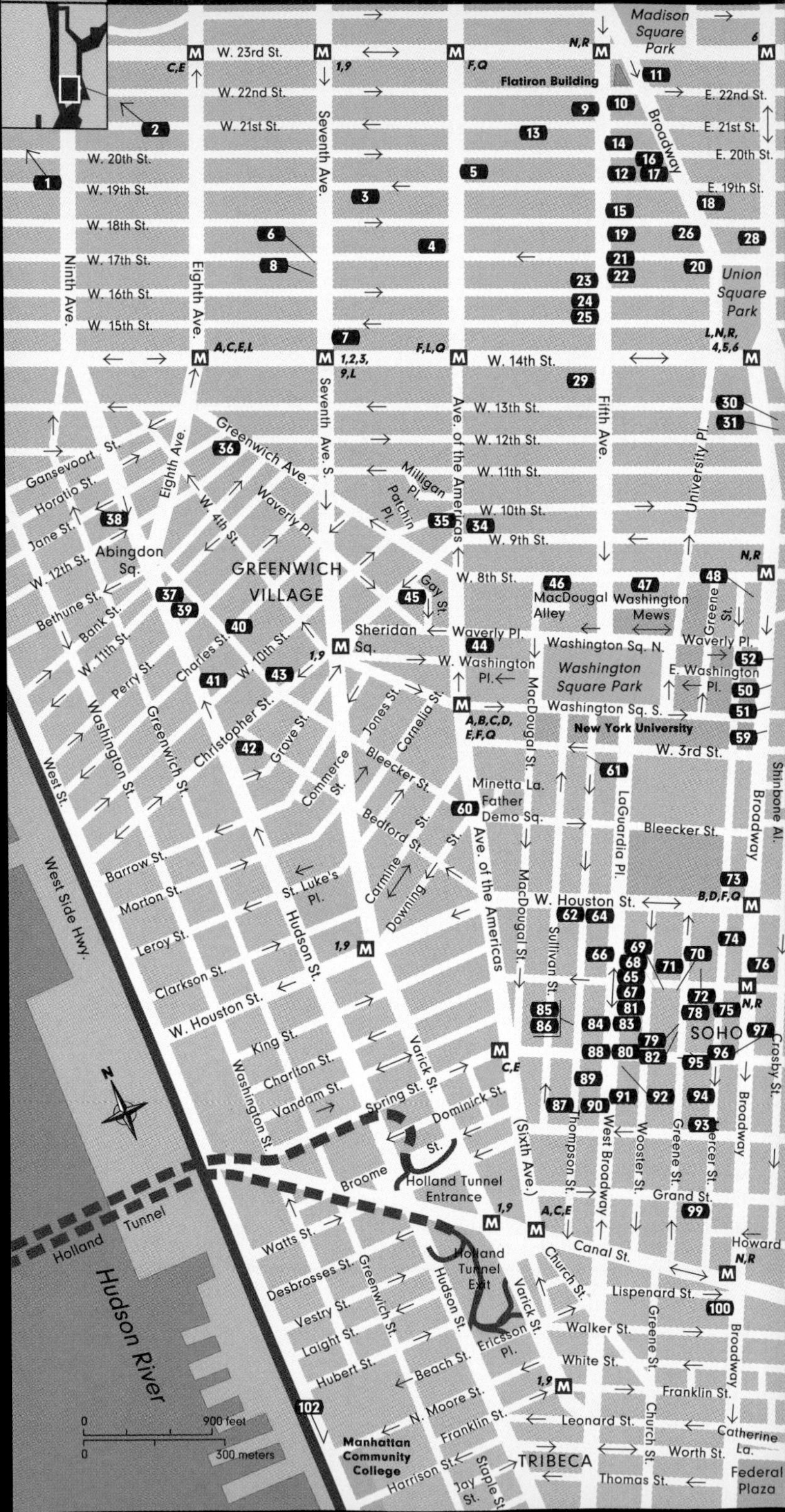
W. 23rd St.
W. 22nd St.
W. 21st St.
W. 20th St.
W. 19th St.
W. 18th St.
W. 17th St.
W. 16th St.
W. 15th St.
W. 14th St.
W. 13th St.
W. 12th St.
W. 11th St.
W. 10th St.
W. 9th St.
W. 8th St.
E. 22nd St.
E. 21st St.
E. 20th St.
E. 19th St.
Madison Square Park
Flatiron Building
Broadway
Union Square Park
Ninth Ave.
Eighth Ave.
Seventh Ave.
Seventh Ave. S.
Ave. of the Americas
Fifth Ave.
University Pl.
Gansevoort St.
Horatio St.
Jane St.
W. 12th St.
Abingdon Sq.
Bethune St.
Bank St.
W. 11th St.
Perry St.
Charles St.
W. 10th St.
Christopher St.
Grove St.
W. 4th St.
Greenwich Ave.
Waverly Pl.
Milligan Pl.
Patchin Pl.
GREENWICH VILLAGE
Gay St.
Sheridan Sq.
MacDougal Alley
Washington Mews
Greene St.
Waverly Pl.
W. Washington Pl.
Washington Sq. N.
Washington Square Park
E. Washington Pl.
Washington Sq. S.
New York University
W. 3rd St.
MacDougal St.
Jones St.
Cornelia St.
Commerce St.
Bleecker St.
Bedford St.
Minetta La.
Father Demo Sq.
LaGuardia Pl.
Bleecker St.
Shinbone Al.
Broadway
West St.
Washington St.
Greenwich St.
Barrow St.
Morton St.
St. Luke's Pl.
Carmine St.
Downing St.
Leroy St.
Clarkson St.
W. Houston St.
Hudson St.
Sullivan St.
W. Houston St.
King St.
Charlton St.
Vandam St.
Varick St.
Spring St.
Dominick St.
Broome St.
Holland Tunnel Entrance
SOHO
Crosby St.
(Sixth Ave.)
Thompson St.
West Broadway
Wooster St.
Greene St.
Mercer St.
Grand St.
Canal St.
Howard
Church St.
Lispenard St.
Walker St.
White St.
Franklin St.
Leonard St.
Worth St.
Catherine La.
Thomas St.
Federal Plaza
TRIBECA
Watts St.
Desbrosses St.
Vestry St.
Laight St.
Hubert St.
Beach St.
Ericsson Pl.
Holland Tunnel Exit
N. Moore St.
Franklin St.
Harrison St.
Jay St.
Staple St.
Manhattan Community College
West Side Hwy.
Hudson River
Holland Tunnel
N
0 900 feet
0 300 meters
C,E
1,9
F,Q
N,R
6
A,C,E,L
1,2,3, 9,L
F,L,Q
L,N,R, 4,5,6
A,B,C,D, E,F,Q
B,D,F,Q
1,9
C,E
A,C,E
1,9
1 2 3 4 5 6 7 8 9 10 11 12 13 14 15 16 17 18 19 20 21 22 23 24 25 26 28 29 30 31 34 35 36 37 38 39 40 41 42 43 44 45 46 47 48 50 51 52 59 60 61 62 64 65 66 67 68 69 70 71 72 73 74 75 76 78 79 80 81 82 83 84 85 86 87 88 89 90 91 92 93 94 95 96 97 99 100 102

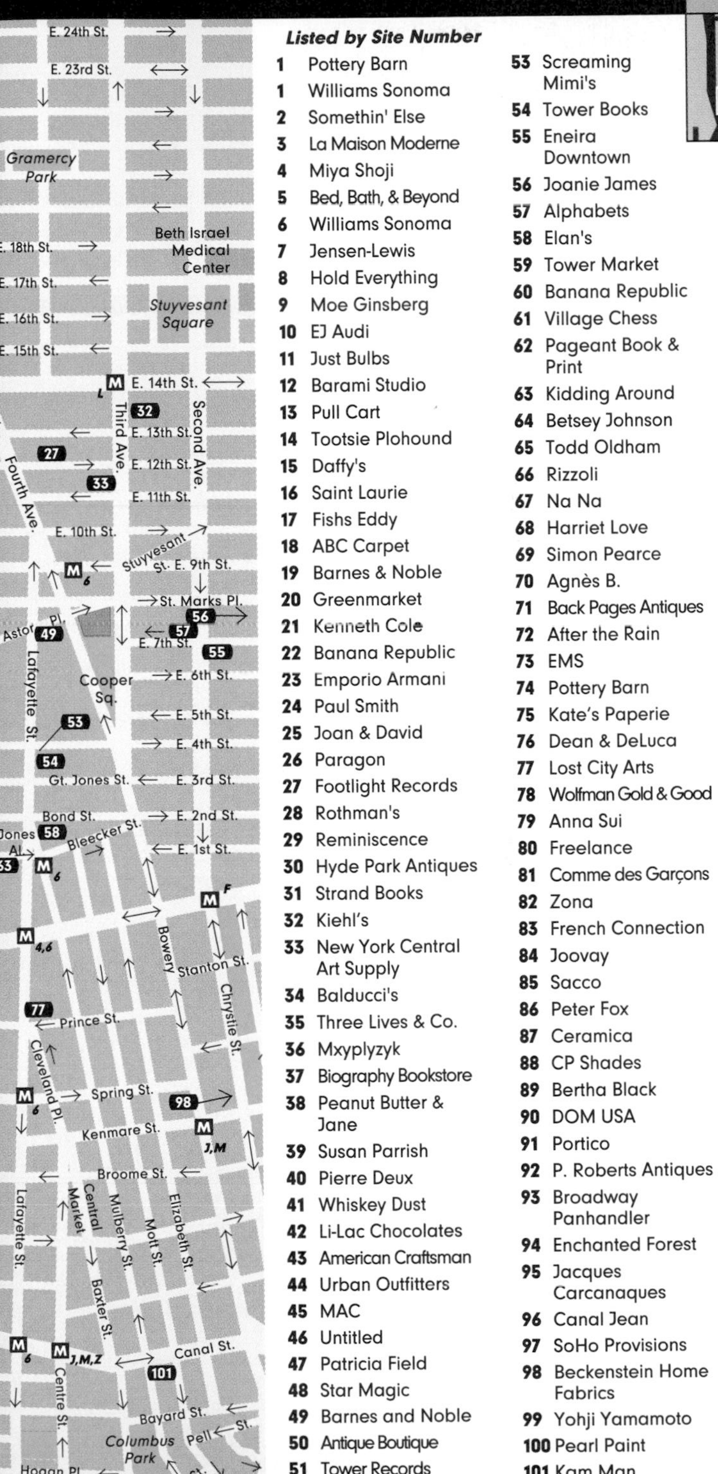

Listed by Site Number

1 Pottery Barn
1 Williams Sonoma
2 Somethin' Else
3 La Maison Moderne
4 Miya Shoji
5 Bed, Bath, & Beyond
6 Williams Sonoma
7 Jensen-Lewis
8 Hold Everything
9 Moe Ginsberg
10 EJ Audi
11 Just Bulbs
12 Barami Studio
13 Pull Cart
14 Tootsie Plohound
15 Daffy's
16 Saint Laurie
17 Fishs Eddy
18 ABC Carpet
19 Barnes & Noble
20 Greenmarket
21 Kenneth Cole
22 Banana Republic
23 Emporio Armani
24 Paul Smith
25 Joan & David
26 Paragon
27 Footlight Records
28 Rothman's
29 Reminiscence
30 Hyde Park Antiques
31 Strand Books
32 Kiehl's
33 New York Central Art Supply
34 Balducci's
35 Three Lives & Co.
36 Mxyplyzyk
37 Biography Bookstore
38 Peanut Butter & Jane
39 Susan Parrish
40 Pierre Deux
41 Whiskey Dust
42 Li-Lac Chocolates
43 American Craftsman
44 Urban Outfitters
45 MAC
46 Untitled
47 Patricia Field
48 Star Magic
49 Barnes and Noble
50 Antique Boutique
51 Tower Records
52 Shakespeare & Co
53 Screaming Mimi's
54 Tower Books
55 Eneira Downtown
56 Joanie James
57 Alphabets
58 Elan's
59 Tower Market
60 Banana Republic
61 Village Chess
62 Pageant Book & Print
63 Kidding Around
64 Betsey Johnson
65 Todd Oldham
66 Rizzoli
67 Na Na
68 Harriet Love
69 Simon Pearce
70 Agnès B.
71 Back Pages Antiques
72 After the Rain
73 EMS
74 Pottery Barn
75 Kate's Paperie
76 Dean & DeLuca
77 Lost City Arts
78 Wolfman Gold & Good
79 Anna Sui
80 Freelance
81 Comme des Garçons
82 Zona
83 French Connection
84 Joovay
85 Sacco
86 Peter Fox
87 Ceramica
88 CP Shades
89 Bertha Black
90 DOM USA
91 Portico
92 P. Roberts Antiques
93 Broadway Panhandler
94 Enchanted Forest
95 Jacques Carcanaques
96 Canal Jean
97 SoHo Provisions
98 Beckenstein Home Fabrics
99 Yohji Yamamoto
100 Pearl Paint
101 Kam Man
102 Century 21

Listed Alphabetically

ABC Carpet, 18. 888 Broadway ☎ 473-3000

After the Rain, 72. 149 Mercer St ☎ 431-1044

Agnès B., 70. 116 Prince St ☎ 925-4649

Alphabets, 57. 115 Avenue A ☎ 475-7250

An American Craftsman, 43. 317 Bleecker St ☎ 727-0841

Anna Sui, 79. 113 Greene St ☎ 941-8406

Antique Boutique, 50. 712 Broadway ☎ 460-8830

Back Pages Antiques, 71. 125 Greene St ☎ 460-5998

Balducci's, 34. 424 Sixth Ave ☎ 673-2600

Banana Republic, 22. 89 Fifth Ave ☎ 366-4691

Banana Republic, 60. 205 Bleecker St ☎ 473-9570

Barami Studio, 13. 119 Fifth Ave ☎ 529-2300

Barnes & Noble, 19. 105 Fifth Ave ☎ 675-5500

Barnes & Noble, 49. 4 Astor Pl ☎ 420-1322

Beckenstein Home Fabrics, 98. 130 Orchard St ☎ 475-4525

Bed, Bath, & Beyond, 5. 620 Sixth Ave ☎ 255-3550

Bertha Black, 89. 80 Thompson St ☎ 966-7116

Betsey Johnson, 64. 130 Thompson St ☎ 420-0169

Biography Bookstore, 37. 400 Bleecker St ☎ 807-8655

Broadway Panhandler, 93. 477 Broome St ☎ 966-3434

Canal Jean, 96. 504 Broadway ☎ 226-1130

Century 21, 102. 22 Cortlandt St ☎ 227-9092

Ceramica, 87. 59 Thompson St ☎ 941-1307

Comme des Garçons, 81. 116 Wooster St ☎ 219-0660

CP Shades, 88. 154 Spring St ☎ 226-4434

Daffy's, 15. 111 Fifth Ave ☎ 529-4477

Dean & DeLuca, 76. 560 Broadway ☎ 431-1691

DOM USA, 90. 382 W Broadway ☎ 334-5580

EJ Audi, 10. 160 Fifth Ave ☎ 337-0700

Elan's, 58. 345 Lafayette ☎ 529-2724

Emporio Armani, 23. 110 Fifth Ave ☎ 727-3240

EMS, 73. 611 B'way ☎ 505-9860

Eneira Downtown, 55. 48 1/2 E 7th St ☎ 473-2454

Enchanted Forest, 94. 85 Mercer St ☎ 925-6677

Fishs Eddy, 17. 889 Broadway ☎ 420-9020

Footlight Records, 27. 113 E 12th St ☎ 533-1572

Freelance, 80. 165 Spring St ☎ 965-9231

French Connection, 83. 435 W Broadway ☎ 219-1197

Greenmarket at Union Square, 20. 17th St at Broadway ☎ 477-3220

Harriet Love, 68. 126 Prince St ☎ 966-2280

Hold Everything, 8. 104 Seventh Ave ☎ 633-1674

Hyde Park Antiques, 30. 836 Broadway ☎ 477-0033

Jacques Carcanaques, 95. 106 Spring St ☎ 925-8110

Jensen-Lewis, 7. 89 Seventh Ave ☎ 929-4880

Joan & David, 25. 104 Fifth Ave ☎ 627-1780

Joanie James, 56. 117 E 7th St ☎ 505-9653

Joovay, 84. 436 W Broadway ☎ 431-6386

Just Bulbs, 11. 936 Broadway ☎ 228-7820

Kam Man, 101. 200 Canal St ☎ 571-0330

Kate's Paperie, 75. 561 Broadway ☎ 941-9816

Kenneth Cole, 21. 95 Fifth Ave ☎ 675-2550

Kidding Around, 63. 68 Bleecker St ☎ 598-0228

Kiehl's, 32. 109 Third Ave ☎ 677-3171

La Maison Moderne, 3. 144 W 19th St ☎ 691-9603

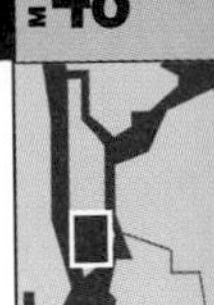

Listed Alphabetically (cont.)

Li-Lac Chocolates, 42. 120 Christopher St ☎ 242-7374

Lost City Arts, 77. 275 Lafayette St ☎ 941-8025

MAC, 45. 14 Christopher St ☎ 243-4150

Miya Shoji, 4. 109 W 17th St ☎ 243-6774.

Moe Ginsberg, 9. 162 Fifth Ave ☎ 242-3482

Mxyplyzyk, 36. 125 Greenwich Ave ☎ 989-4300

Na Na, 67. 138 Prince St ☎ 274-0749

New York Central Art Supply, 33. 62 Third Ave ☎ 473-7705

Pageant Book & Print, 62. 114 W Houston ☎ 674-5296

Paragon, 26. 867 Broadway ☎ 255-8036

Patricia Field, 47. 10 E 8th St ☎ 254-1699

Paul Smith, 24. 108 Fifth Ave ☎ 627-9770

Peanut Butter & Jane, 38. 617 Hudson St ☎ 620-7952

Pearl Paint, 100. 308 Canal St ☎ 431-7932

Peter Fox, 86. 105 Thompson St ☎ 431-7426

Peter Roberts Antiques, 92. 134 Spring St ☎ 226-4777

Pierre Deux, 40. 369 Bleecker St ☎ 243-7740

Portico, 91. 379 W B'way ☎ 941-7800

Pottery Barn Outlet, 1. 231 Tenth Ave ☎ 206-8118

Pottery Barn, 74. 600 Broadway ☎ 219-2420

Pull Cart, 13. 31 W 21st St ☎ 727-7089

Reminiscence, 29. 74 Fifth Ave ☎ 243-2292

Rizzoli, 66. 454 W Broadway ☎ 674-1616

Rothman's, 28. 200 Park Ave S ☎ 777-7400

Sacco, 85. 111 Thompson St ☎ 925-8010

Saint Laurie, 16. 895 Broadway ☎ 473-0100

Screaming Mimi's, 53. 382 Lafayette St ☎ 677-6464

Shakespeare & Co, 52. 716 Broadway ☎ 529-1330

Simon Pearce, 69. 120 Wooster St ☎ 334-2393

SoHo Provisions, 97. 518 Broadway ☎ 334-4311

Somethin' Else, 2. 182 Ninth Ave ☎ 924-0006

Star Magic, 48. 745 Broadway ☎ 228-7770

Strand Books, 31. 828 Broadway ☎ 473-1452

Susan Parrish, 39. 390 Bleecker St ☎ 645-5020

Three Lives & Co., 35. 154 W 10th St ☎ 741-2069

Todd Oldham, 65. 123 Wooster St ☎ 219-3531

Tootsie Plohound, 14. 137 Fifth Ave ☎ 460-8650

Tower Books, 54. 383 Lafayette St ☎ 228-5100

Tower Market, 59. Broadway, between W 4th & Great Jones

Tower Records, 51. 692 Broadway ☎ 505-1500

Untitled, 46. 26 W Eighth St ☎ 505-9725

Urban Outfitters, 44. 374 Sixth Ave ☎ 677-9350

Village Chess, 61. 230 Thompson St ☎ 475-9580

Whiskey Dust, 41. 526 Hudson St ☎ 691-5576

Williams Sonoma, 6. 110 Seventh Ave ☎ 633-2203

Williams Sonoma Outlet, 1. 231 Tenth Ave ☎ 206-8118

Wolfman Gold & Good Company, 78. 117 Mercer St ☎ 431-1888

Yohji Yamamoto, 99. 103 Grand St ☎ 966-9066

Zona, 82. 97 Greene St ☎ 925-6750

Restaurants/Midtown

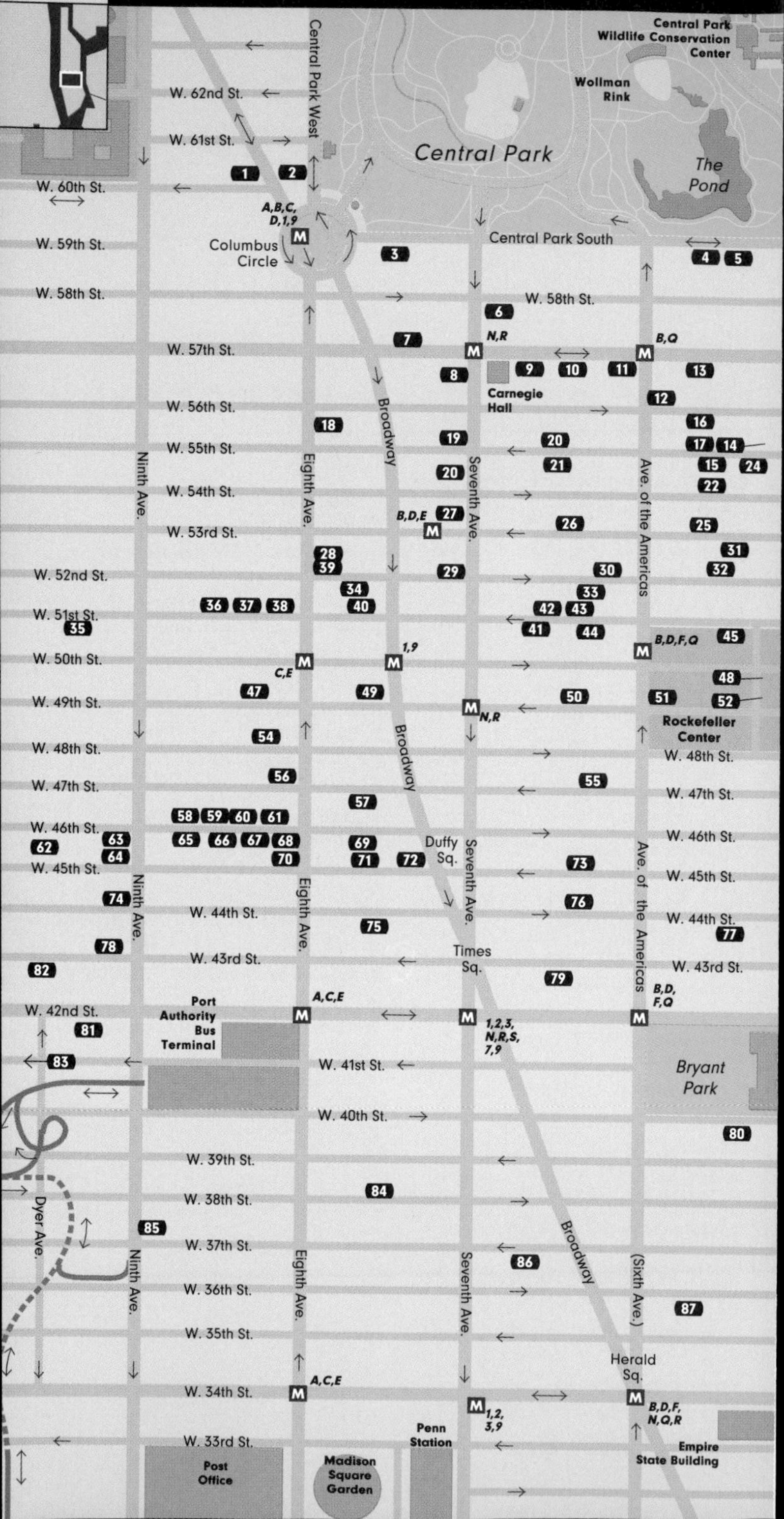

E. 63rd St.
B,Q
E. 62nd St.
E. 61st St.
E. 60th St.
TRAMWAY TO ROOSEVELT ISLAND
4,5,6, N,R
Grand Army Plaza
N,R
E. 59th St.
E. 58th St.
E. 57th St.
E. 56th St.
E. 55th St.
E. 54th St.
E,F
E. 53rd St.
E. 52nd St.
St. Patrick's Cathedral
E. 51st St.
6
E. 50th St.
E. 49th St.
E. 48th St.
E. 47th St.
E. 46th St.
E. 45th St.
E. 44th St.
Grand Central Terminal
E. 43rd St.
E. 42nd St.
S
4,5, 6,7
Chrysler Building
N.Y. Public Library (Main)
E. 41st St.
E. 40th St.
E. 39th St.
E. 38th St.
E. 37th St.
E. 36th St.
E. 35th St.
E. 34th St.
E. 33rd St.
E. 32nd St.
Fifth Ave.
Madison Ave.
Park Ave.
Vanderbilt Ave.
Lexington Ave.
Third Ave.
Second Ave.
First Ave.
United Nations Plaza
Beekman Pl.
United Nations Headquarters
FDR Dr.
Kips Bay Plaza
NYU Medical Center
N
0 7500 feet
0 250 meters
88 89 90 91 92 93 94 95 96 97 98 99 100 101 102 103 104 105 106 107 108 109 110 111 112 113 114 115 116 117 118 119 120 121 122 123 124 125 126 127 128 129 130 131 132 133 134 135 136 137 138 139 140 141 142 143 144 145 146 147 23 46 53

Restaurants/Midtown

Listed by Site Number

1 Gabriel's
2 Jean-Georges
3 San Domenico
4 Mickey Mantle
5 Nirvana
6 Petrossian
7 Hard Rock Café
8 Trattoria dell'Arte
9 Russian Tea Room
10 Planet Hollywood
11 Motown Café
12 Harley Davidson Café
13 Mangia
14 La Caravelle
15 La Côte Basque
16 Darbar
17 Allegria
18 Tapika
19 Carnegie Deli
20 Christer's
21 Osteria del Circo
22 Ciao Europa
23 Aquavit
24 La Bonne Soupe
25 Raphael
26 Remi
27 Stage Deli
28 Caffe Cielo
29 Rosie O'Grady's
30 Ben Benson's
31 China Grill
32 21 Club
33 Victor's Café 52
34 Gallagher's
35 Hallo Berlin
36 Café des Sports
37 Rene Pujol
38 Tout Va Bien
39 Bangkok Cuisine
40 Les Pyrénées
41 Ruth's Chris Steakhouse
42 Le Bernardin
43 Palio
44 La Cité
45 Fashion Café
46 The Assembly
47 New World Grill
48 Sea Grill
49 Wally's & Joseph's
50 Iroha
51 Hurley's
52 American Festival Café
53 La Reserve
54 Swiss Inn
55 Dish of Salt
56 B Smith's
57 Pierre au Tunnel
58 Crepes Suzette
59 Barbetta
60 Becco
61 Broadway Joe
62 Mike's American Bar and Grill
63 Zen Palate
64 Film Center Café
65 Le Rivage
66 Joe Allen's
67 Orso
68 Beefsteak Charlie's
69 Pergola Des Artistes
70 Kodama
71 Frankie & Johnny's
72 Charley O's
73 Cabana Carioca
74 Westbank Café
75 Sardi's
76 Café Un Deux Trois
77 44
78 Le Madeleine
79 Century Cafe
80 Bryant Park Cafe
80 Bryant Park Grill
81 Chez Josephine
82 Cafe St. Francis
83 World Yacht Cruises
84 Lou G Siegel
85 Market Café
86 Hideaway
87 Keen's
88 Harry Cipriani
89 Mad 61
90 Yellowfingers
91 Arizona 206
92 Rosa Mexicano
93 March
94 L'Entrecote
95 Dawat
96 Felidia
97 Le Chantilly
98 Akbar
99 Adrienne
100 5757
101 Benihana of Tokyo
102 Lespinasse
103 Shun Lee Palace
104 PJ Clarke's
105 Oceana
106 Cellini
107 San Pietro
108 Seryna
109 Vong
110 Lipstick Cafe
111 Il Nido
112 Solera
113 Maple Garden Duckhouse
114 Eamonn Doran
115 Billy's
116 Le Perigord
117 La Grenouille
118 Four Seasons
119 Nippon
120 Wylie's Ribs & Co
121 Tsukiji Sushisay
122 Tatou
123 Al Bustan
124 Zarela
125 Lutèce
126 Sushiden
127 San Giusto
128 David K's
129 Smith & Wollensky
130 Chin Chin
131 Box Tree
132 Inagiku
133 Peacock Alley
134 Giambelli
135 Hatsuhana
136 Dolce
137 Rusty Staub's
138 Morton's of Chicago
139 Bienvenue
140 Grand Central Oyster Bar
141 Nanni
142 Captain's Table
143 Spark's Steakhouse
144 Palm
145 Ambassador Grill
146 Sichuan Pavilion
147 Dock's on Third

Listed Alphabetically

Adrienne, 99. 700 Fifth Ave ☎ 903-3918. Continental. $$$$

Allegria, 17. 66 W 55th St ☎ 956-7755. Italian. $$$

Akbar, 98. 475 Park Ave ☎ 838-1717. Indian. $$$

Al Bustan, 123. 827 Third Ave ☎ 759-8439. Lebanese. $$

Ambassador Grill, 145. UN Plaza-Park Hyatt ☎ 702-5014. Continental. $$$

American Festival Café, 52. Rockefeller Center, 20 W 50th St ☎ 332-7620. American. $$

Aquavit, 23. 13 W 54th St ☎ 307-7311. Scandinavian. $$$$

Arizona 206, 91. 206 E 60th St ☎ 838-0440. Southwestern. $$

The Assembly, 46. 16 W 51st St ☎ 581-3580. Steakhouse. $$$

B Smith's, 56. 771 Eighth Ave ☎ 247-2222. Continental. $$$

Bangkok Cuisine, 39. 885 Eighth Ave ☎ 581-6370. Thai. $$

Barbetta, 59. 321 W 46th St ☎ 246-9171. Italian. $$$$

Becco, 60. 355 W 46th St ☎ 397-7597. Italian. $$

Beefsteak Charlie's, 68. 709 Eighth Ave ☎ 757-3110. Steakhouse. $

Ben Benson's, 30. 123 W 52nd St ☎ 581-8888. Steakhouse. $$$$

Benihana of Tokyo, 101. 120 E 56th St ☎ 593-1627. Japanese. $$

Bienvenue, 139. 21 E 36th St. ☎ 684-0215. French. $$

Billy's, 115. 948 First Ave ☎ 355-8920. American. $$$

Box Tree, 131. 250 E 49th St ☎ 758-8320. Continental. $$$$

Broadway Joe, 61. 315 W 46th St ☎ 246-6513. American. $$

Bryant Park Café, 80. 25 W 40th St ☎ 840-6500. American. $$

Bryant Park Grill, 80. 25 W 40th St ☎ 840-6500. American. $$$

Cabana Carioca, 73. 123 W 45th St ☎ 581-8088. Brazilian. $$

Café des Sports, 36. 329 W 51st St ☎ 974-9052. French. $$

Café Un Deux Trois, 76. 123 W 44th St ☎ 354-4148. French. $$

Café St Francis, 82. 482 W 43rd St ☎ 947-6430. American. $$

Caffe Cielo, 28. 881 Eighth Ave ☎ 246-9555. Italian. $$

Captain's Table, 142. 860 Second Ave ☎ 697-9538. Seafood. $$$

Carnegie Deli, 19. 854 Seventh Ave ☎ 757-2245. Deli. $$

Cellini, 106. 65 E 54th St ☎ 751-1555. Italian. $$$

Century Café, 79. 132 W 43rd St ☎ 398-1988. American. $$$

Charley O's, 72. 218 W 45th St ☎ 563-7440. Continental. $$

Chez Josephine, 81. 414 W 42nd St ☎ 594-1925. International. $$$

Chin Chin, 130. 216 E 49th St ☎ 888-4555. Chinese. $$$

China Grill, 31. 52 W 53rd St ☎ 333-7788. Asian. $$$

Christer's, 20. 145 W 55th St ☎ 974-7224. Scandinavian. $$$

Ciao Europa, 22. 63 W 54th St ☎ 247-1200. Italian. $$$

Crepes Suzette, 58. 363 W 46th St ☎ 581-9717. French. $$$

Darbar, 16. 44 W 56th St ☎ 432-7227. Indian. $$$

David K's, 128. 209 E 49th St ☎ 800/357-1802. Chinese. $$

Dawat, 95. 210 E 58th St ☎ 355-7555. Indian. $$$

Dish of Salt, 55. 133 W 47th St ☎ 921-4242. Cantonese. $$

Dock's on Third, 147. 633 Third Ave ☎ 986-8080. Seafood. $$

Dolce, 136. 60 E 49th St ☎ 692-9292. Italian. $$

Eamonn Doran, 114. 998 Second Ave ☎ 752-8088. Continental. $$

Fashion Café, 45. 51 Rockefeller Plaza ☎ 758-1479. American. $$

Felidia, 96. 243 E 58th St ☎ 758-1479. Italian. $$$$

5757, 100. 57 E 57th St ☎ 758-5757. American. $$$$

Film Center Café, 64. 635 Ninth Ave ☎ 262-2525. American. $$

$$$$ = ***over $50*** $$$ = ***$30–$50*** $$ = ***$20–$30*** $ = ***under $20***

Based on cost per person, excluding drinks, service, and 8 1/4% sales tax.

Listed Alphabetically (Cont.)

44, 77. 44 W 44th St ☎ 944-8844. American. $$$

Four Seasons, 118. 99 E 52nd St ☎ 754-9494. Continental. $$$$

Frankie & Johnny's, 71. 269 W 45th St ☎ 997-9494. American. $$$

Gabriel's, 1. 11 W 60th St ☎ 956-4600. Italian. $$$

Gallagher's, 34. 228 W 52nd St ☎ 245-5336. Steakhouse. $$$

Giambelli, 134. 46 E 50th St ☎ 688-2760. Italian. $$$$

Grand Central Oyster Bar, 140. Grand Central Terminal ☎ 490-6650. Seafood. $$$

Hallo Berlin, 35. 402 W 51st St ☎ 541-6248. German. $

Hard Rock Café, 7. 221 W 57th St ☎ 489-6565. American. $$

Harley Davidson Café, 12. 1370 Ave of the Americas ☎ 245-6000. American. $$

Harry Cipriani, 88. 781 Fifth Ave ☎ 753-5566. Italian. $$$$

Hatsuhana, 135. 17 E 48th St ☎ 355-3345. Japanese. $$$

Hideaway, 86. 32 W 37th St ☎ 947-8940. Italian. $$$

Hurley's, 51. 1240 Ave of the Americas ☎ 765-8981. American. $$

Il Nido, 111. 251 E 53rd St ☎ 753-8450. Italian. $$$$

Inagiku, 132. 111 E 49th St ☎ 355-0440. Japanese. $$$

Iroha, 50. 152 W 49th St ☎ 398-9049. Japanese. $$

Jean-Georges, 2. 1 Central Park West ☎ 299-3900. French. $$$$

Joe Allen's, 66. 326 W 46th St ☎ 581-6464. American. $$

Keen's, 87. 72 W 36th St ☎ 947-3636. Steakhouse. $$$

Kodama, 70. 301 W 45th St ☎ 582-8065. Japanese. $$

La Bonne Soupe, 24. 48 W 55th St ☎ 586-7650. French. $$

La Caravelle, 14. 33 W 55th St ☎ 586-4252. French. $$$$

La Cité, 44. 120 W 51st St ☎ 956-7100. Steakhouse. $$$

La Côte Basque, 15. 60 W 55th St ☎ 688-6525. French. $$$$

La Grenouille, 117. 3 E 52nd St ☎ 752-1495. French. $$$$

La Reserve, 53. 4 W 49th St ☎ 247-2993. French. $$$

Le Bernardin, 42. 155 W 51st St ☎ 489-1515. Seafood. $$$$

Le Chantilly, 97. 106 E 57th St ☎ 751-2931. French. $$$$

Le Madeleine, 78. 403 W 43rd St ☎ 246-2993. French. $$$

L'Entrecote, 94. 1057 First Ave ☎ 755-0080. French. $$$

Le Perigord, 116. 405 E 52nd St ☎ 755-6244. French. $$$

Le Rivage, 65. 340 W 46th St ☎ 765-7374. French. $$

Les Pyrénées, 40. 251 W 51st St ☎ 246-0044. French. $$$

Lespinasse, 102. 2 E 55th St ☎ 339-6719. French. $$$$

Lipstick Café, 110. 885 Third Ave ☎ 486-8664. Continental. $$

Lou G Siegel, 84. 209 W 38th St ☎ 921-4433. Kosher. $

Lutèce, 125. 249 E 50th St ☎ 752-2225. French. $$$$

Mad 61, 89. 660 Madison Ave ☎ 833-2200. Italian. $$$

Mangia, 13. 50 W 57th St ☎ 582-3061. Italian. $

Maple Garden Duckhouse, 113. 236 E 53rd St ☎ 759-8260. Chinese. $

March, 93. 405 E 58th St ☎ 754-6272. American. $$$$

Market Café, 85. 496 Ninth Ave ☎ 967-3892. American. $$

Mickey Mantle's, 4. 42 Central Park S ☎ 688-7777. American. $$

Mike's American Bar and Grill, 62. 650 10th Ave ☎ 246-4115. American. $$

Morton's of Chicago, 138. 551 Fifth Ave ☎ 972-3315. Steakhouse. $$$$

Motown Café, 11. 104 W 57th St ☎ 581-8030. American. $$

Nanni, 141. 146 E 46th St ☎ 697-4161. Italian. $$$$

New World Grill, 47. 329 W 49th St ☎ 957-4757. Eclectic. $$

Nippon, 119. 155 E 52nd St ☎ 355-9020. Japanese. $$$

Listed Alphabetically (cont.)

Nirvana, 5. 30 Central Park S ☎ 486-5700. Indian. $$

Oceana, 105. 55 E 54th St ☎ 759-5941. Seafood. $$$$

Orso, 67. 322 W 46th St ☎ 489-7212. Italian. $$$

Osteria del Circo, 21. 120 W 55th St ☎ 265-3636. Italian. $$$

Palio, 43. 151 W 51st St ☎ 245-4850. Italian. $$$$

Palm, 144. 837 Second Ave ☎ 687-2953. Steakhouse. $$$$

Peacock Alley, 133. 301 Park Ave ☎ 872-4895. French. $$$

Pergola Des Artistes, 69. 252 W 46th St ☎ 302-7500. French. $

Petrossian, 6. 182 W 58th St ☎ 245-2214. French. $$$$

Pierre au Tunnel, 57. 250 W 47th St ☎ 575-1220. French. $$

PJ Clarke's, 104. 915 Third Ave ☎ 759-1650. American. $

Planet Hollywood, 10. 140 W 57th St ☎ 333-7827. American. $$$

Raphael, 25. 33 W 54th St ☎ 582-8993. French. $$$

Remi, 26. 145 W 53rd St ☎ 581-4242. Italian. $$$

Rene Pujol, 37. 321 W 51st St ☎ 246-3023. French. $$$

Rosa Mexicano, 92. 1063 First Ave ☎ 753-7407. Mexican. $$$

Rosie O'Grady's, 29. 800 Seventh Ave ☎ 582-2975. Irish. $$

Russian Tea Room, 9. 150 W 57th St ☎ 265-0947. Russian. $$$

Rusty Staub's, 137. 575 Fifth Ave ☎ 682-1000. American. $$$

Ruth's Chris Steakhouse, 41. 148 W 51st St ☎ 245-9600. American. $$$

San Domenico, 3. 240 Central Park S ☎ 265-5959. Italian. $$$$

San Giusto, 127. 935 Second Ave ☎ 319-0900. Italian. $$$

San Pietro, 107. 18 E 54th St ☎ 753-9015. Italian. $$$

Sardi's, 75. 234 W 44th St ☎ 221-8444. Continental. $$$

Sea Grill, 48. Rockefeller Ctr, 19 W 49th St ☎ 332-7610. Seafood. $$$$

Seryna, 108. 11 E 53rd St ☎ 980-9393. Japanese. $$$

Shun Lee Palace, 103. 155 E 55th St ☎ 371-8844. Chinese. $$$

Sichuan Palace, 146. 310 E 44th St ☎ 972-7377. Chinese. $$

Smith & Wollensky, 129. 797 Third Ave ☎ 753-1530. Steakhouse. $$$

Solera, 112. 216 E 53rd St ☎ 644-1166. Spanish. $$

Spark's Steakhouse, 143. 210 E 46th St ☎ 687-4855. Steakhouse. $$$

Stage Deli, 27. 834 Seventh Ave ☎ 245-7850. Deli. $

Sushiden, 126. 19 E 49th St ☎ 758-2700. Japanese. $$$

Swiss Inn, 54. 311 W 48th St ☎ 459-9280. Swiss. $$$

Tapika, 18. 950 Eighth Ave ☎ 397-3737. Southwest. $$$

Tatou, 122. 151 E 50th St ☎ 753-1144. American. $$$

Tout Va Bien, 38. 311 W 51st St ☎ 265-0190. French. $$

Trattoria dell'Arte, 8. 900 Seventh Ave ☎ 245-9800. Italian. $$$.

Tsukiji Sushisay, 121. 38 E 51st St ☎ 755-1780. Japanese. $$

21 Club, 32. 21 W 52nd St ☎ 582-7200. Continental. $$$$

Victor's Café 52, 33. 236 W 52nd St ☎ 586-7714. Cuban. $$

Vong, 109. 200 E 54th St ☎ 486-9592. Thai. $$$

Wally's & Joseph's, 49. 249 W 49th St ☎ 582-0460. Steakhouse. $$$

Westbank Café, 74. 407 W 42nd St ☎ 695-6909. Continental. $$

World Yacht Cruises, 83. Pier 81, W 41st St ☎ 630-8100. Continental. $$$$

Wylie's Ribs & Co, 120. 891 First Ave ☎ 751-0700. Barbecue. $$

Yellowfingers, 90. 200 E 60th St ☎ 751-8615. Italian. $$

Zarela, 124. 953 Second Ave ☎ 644-6740. Mexican. $$

Zen Palate, 63. 663 Ninth Ave ☎ 582-1669. Vegetarian. $$

$$$$ = ***over $50*** $$$ = ***$30–$50*** $$ = ***$20–$30*** $ = ***under $20***

Based on cost per person, excluding drinks, service, and 8 1/4% sales tax.

Restaurants/Upper West Side

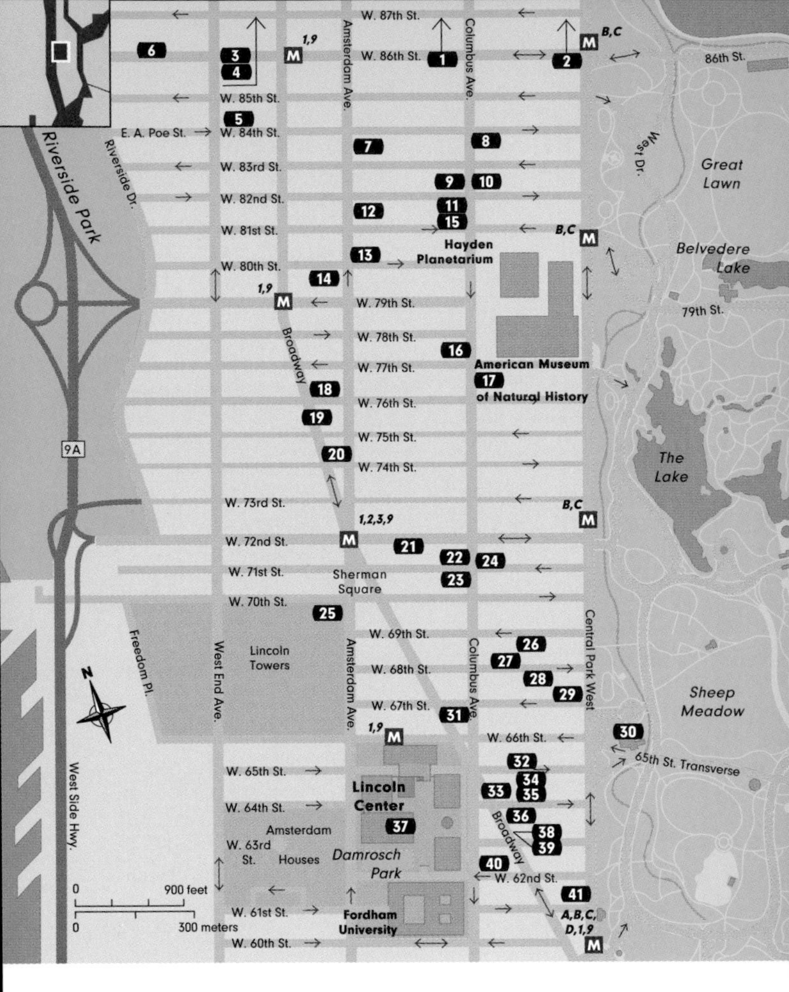

Listed by Site Number

1 Terrace
2 Sylvia's
3 Dock's Oyster Bar & Grill
4 Carmine's
5 Edgar's Cafe
6 La Mirabelle
7 Good Enough to Eat
8 Isola
9 Columbus Bakery
10 Fujiyama Mama
11 Rain
12 EJ's Luncheonette
13 Sarabeth's Kitchen
14 Savann
15 Main Street
16 Museum Cafe
17 Isabella's
18 Harry's Burrito Junction
19 Ernie's
20 Josie's
21 Fine & Shapiro
22 Penang
23 China Fun
24 Fishin Eddie
25 Café Luxembourg
26 Santa Fe
27 La Boîte en Bois
28 Vince & Eddie's
29 Café des Artistes
30 Tavern on the Green
31 Ollie's
32 Shun Lee West
33 The Saloon
34 John's Pizza
35 O'Neal's
36 Picholine
37 Grand Tier
38 Fiorello's Roman Cafe
39 Josephina
40 Merlot Bar & Grill
41 Conservatory

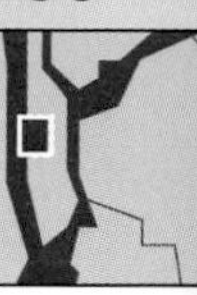

Listed Alphabetically

Café des Artistes, 29. 1 W 67th St ☎ 877-3500. French. $$$$

Café Luxembourg, 25. 200 W 70th St ☎ 873-7411. American. $$$$

Carmine's, 4. 2450 Broadway ☎ 362-2200. Italian. $$

China Fun, 23. 246 Columbus Ave ☎ 580-1516. Dim Sum. $

Columbus Bakery, 9. 474 Columbus Ave ☎ 724-6880. American. $

Conservatory, 41. 15 Central Park W ☎ 581-0896. Continental. $$$

Dock's Oyster Bar & Grill, 3. 2427 B'way ☎ 724-5588. Seafood. $$$

EJ's Luncheonette, 12. 447 Amsterdam Ave ☎ 873-3444. American. $

Edgar's Cafe, 5. 255 W 84th Street ☎ 496-6126. Dessert. $

Ernie's, 19. 2150 Broadway ☎ 496-1588. Italian. $$$

Fine & Shapiro, 21. 138 W 72nd St ☎ 877-2874. Deli. $$

Fiorello's Roman Cafe, 38. 1900 Broadway ☎ 595-5330. Italian. $$$

Fishin Eddie, 24. 73 W 71st St ☎ 874-3474. Seafood. $$$

Fujiyama Mama, 10. 467 Columbus Ave ☎ 769-1144. Japanese. $$$

Good Enough to Eat, 7. 483 Amsterdam Ave ☎ 496-0163. American. $$

Grand Tier, 37. Lincoln Center, Broadway & W 64th St ☎ 799-3400. Continental. $$$$

Harry's Burrito Junction 18. 2160 Broadway ☎ 362-2500. Mexican. $

Isabella's, 17. 359 Columbus Ave ☎ 724-2100. Mediterranean. $$

Isola, 8. 485 Columbus Ave ☎ 362-7400. Italian. $$

John's Pizza, 34. 48 W 65th St ☎ 721-7001. Italian. $

Josephina, 39. 1900 Broadway ☎ 799-1000. American. $$

Josie's, 20. 300 Amsterdam ☎ 769-1212. American, $$

La Boîte en Bois, 27. 75 W 68th St ☎ 874-2705. French. $$$

La Mirabelle, 6. 333 W 86th St ☎ 496-0458. French. $$$

Main Street, 15. 446 Columbus Ave ☎ 873-5025. American. $$

Merlot Bar & Grill, 40. 48 W 63rd St ☎ 363-7568. French/American.

Museum Cafe, 16. 366 Columbus Ave ☎ 799-0150. American. $$

Ollie's, 31. 1991 Broadway ☎ 595-8181. Chinese. $

O'Neal's, 35. 49 W 64th St ☎ 787-4663. Continental. $$

Penang, 22. 240 Columbus Ave ☎ 769-3988. Malaysian. $

Picholine, 36. 35 W 64th St ☎ 724-8585. French. $$$$

Rain, 11. 100 W 82nd St ☎ 501-0776. South Asian. $$

The Saloon, 33. 1920 B'way ☎ 874-1500. American. $$$

Santa Fe, 26. 72 W 69th St ☎ 724-0822. Mexican. $$$

Sarabeth's Kitchen, 13. 423 Amsterdam Ave ☎ 496-6280. American. $$

Savann, 14. 414 Amsterdam Ave ☎ 580-0202. American. $

Shun Lee West, 32. 43 W 65th St ☎ 595-8895. Chinese. $$$

Sylvia's, 2. 328 Lenox Ave ☎ 996-0660. Soul. $$

Tavern on the Green, 30. Central Park W & 67th St ☎ 873-3200. Continental. $$$$

Terrace, 1. 400 W 119th St ☎ 666-9490. French. $$$$

Vince & Eddie's, 28. 70 W 68th St ☎ 721-0068. American. $$$

MAP 51 Restaurants/Upper East Side

Listed by Site Number

1 Table d'Hote
2 Bistro de Nord
3 Elaine's
4 Heidelberg
5 Tombola
6 Wilkinson's
7 Mocca
8 Divino
9 Pig Heaven
10 Sistina
11 La Metairie
12 Miss Saigon
13 The Lobster Club
14 E.A.T.
15 Mark's Restaurant
16 Carlyle Restaurant
17 Daniel
18 Sarabeth's Kitchen-Whitney
19 First Wok
20 Caffé Buon Gusto
21 Lusardi's
22 Bankok House
23 Szechuan Kitchen
24 Canyon Road
25 Dresner's
26 Red Tulip
27 Pamir
28 JG Melon
29 Mezzaluna
30 Café Crocodile
31 Petaluma
32 Allora
33 Polo
34 Right Bank
35 7th Regiment Mess
36 Sign of the Dove
37 Le Cirque 2000
38 Le Regence
39 Jo Jo
40 Post House
41 Bravo Gianni
42 Park Avenue Café
43 Madame Romaine
44 Brio
45 Maxim's
46 Arcadia
47 Aureole
48 Serendipity 3

Listed Alphabetically

Arcadia, 46. 21 E 62nd St ☎ 223-2900 American $$$$

Allora, 32. 1321 First Ave ☎ 570-0384. Italian. $$

Aureole, 47. 34 E 61st St ☎ 319-1660. French. $$$$

Bangkok House, 22. 1485 First Ave ☎ 581-6370. Thai. $$

Bistro du Nord, 2. 1312 Madison Ave ☎ 289-0997. French. $$$

Bravo Gianni, 41. 230 E 63rd St ☎ 752-7272. Italian. $$$

Brio, 44. 786 Lexington Ave ☎ 980-2300. Italian. $$

Café Crocodile, 30. 354 E 74th St ☎ 249-6619. French. $$$

Caffé Buon Gusto, 20. 236 E 77th St ☎ 535-6884. Italian $

Canyon Road, 24. 1470 First Ave ☎ 734-1600. Southwestern. $$$

Carlyle Restaurant, 16. Carlyle Hotel, 35 E 76th St ☎ 744-1600. Continental. $$$$

Daniel, 17. 20 E 76th St ☎ 288-0033. French. $$$$

Divino, 8. 1556 Second Ave ☎ 861-1096. Italian. $$$

Dresner's, 25. 1479 York Ave ☎ 988-5153. American. $$

E.A.T., 14. 1064 Madison Ave ☎ 772-0022. Continental. $$$

Elaine's, 3. 1703 Second Ave ☎ 534-8103. Italian. $$$

First Wok, 19. 1374 Third Ave ☎ 861-2600. Chinese. $

Heidelberg, 4. 1648 Second Ave ☎ 628-3232. German. $$

JG Melon, 28. 1291 Third Ave ☎ 744-0585. American. $$

Jo Jo, 39. 160 E 64th St ☎ 223-5656. French. $$$

La Metairie, 11. 1442 Third Ave ☎ 988-1800. French. $$$$

Le Cirque 2000, 37. 58 E 65th St ☎ 794-9292. French. $$$$

Le Regence, 38. 37 E 64th St ☎ 607-4647. French. $$$$

The Lobster Club, 13. 24 E 80th St ☎ 249-6500. American. $$$

Lusardi's, 21. 1494 Second Ave ☎ 249-2020. Italian. $$$$

Madame Romaine, 43. 132 E 61st St ☎ 758-2422. French. $$

Mark's Restaurant, 15. 25 E 77th St ☎ 879-1864. Continental. $$$

Maxim's, 45. 680 Madison Ave ☎ 751-5111. French. $$$$

Mezzaluna, 29. 1295 Third Ave ☎ 535-9600. Italian. $$$

Miss Saigon, 12. 1425 Third Ave ☎ 988-8828. Vietnamese. $

Mocca, 7. 1588 Second Ave ☎ 734-6470. Hungarian. $$

Pamir, 27. 1437 Second Ave ☎ 650-1095. Afghan. $$

Park Avenue Café, 42. 100 E 63rd St ☎ 644-1900. American. $$$$

Petaluma, 31. 1356 First Ave ☎ 772-8800. Italian. $$$

Pig Heaven, 9. 1540 Second Ave ☎ 744-4333. Chinese. $$

Polo, 33. Westbury Hotel, 840 Madison Ave ☎ 439-4907. French/Continental. $$$

Post House, 40. 28 E 63rd St ☎ 935-2888. American. $$$$

Red Tulip, 26. 439 E 75th St ☎ 734-4893. Hungarian. $$$

Right Bank, 34. 822 Madison Ave ☎ 737-2811. American. $$

Sarabeth's Kitchen-Whitney, 18. 1295 Madison Ave ☎ 570-3670. American. $

Serendipity 3, 48. 225 E 60th St ☎ 838-3531. American. $$

7th Regiment Mess, 35. 643 Park Ave ☎ 744-4107. American. $$

Sign of the Dove, 36. 1110 Third Ave ☎ 861-8080. Continental. $$$

Sistina, 10. 1555 Second Ave ☎ 861-7660. Italian. $$$$

Szechuan Kitchen, 23. 1460 First Ave ☎ 249-4615. Szechuan. $

Table d'Hote, 1. 44 E 92nd St ☎ 348-8125. Continental. $$$

Tombola, 5. 1603 Second Ave ☎ 772-2161. Italian. $$

Wilkinson's, 6. 1573 York Ave ☎ 535-5454. Seafood. $$$

$$$$ = ***over $50*** $$$ = ***$30–$50*** $$ = ***$20–$30*** $ = ***under $20***

Based on cost per person, excluding drinks, service, and 8 1/4% sales tax.

MAP 52 Restaurants/Chelsea & Gramercy Park

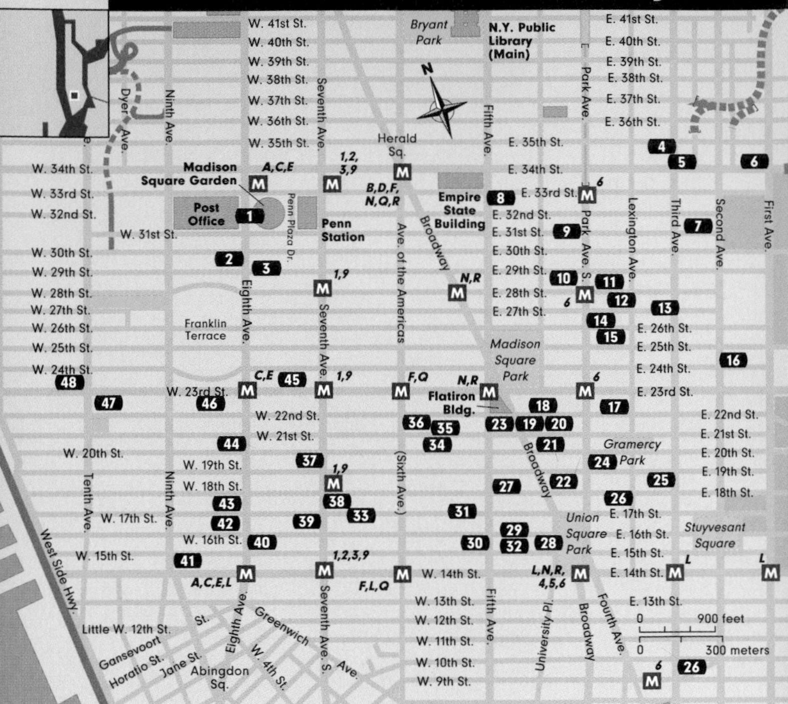

Listed by Site Number

1 Charley O's
2 San Remo
3 Estoril Sol
4 Patsy's Pizza
5 Nicola Paone
6 El Parador
7 Marchi's
8 Hunan Fifth Ave
9 An American Place
10 Park Bistro
11 Les Halles
12 La Petite Auberge
13 Albuquerque Eats
14 Park Ave Country Club
15 La Colombe d'Or
16 Ole
17 Novitá
18 Bolo
19 Rascals
20 Alva
21 Gramercy Tavern
22 Patria
23 Aja
24 City Crab
25 Pitchoune
26 Rectangles
27 America
28 Coffee Shop
29 Union Square Café
30 Mesa Grill
31 Flowers
32 Chat n' Chew
33 Da Umberto
34 Periyali
35 Cal's
36 Lola
37 Claire
38 Le Madri
39 Merchants NY
40 Chelsea Trattoria Italiana
41 Old Homestead
42 Eighteenth and Eighth
43 Food Bar
44 Bendix
45 El Quijote
46 Chelsea Bistro
47 Empire Diner
48 Zucca

Listed Alphabetically

Aja, 23. 937 Broadway ☎ 473-8388. American. $$$

Albuquerque Eats, 13. 375 Third Ave☎ 683-6500. Mexican. $

Alva, 20. 36 E 22nd St ☎ 228-4399. American. $$$

America, 27. 9 E 18th St ☎ 505-2110. American. $$

An American Place, 9. 2 Park Ave ☎ 684-2122. American. $$$$

Bendix, 44. 219 Eighth Ave ☎ 366-0560. Thai/American. $

Bolo, 18. 23 E 22nd St ☎ 228-2200. Italian. $$$

Cal's, 35. 55 W 21st St ☎ 929-0740. French. $$$

Charley O's, 1. 9 Penn Plaza ☎ 630-0343. Irish. $$

Chat 'n Chew, 32. 10 E 16th St. 243-1616. American. $

Chelsea Bistro, 46. 358 W 23rd St ☎ 727-2026. French. $$$

Chelsea Trattoria Italiana, 40. 108 Eighth Ave ☎ 924-7786. Italian. $$$

City Crab, 24. 235 Park Ave S ☎ 529-3800. Seafood. $$

Claire, 37. 156 Seventh Ave ☎ 255-1955. Seafood. $$

Coffee Shop, 28. 29 Union Sq W ☎ 243-7969. Brazilian-American. $$

Da Umberto, 33. 107 W 17th St ☎ 989-0303. Italian. $$$

Eighteen and Eighth, 43. 159 Eighth Ave ☎ 242-5000. American. $

El Quijote, 45. 226 W 23rd St. 929-1855. Spanish. $$$

El Parador, 6. 325 E 34th St ☎ 679-6812. Mexican. $$

Empire Diner, 47. 210 Tenth Ave ☎ 243-2736. American. $$

Estoril Sol, 3. 382 Eighth Ave ☎ 947-1043. Portuguese. $

Flowers, 31. 21 W 17th St ☎ 691-8888. Continental. $$$

Food Bar, 42. 149 Eighth Ave. 243-2020. American. $$

Gramercy Tavern, 21. 42 E 20th St. 477-0777. American. $$$$

Hunan Fifth Ave, 8. 323 Fifth Ave ☎ 686-3366. Chinese. $

La Colombe d'Or, 15. 134 E 26th St ☎ 689-0666. French. $$$

La Petite Auberge, 12. 116 Lexington Ave ☎ 689-5003. French. $$$

Le Madri, 38. 168 W 18th St ☎ 727-8022. Italian. $$$

Les Halles, 11. 411 Park Ave S ☎ 679-4111. French. $$$

Lola, 36. 30 W 22nd St ☎ 675-6700. Caribbean. $$$

Marchi's, 7. 251 E 31st St ☎ 679-2494. Italian. $$$

Merchants NY, 39. 112 Seventh Ave ☎ 366-7267. American. $$

Mesa Grill, 30. 102 Fifth Ave ☎ 807-7400. Southwestern. $$

Nicola Paone, 5. 207 E 34th St ☎ 889-3239. Italian. $$$$

Novitá, 17. 102 E 22nd St. 677-2222. Italian. $$$

Old Homestead, 41. 56 Ninth Ave ☎ 242-9040. Steakhouse. $$$

Ole, 16. 434 Second Ave ☎ 725-1953. Spanish. $$

Patria, 22. 250 Park Ave S. 777-6211. Nuevo Latino. $$$$

Park Ave Country Club, 14. 381 Park Ave S ☎ 685-3636. American. $$$

Park Bistro, 10. 414 Park Ave S ☎ 689-1360. French. $$$

Patsy's Pizza, 4. 509 Third Ave. 689-7500. Pizza. $

Periyali, 34. 35 W 20th St ☎ 463-7890. Greek. $$$

Pitchoune, 25. 226 Third Ave. 614-8641. French. $$$

Rascals, 19. 12 E 22nd St ☎ 420-1777. American. $$

Rectangles, 26. 159 Second Ave. 677-8410. Israeli. $$

San Remo, 2. 393 Eighth Ave ☎ 564-1819. Italian. $

Union Square Café, 29. 21 E 16th St ☎ 243-4020. European. $$$$

Zucca, 48. 227 10th Ave ☎ 741-1970. Mediterranean. $$

$$$$ = ***over $50*** $$$ = ***$30–$50*** $$ = ***$20–$30*** $ = ***under $20***

Based on cost per person, excluding drinks, service, and 8 1/4% sales tax.

Restaurants/The Village & Downtown

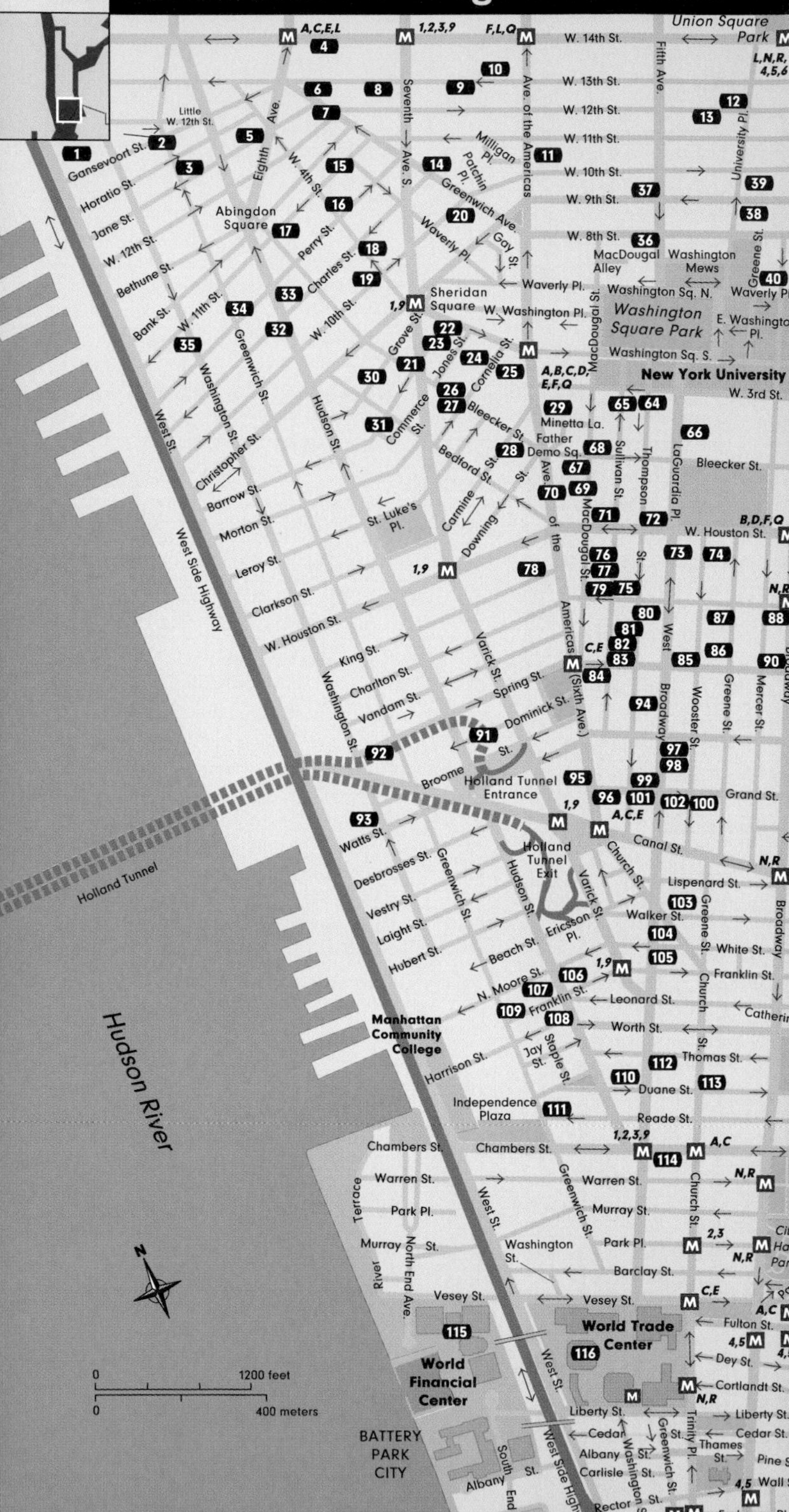

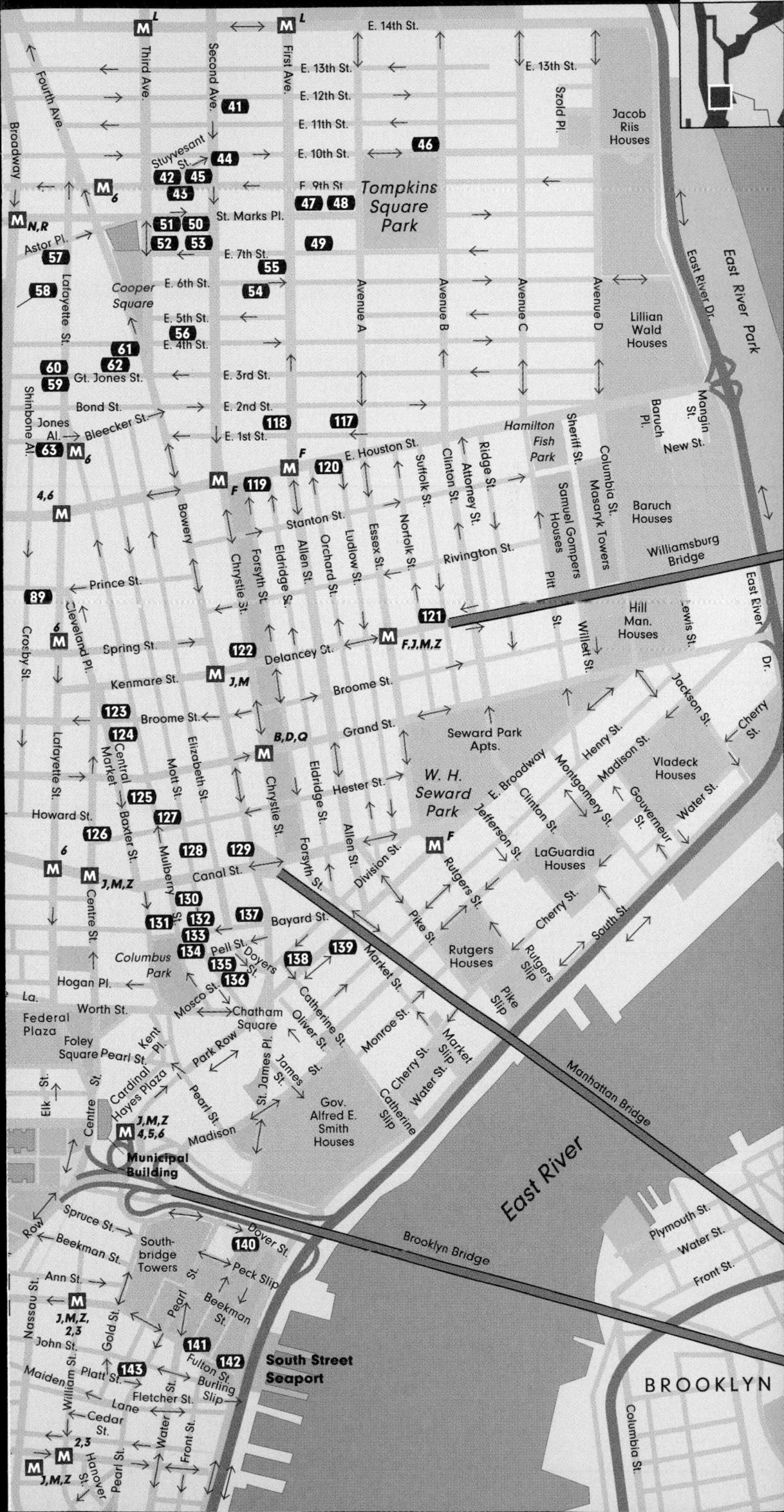

E. 14th St.
E. 13th St.
E. 12th St.
E. 11th St.
E. 10th St.
E. 9th St.
St. Marks Pl.
E. 7th St.
E. 6th St.
E. 5th St.
E. 4th St.
E. 3rd St.
E. 2nd St.
E. 1st St.
E. Houston St.
Stanton St.
Rivington St.
Delancey St.
Broome St.
Grand St.
Hester St.
Canal St.
Bayard St.
Tompkins Square Park
Cooper Square
Hamilton Fish Park
W. H. Seward Park
Seward Park Apts.
Columbus Park
Chatham Square
Jacob Riis Houses
Lillian Wald Houses
Baruch Houses
Samuel Gompers Houses
Masaryk Towers
Hill Man. Houses
Vladeck Houses
LaGuardia Houses
Rutgers Houses
Gov. Alfred E. Smith Houses
Southbridge Towers
Municipal Building
South Street Seaport
Williamsburg Bridge
Manhattan Bridge
Brooklyn Bridge
East River
East River Park
East River Dr.
BROOKLYN
Federal Plaza
Foley Square
Cardinal Hayes Plaza
Broadway
Fourth Ave.
Third Ave.
Second Ave.
First Ave.
Avenue A
Avenue B
Avenue C
Avenue D
Bowery
Lafayette St.
Centre St.
Mott St.
Mulberry St.
Elizabeth St.
Chrystie St.
Forsyth St.
Eldridge St.
Allen St.
Orchard St.
Ludlow St.
Essex St.
Norfolk St.
Suffolk St.
Clinton St.
Attorney St.
Ridge St.
Pitt St.
Willett St.
Sheriff St.
Columbia St.
Baruch Pl.
Mangin St.
New St.
Lewis St.
Szold Pl.
Stuyvesant St.
Astor Pl.
Gt. Jones St.
Bond St.
Bleecker St.
Jones Al.
Shinbone Al.
Prince St.
Spring St.
Kenmare St.
Cleveland Pl.
Crosby St.
Howard St.
Baxter St.
Central Market
Hogan Pl.
Worth St.
Pell St.
Doyers St.
Mosco St.
Park Row
Pearl St.
Kent Pl.
James St.
St. James Pl.
Oliver St.
Catherine St.
Catherine Slip
Madison St.
Market St.
Market Slip
Monroe St.
Cherry St.
Water St.
Division St.
E. Broadway
Rutgers St.
Rutgers Slip
Pike St.
Pike Slip
Jefferson St.
Montgomery St.
Henry St.
Gouverneur St.
Jackson St.
South St.
Elk St.
La.
Spruce St.
Beekman St.
Ann St.
Nassau St.
Gold St.
John St.
Platt St.
Maiden Lane
William St.
Cedar St.
Fletcher St.
Fulton St.
Burling Slip
Peck Slip
Dover St.
Front St.
Hanover St.
Plymouth St.
Row
M L
M N,R
M 6
M F
M F,J,M,Z
M J,M
M B,D,Q
M J,M,Z
M J,M,Z 4,5,6
M J,M,Z, 2,3
M 2,3
41
42 43 44 45 46 47 48 49 50 51 52 53 54 55 56 57 58 59 60 61 62 63
89
117 118 119 120 121 122 123 124 125 126 127 128 129 130 131 132 133 134 135 136 137 138 139 140 141 142 143

Restaurants/The Village & Downtown

Listed by Site Number

1 Florent
2 Tortilla Flats
3 El Faro
4 One City Café
5 Jane St Seafood Café
6 Café de Bruxelles
7 Benny's Burritos
8 Cuisine de Saigon
9 Zinno
10 Café Loup
11 French Roast
12 Japonica
13 Gotham Bar & Grill
14 Elephant & Castle
15 Ye Waverly Inn
16 Patisserie Lanciani
17 Cottonwood Café
18 Sevilla
19 La Metairie
20 Indigo
21 Ithaka
22 Boxer's
23 One If By Land, Two If By Sea
24 Po
25 Home
26 Cucina Stagionale
27 John's of Bleecker Street
28 Cent' Anni
29 La Boheme
30 Pink Tea Cup
31 Chumley's
32 Sazerac House Bar & Grill
33 White Horse Tavern
34 Caribe
35 Black Sheep
36 Clementine
37 Rose Café
38 Knickerbocker
39 Il Cantinori
40 Waverly Coffee Shop
41 Angelica Kitchen
42 Around the Clock
43 Café Tabac
44 Second Ave Kosher Delicatessen
45 Telephone Bar & Grill
46 Life Café
47 Yaffa Café
48 Stingy Lu Lu's
49 Harry's Burrito
50 Khyber Pass
51 DoJo
52 McSorley's Old Ale House
53 Circa
54 Mitali East
55 Teresa's
56 Cucina di Pesce
57 Indochine
58 Bayamo
59 Acme Bar & Grill
60 Time Café
61 Marion's
62 Great Jones St Café
63 Noho Star
64 Il Mulino
65 Quantum Leap
66 Ennio & Michael
67 Chez Jacqueline
68 Le Figaro
69 Villa Mosconi
70 Da Silvano
71 Aggie's
72 Arturo's
73 I Tre Merli
74 Casa La Femme
75 Jean Claude
76 Le Gamin
77 Provence
78 Le Pescadou
79 Frontière
80 Raoul's
81 Omen
82 Blue Ribbon
83 Mezzogiorno
84 Aqua Grill
85 Tennesse Mountain
86 Five & Ten No Exaggeration
87 Soho Kitchen
88 Zoë
89 Savoy
90 Balthazar
91 Alison on Dominick Street
92 Ear Inn
93 Capsouto Frères
94 Barolo
95 Triplet's Roumanian
96 Moondance Diner
97 Cupping Room Café
98 West Broadway
99 Felix
100 Lucky Strike
101 Abyssinia
102 Aj's Niota
103 Barocco
104 Montrachet
105 El Teddy's
106 Bubby's
107 Nobu
108 Chanterelle
109 TriBeCa Grill
110 Duane Park Café
111 Salaam Bombay
112 Odeon
113 Arqua
114 Ecco
115 Hudson River Club
116 Windows on the World
117 Mekka
118 Boca Chica
119 Yonah Schimmel's Knishery
120 Katz's Delicatessen
121 Ratner's
122 Sammy's Roumanian
123 Grotta Azzurra
124 Benito's II
125 Angelo's
126 Puglia
127 Vincent's Clam Bar
128 Wong Kee
129 Silver Palace
130 Mandarin Court
131 Thailand
132 Eastern Villa
133 Bo Ky
134 Saigon
135 Peking Duck House
136 20 Mott St
137 Joe's Shanghai
138 Canton
139 Nice
140 Bridge Café
141 Gianni's
142 Sloppy Louie's
143 Fraunces Tavern

Listed Alphabetically

Abyssinia, 101. 35 Grand St ☎ 226-5959. Ethiopian. $

Acme Bar & Grill, 59. 9 Great Jones St ☎ 420-1934. Southern. $

Aggie's, 71. 146 W Houston St ☎ 673-8994. American. $

AJ Niota's, 102. 337 W Broadway. ☎ 431-6222. Indian. $

Alison on Dominick Street, 91. 38 Dominick St ☎ 727-1188. French. $$$

Angelica Kitchen, 41. 300 E 12th St ☎ 228-2909. Vegetarian. $

Angelo's, 125. 146 Mulberry St ☎ 966-1277. Italian. $$

Aqua Grill, 84. 210 Spring St. ☎ 274-0505. Seafood. $$$

Around the Clock, 42. 8 Stuyvesant St ☎ 598-0402. American. $

Arqua, 113. 281 Church St ☎ 334-1888. Italian. $$$

Arturo's, 72. 106 Houston St ☎ 677-3820. Italian. $$

Balthazar, 90. 80 Spring St ☎ 965-1414. French. $$$

Barocco, 103. 301 Church St ☎ 431-1445. Italian. $$$

Barolo, 94. 398 W Broadway ☎ 226-1102. Italian. $$$

Bayamo, 58. 704 Broadway ☎ 475-5151. Cuban/Chinese. $$

Benito's II, 124. 163 Mulberry St ☎ 226-9012. Italian. $$$

Benny's Burritos, 7. 113 Greenwich Ave ☎ 727-0584. Mexican. $

Black Sheep, 35. 344 W 11th St ☎ 242-1010. French. $$

Blue Ribbon, 82. 97 Sullivan St ☎ 274-0404. Eclectic. $$$

Bo Ky, 133. 80 Bayard St ☎ 406-2292. Chinese. $

Boca Chica, 118. 13 First Ave ☎ 473-0108. Latin. $$

Boxer's, 22. 190 W 4th St ☎ 633-2275. American. $$

Bridge Café, 140. 279 Water St ☎ 227-3344. American. $$

Bubby's, 106. 120 Hudson St ☎ 219-0666. American. $

Café de Bruxelles, 6. 118 Greenwich Ave ☎ 206-1830. Belgian. $$$

Café Loup, 10. 105 W 13th St ☎ 255-4746. Continental. $$

Café Tabac, 43. 232 E 9th St ☎ 674-7072. American. $$

Canton, 138. 45 Division St ☎ 226-4441. Chinese. $$

Capsouto Frères, 93. 451 Washington St ☎ 966-4900. French. $$$$

Caribe, 34. 117 Perry St ☎ 255-9191. Jamaican. $

Casa La Femme, 74. 150 Wooster St ☎ 505-0005. Mediterranean. $$$

Cent' Anni, 28. 50 Carmine St ☎ 989-9494. Italian. $$$

Chez Jacqueline, 67. 72 McDougal St ☎ 505-0727. $$$

Chanterelle, 108. 2 Harrison St ☎ 966-6960. French. $$$$

Chumley's, 31. 86 Bedford St ☎ 675-4449. American. $

Circa, 53. 103 Second Ave. ☎ 777-4120. Continental. $$$

Clementine, 36. 1 Fifth Ave. ☎ 253-0003. American. $$$

Cottonwood Café, 17. 415 Bleecker St ☎ 924-6271. Southwestern. $

Cucina di Pesce, 56. 87 E 4th St ☎ 260-6800. Italian. $

Cucina Stagionale, 26. 275 Bleecker St ☎ 924-2707. Italian. $

Cuisine de Saigon, 8. 154 W 13th St ☎ 255-6003. Vietnamese. $$

Cupping Room Café, 97. 359 W B'way ☎ 925-2898. Australian. $$

Da Silvano, 70. 260 Sixth Ave ☎ 982-2343. Italian. $$$

Diva, 98. 349 W B'way ☎ 941-9024. Seafood. $$$

DoJo, 51. 24 St Mark's Pl ☎ 674-9821. Vegetarian. $

Duane Park Café, 110. 157 Duane St ☎ 732-5555. American. $$$

Ear Inn, 92. 326 Spring St ☎ 226-9060. American. $$

Eastern Villa, 132. 66 Mott Street ☎ 226-4675. Chinese/Seafood. $$

Ecco, 114. 124 Chambers St ☎ 227-7074. Italian. $$$

El Faro, 3. 823 Greenwich St.

$$$$ = ***over $50*** $$$ = ***$30–$50*** $$ = ***$20–$30*** $ = ***under $20***

Based on cost per person, excluding drinks, service, and 8 1/4% sales tax.

Listed Alphabetically (cont.)

☎ 929-8210. Spanish. $$

El Teddy's, 105. 219 W Broadway ☎ 941-7070. Mexican. $$

Elephant & Castle, 14. 68 Greenwich Ave ☎ 243-1400. American. $$

Ennio & Michael, 66. 539 LaGuardia Pl ☎ 677-8577. Italian. $$

Felix, 99. 340 W Broadway ☎ 431-0021. French. $$

Five & Ten No Exaggeration, 86. 77 Greene St ☎ 925-7414. American. $$

Florent, 1. 69 Gansevoort St ☎ 989-5779. French. $$

Fraunces Tavern, 143. 54 Pearl St ☎ 269-0144. American/ Continental. $$$

French Roast, 11. 458 Ave of the Americas ☎ 533-2233. French. $

Frontière, 79. 199 Prince St. ☎ 387-0898. French/Italian. $$$

Gianni's, 141. 15 Fulton St ☎ 608-7300. Italian. $$$

Gotham Bar & Grill, 13. 12 E 12th St ☎ 620-4020. American. $$$$

Great Jones St Café, 62. 54 Great Jones St ☎ 674-9304. American. $$

Grotta Azzurra, 123. 387 Broome St ☎ 925-8775. Italian. $$

Harry's Burrito, 49. 91 E 7th St ☎ 477-0773. Mexican. $

Home, 25. 20 Cornelia St ☎ 243-9579. American. $$$

Hudson River Club, 115. 4 World Financial Ctr ☎ 786-1500. American. $$$$

I Tre Merli, 73. 463 W Broadway ☎ 254-8699. Italian. $$$$

Il Cantinori, 39. 32 E 10th St ☎ 673-6044. Italian. $$$

Il Mulino, 64. 86 W 3rd St ☎ 673-3783. Italian. $$$$

Indigo, 20. 142 W 10th St. ☎ 691-7757. American/Eclectic. $$$

Indochine, 57. 430 Lafayette St ☎ 505-5111. Viet/Cambodian. $$$$

Ithaka, 21. 48 Barrow St☎ 727-8886. Greek. $$$

Jane St Seafood Café, 5. 575 Hudson St ☎ 242-0003. Seafood. $$$$

Japonica, 12. 100 University Place ☎ 243-7752. Japanese. $$

Jean Claude, 75. 137 Sullivan St ☎ 475-9232. French. $$

Joe's Shanghai, 137. 9 Pell St. ☎ 233-8888. Chinese. $$

John's of Bleecker Street, 27. 278 Bleecker St ☎ 243-1680. Pizza. $

Katz's Delicatessen, 120. 205 E Houston St ☎ 254-2246. Deli. $

Khyber Pass, 50. 34 St Mark's Pl ☎ 473-0989. Afghan. $$

Knickerbocker, 38. 33 University Pl ☎ 228-8490. American. $$

La Boheme, 29. 24 Minetta La ☎ 473-6447. American. $$

La Metairie, 19. 189 W 10th St ☎ 989-0343. French. $$

Le Figaro, 68. 184 Bleecker St ☎ 677-1100. American. $

Le Gamin, 76. 50 MacDougal St ☎ 254-4678. French. $

Le Pescadou, 78. 16 King St ☎ 924-3434. French. $$$

Life Cafe, 46. 343 E 10th St ☎ 477-8791. Vegetarian. $

Lucky Strike, 100. 59 Grand St ☎ 941-0479. Continental. $$

Mandarin Court, 130. 61 Mott St ☎ 608-3838. Chinese. $$

Marion's, 61. 354 Bowery ☎ 475-7621. Italian. $$$

McSorley's Old Ale House, 52. 15 E 7th St ☎ 473-9148. American. $

Mekka, 117. 14 Avenue A. ☎ 475-8500. Soul Food. $$

Mezzogiorno, 83. 195 Spring St ☎ 334-2112. Italian. $$$

Mitali East, 54. 334 E 6th St ☎ 533-2508. Indian. $

Montrachet, 104. 239 W Broadway ☎ 219-2777. French. $$$

Moondance Diner, 96. 80 Sixth Ave ☎ 226-1191. American. $

Nice, 139. 35 E Broadway ☎ 406-9510. Chinese. $$

Nobu, 107. 105 Hudson ☎ 219-0050. Japanese. $$$

Noho Star, 63. 330 Lafayette St ☎ 925-0070. American. $

Odeon, 112. 145 W Broadway ☎ 233-0507. Continental. $$$

Omen, 81. 113 Thompson St ☎ 925-8923. Japanese. $$$

One City Café, 4. 240 W 14th St

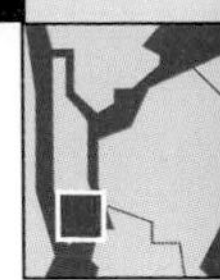

Listed Alphabetically (cont.)

☎ 807-1738. American. $$

One If By Land, Two If By Sea, 23. 17 Barrow St ☎ 228-0822. Continental. $$$$

Patisserie Lanciani, 16. 271 W 4th St ☎ 989-1213. French. $

Peking Duck House, 135. 22 Mott St ☎ 227-1810. Chinese. $$

Pink Tea Cup, 30. 42 Grove St ☎ 807-6755. Soul. $

Po, 24. 31 Cornelia St ☎ 645-2189. Italian. $$$

Provence, 77. 38 MacDougal St ☎ 475-7500. French. $$$

Puglia, 126. 189 Hester St ☎ 226-8912. Italian. $$

Quantum Leap, 65. 88 W 3rd St ☎ 677-8050. Vegetarian. $$

Raoul's, 80. 180 Prince St ☎ 966-3518. French. $$$

Ratner's, 121. 138 Delancey St ☎ 677-5588. Kosher. $

Rose Café, 37. 24 Fifth Ave ☎ 260-4118. American. $$

Saigon, 134. 89-91 Bayard St ☎ 732-8988. Vietnamese. $

Salaam Bombay, 111. 317 Greenwich St ☎ 226-9400. Indian. $$

Sammy's Roumanian, 122. 157 Chrystie St ☎ 673-0030. Eastern European. $$$$

Savoy, 89. 70 Prince St. ☎ 219-8570. Mediterranean/American. $$$

Sazerac House Bar & Grill, 32. 533 Hudson St ☎ 989-0313. American. $$

Second Ave Kosher Delicatessen, 44. 156 Second Ave ☎ 677-0606. Deli. $$

Sevilla, 18. 62 Charles St ☎ 243-3189. Spanish. $$

Silver Palace, 129. 50 Bowery ☎ 964-1204. Chinese. $

Sloppy Louie's, 142. 92 South St ☎ 509-9694. Seafood. $$

Soho Kitchen, 87. 103 Greene St ☎ 925-1866. American. $$$

Stingy Lu Lu's, 48. 129 St Marks Pl ☎ 674-3545. American. $

Telephone Bar & Grill, 45. 149 Second Ave ☎ 529-5000. Continental. $$

Tennessee Mountain, 85. 143 Spring St ☎ 431-3993. American. $

Teresa's, 55. 103 First Ave ☎ 228-0604. Polish/Deli. $

Thailand, 131. 106 Bayard St ☎ 349-3132. Thai. $

Time Café, 60. 380 Lafayette St ☎ 533-7000. American. $$

Tortilla Flats, 2. 767 Washington St ☎ 243-1053. Mexican. $

TriBeCa Grill, 109. 375 Greenwich St ☎ 941-3900. Seafood. $$$

Triplet's Roumanian, 95. 11–17 Grand St ☎ 925-9303. Eastern European. $$$

20 Mott St, 136. 20 Mott St ☎ 964-0380. Chinese. $$

Villa Mosconi, 69. 69 MacDougal St ☎ 673-0390. Italian. $$

Vincent's, 127. 119 Mott St ☎ 226-8133. Italian. $

Waverly Coffee Shop, 40. 19 Waverly Pl ☎ 674-3760. American. $

White Horse Tavern, 33. 567 Hudson St ☎ 989-39560. American. $

Windows on the World, 116. 1 World Trade Center, 107th Floor. ☎ 524-7000. American. $$$$

Wong Kee, 128. 113 Mott St ☎ 966-1160. Chinese. $

Yaffa Café, 47. 97 St Mark's Pl ☎ 674-9302. Vegetarian. $

Ye Waverly Inn, 15. 16 Bank St ☎ 929-4377. American. $$

Yonah Schimmel's Knishery, 119. 137 E Houston St ☎ 477-2858. Jewish. $

Zinno, 9. 126 W 13th St ☎ 924-5182. Italian. $$$

Zoë, 88. 90 Prince St ☎ 966-6722. American. $$$

$$$$ = over $50 $$$ = $30–$50 $$ = $20–$30 $ = under $20

Based on cost per person, excluding drinks, service, and 8 1/4% sales tax.

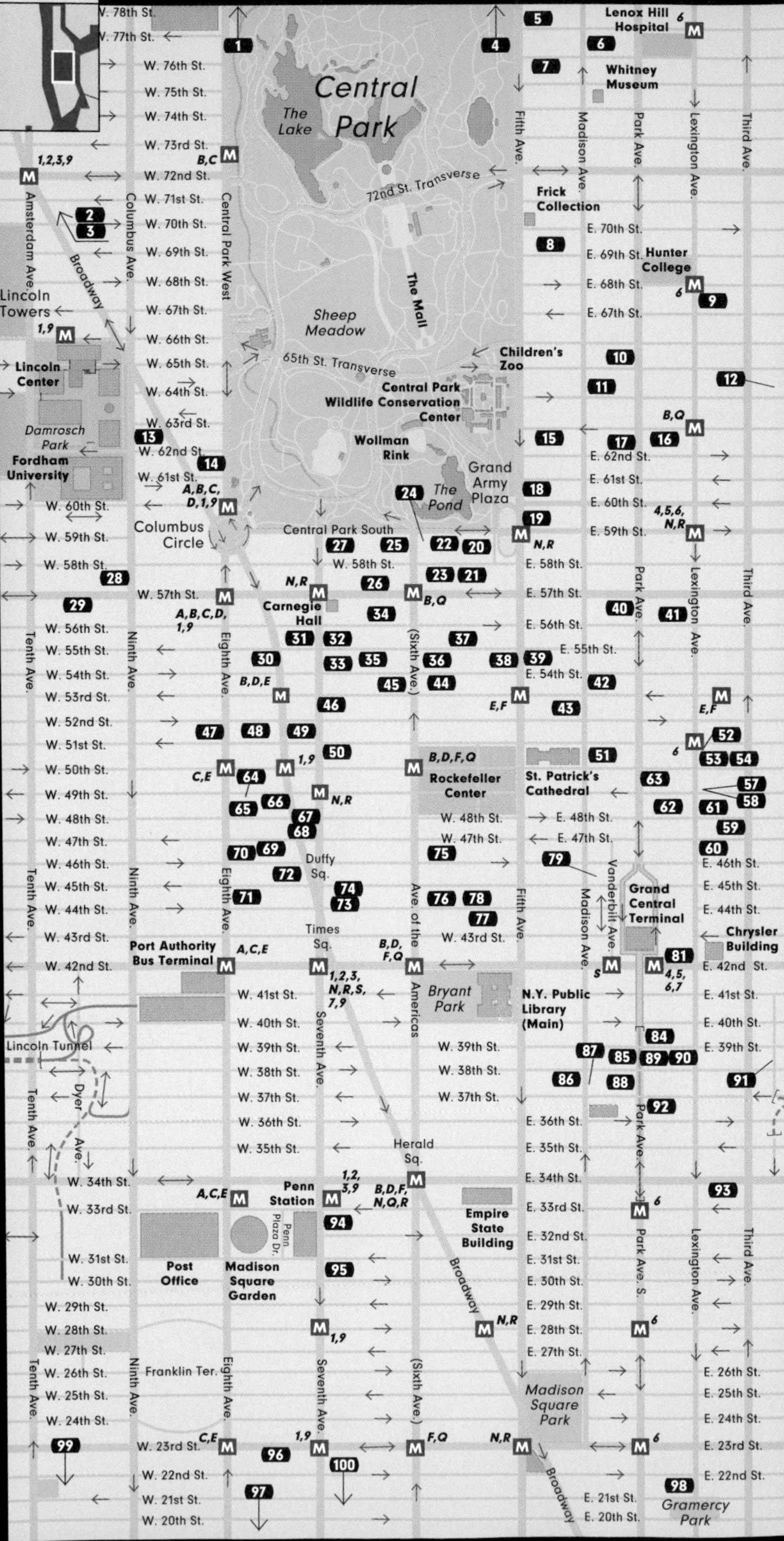

Central Park
The Lake
72nd St. Transverse
The Mall
Sheep Meadow
65th St. Transverse
Children's Zoo
Central Park Wildlife Conservation Center
Wollman Rink
The Pond
Grand Army Plaza
Central Park South
Columbus Circle
Lincoln Towers
Lincoln Center
Damrosch Park
Fordham University
Frick Collection
Whitney Museum
Lenox Hill Hospital
Hunter College
Carnegie Hall
Rockefeller Center
St. Patrick's Cathedral
Duffy Sq.
Times Sq.
Port Authority Bus Terminal
Grand Central Terminal
Chrysler Building
Bryant Park
N.Y. Public Library (Main)
Lincoln Tunnel
Herald Sq.
Penn Station
Penn Plaza Dr.
Post Office
Madison Square Garden
Empire State Building
Franklin Ter.
Madison Square Park
Gramercy Park
Amsterdam Ave.
Broadway
Columbus Ave.
Central Park West
Fifth Ave.
Madison Ave.
Park Ave.
Lexington Ave.
Third Ave.
Tenth Ave.
Ninth Ave.
Eighth Ave.
Seventh Ave.
(Sixth Ave.)
Ave. of the Americas
Vanderbilt Ave.
Dyer Ave.
Park Ave. S.
W. 78th St.
W. 77th St.
W. 76th St.
W. 75th St.
W. 74th St.
W. 73rd St.
W. 72nd St.
W. 71st St.
W. 70th St.
W. 69th St.
W. 68th St.
W. 67th St.
W. 66th St.
W. 65th St.
W. 64th St.
W. 63rd St.
W. 62nd St.
W. 61st St.
W. 60th St.
W. 59th St.
W. 58th St.
W. 57th St.
W. 56th St.
W. 55th St.
W. 54th St.
W. 53rd St.
W. 52nd St.
W. 51st St.
W. 50th St.
W. 49th St.
W. 48th St.
W. 47th St.
W. 46th St.
W. 45th St.
W. 44th St.
W. 43rd St.
W. 42nd St.
W. 41st St.
W. 40th St.
W. 39th St.
W. 38th St.
W. 37th St.
W. 36th St.
W. 35th St.
W. 34th St.
W. 33rd St.
W. 31st St.
W. 30th St.
W. 29th St.
W. 28th St.
W. 27th St.
W. 26th St.
W. 25th St.
W. 24th St.
W. 23rd St.
W. 22nd St.
W. 21st St.
W. 20th St.
E. 70th St.
E. 69th St.
E. 68th St.
E. 67th St.
E. 62nd St.
E. 61st St.
E. 60th St.
E. 59th St.
E. 58th St.
E. 57th St.
E. 56th St.
E. 55th St.
E. 54th St.
E. 48th St.
E. 47th St.
E. 46th St.
E. 45th St.
E. 44th St.
E. 42nd St.
E. 41st St.
E. 40th St.
E. 39th St.
E. 36th St.
E. 35th St.
E. 34th St.
E. 33rd St.
E. 32nd St.
E. 31st St.
E. 30th St.
E. 29th St.
E. 28th St.
E. 27th St.
E. 26th St.
E. 25th St.
E. 24th St.
E. 23rd St.
E. 22nd St.
E. 21st St.
E. 20th St.
1 2 3 4 5 6 7 8 9 10 11 12 13 14 15 16 17 18 19 20
21 22 23 24 25 26 27 28 29 30 31 32 33 34 35 36 37 38 39 40
41 42 43 44 45 46 47 48 49 50 51 52 53 54 57 58 59 60 61 62 63 64 65 66 67 68 69 70
71 72 73 74 75 76 77 78 79 81 84 85 86 87 88 89 90 91 92 93 94 95 96 97 98 99 100
1,2,3,9
B,C
1,9
A,B,C, D,1,9
A,B,C,D, 1,9
N,R
B,Q
B,D,E
C,E
N,R
B,D,F,Q
E,F
4,5,6, N,R
A,C,E
B,D, F,Q
1,2,3, N,R,S, 7,9
S
4,5, 6,7
A,C,E
1,2, 3,9
B,D,F, N,Q,R
1,9
N,R
C,E
F,Q
6

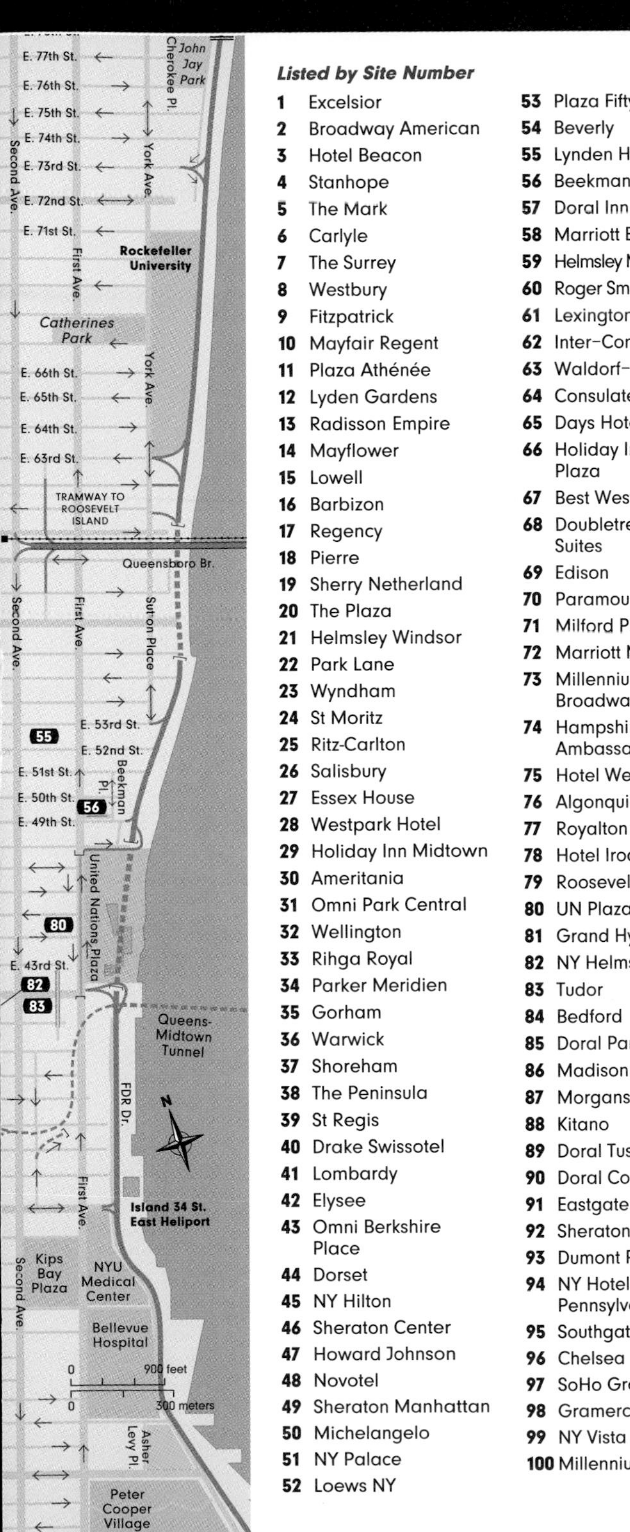

Listed by Site Number

- **1** Excelsior
- **2** Broadway American
- **3** Hotel Beacon
- **4** Stanhope
- **5** The Mark
- **6** Carlyle
- **7** The Surrey
- **8** Westbury
- **9** Fitzpatrick
- **10** Mayfair Regent
- **11** Plaza Athénée
- **12** Lyden Gardens
- **13** Radisson Empire
- **14** Mayflower
- **15** Lowell
- **16** Barbizon
- **17** Regency
- **18** Pierre
- **19** Sherry Netherland
- **20** The Plaza
- **21** Helmsley Windsor
- **22** Park Lane
- **23** Wyndham
- **24** St Moritz
- **25** Ritz-Carlton
- **26** Salisbury
- **27** Essex House
- **28** Westpark Hotel
- **29** Holiday Inn Midtown
- **30** Ameritania
- **31** Omni Park Central
- **32** Wellington
- **33** Rihga Royal
- **34** Parker Meridien
- **35** Gorham
- **36** Warwick
- **37** Shoreham
- **38** The Peninsula
- **39** St Regis
- **40** Drake Swissotel
- **41** Lombardy
- **42** Elysee
- **43** Omni Berkshire Place
- **44** Dorset
- **45** NY Hilton
- **46** Sheraton Center
- **47** Howard Johnson
- **48** Novotel
- **49** Sheraton Manhattan
- **50** Michelangelo
- **51** NY Palace
- **52** Loews NY
- **53** Plaza Fifty
- **54** Beverly
- **55** Lynden House
- **56** Beekman Tower
- **57** Doral Inn
- **58** Marriott East Side
- **59** Helmsley Middletowne
- **60** Roger Smith Winthrop
- **61** Lexington
- **62** Inter-Continental NY
- **63** Waldorf-Astoria
- **64** Consulate
- **65** Days Hotel
- **66** Holiday Inn Crowne Plaza
- **67** Best Western
- **68** Doubletree Guest Suites
- **69** Edison
- **70** Paramount
- **71** Milford Plaza
- **72** Marriott Marquis
- **73** Millennium Broadway
- **74** Hampshire Ambassador
- **75** Hotel Wentworth
- **76** Algonquin
- **77** Royalton
- **78** Hotel Iroquois
- **79** Roosevelt
- **80** UN Plaza
- **81** Grand Hyatt NY
- **82** NY Helmsley
- **83** Tudor
- **84** Bedford
- **85** Doral Park
- **86** Madison Towers
- **87** Morgans
- **88** Kitano
- **89** Doral Tuscany
- **90** Doral Court
- **91** Eastgate Tower
- **92** Sheraton Park Ave
- **93** Dumont Plaza
- **94** NY Hotel Pennsylvania
- **95** Southgate Tower
- **96** Chelsea Hotel
- **97** SoHo Grand
- **98** Gramercy Park
- **99** NY Vista
- **100** Millennium Hilton

Listed Alphabetically

Algonquin, 76. 59 W 44th St ☎ 840-6800. FAX 944-1419. $$

Ameritania, 30. 1701 B'way ☎ 247-5000. FAX 247-3316. $

Barbizon, 16. 140 E 63rd St ☎ 838-5700. FAX 888-4271. $$

Bedford, 84. 118 E 40th St ☎ 697-4800. FAX 697-1093. $$

Beekman Tower, 56. 3 Mitchell Pl ☎ 355-7300. FAX 753-9366. $$

Best Western, 67. 234 W 48th St ☎ 246-8800. FAX 974-3922. $

Beverly, 54. 125 E 50th St ☎ 753-2700. FAX 759-7300. $

Broadway American, 2. 2178 B'way ☎ 362-1100. FAX 787-9521. $

Carlyle, 6. 35 E 76th St ☎ 744-1600. FAX 717-4682. $$$$

Chelsea Hotel, 96. 222 W 23rd St ☎ 243-3700. FAX 243-3700. $

Consulate, 64. 224 W 49th St ☎ 246-5252. FAX 245-2305. $

Days Hotel, 65. 790 Eighth Avenue ☎ 581-7000. FAX 974-0291. $

Doral Court, 90. 130 E 39th St ☎ 685-1100. FAX 889-0287. $$

Doral Inn, 57. 541 Lexington Ave ☎ 755-1200. FAX 319-8344. $

Doral Park, 85. 70 Park Ave ☎ 973-2400. FAX 808-9029. $$$

Doral Tuscany, 89. 120 E 39th St ☎ 686-1600. FAX 779-7822. $$$

Dorset, 44. 30 W 54th St ☎ 247-7300. FAX 581-0153. $$$

Doubletree Guest Suites, 68. 1568 B'way ☎ 719-1600. FAX 921-5212. $$$$

Drake Swissotel, 40. 440 Park Ave ☎ 753-4500. FAX 371-4190. $$$$

Dumont Plaza, 93. 150 E 34th St ☎ 481-7600. FAX 889-8856. $$

Eastgate Tower, 91. 222 E 39th St ☎ 687-8000. FAX 490-2634. $$

Edison, 69. 228 W 47th St ☎ 840-5000. FAX 596-6850. $

Elysee, 42. 60 E 54th St ☎ 753-1066. FAX 980-9278. $$

Essex House, 27. 160 Central Park S ☎ 247-0300. FAX 315-1839. $$$$

Excelsior, 1. 45 W 81st St ☎ 362-9200. FAX 721-2994. $

Fitzpatrick, 9. 687 Lexington Ave ☎ 355-0100. FAX 355-1371. $$

Gorham, 35. 136 W 55th St ☎ 245-1800. FAX 582-8332. $$

Gramercy Park, 98. 2 Lexington Ave ☎ 475-4320. FAX 505-0535. $

Grand Hyatt NY, 81. Park Ave & 42nd St ☎ 883-1234. FAX 697-3772. $$$$

Hampshire Ambassador, 74. 132 W 45th St. ☎ 921-7600 FAX 719-0171. $$

Helmsley Middletowne, 59. 148 E 48th St ☎ 755-3000. FAX 832-0261. $$

Helmsley Windsor, 21. 100 W 58th St ☎ 265-2100. FAX 315-0371. $$

Holiday Inn Crowne Plaza, 66. 1605 B'way ☎ 977-4000. FAX 333-7393. $$

Holiday Inn Midtown, 29. 440 W 57th St. ☎ 581-8100 FAX 581-8719. $$

Hotel Beacon, 3. 2130 B'way ☎ 787-1100. FAX 724-0839. $

Hotel Iroquois, 78. 49 W 44th St ☎ 840-3080. FAX 398-1754. $$

Hotel Wentworth, 75. 59 W 46th St ☎ 719-2300. FAX 768-3477. $

Howard Johnson, 47. 851 Eighth Ave ☎ 581-4100. FAX 974-7502. $

Inter-Continental NY, 62. 111 E 48th St ☎ 755-5900. FAX 644-0079. $$$

Kitano, 88. 66 Park Ave ☎ 681-6007. FAX 885-7100. $

Lexington, 61. 511 Lexington Ave ☎ 755-4400. FAX 751-4091. $$

Loews New York, 52. 569 Lexington Ave ☎ 752-7000. FAX 758-6311. $$

Lombardy, 41. 111 E 56th St ☎ 753-8600. FAX 754-5683. $$

Lowell, 15. 28 E 63rd St ☎ 838-1400. FAX 838-9194. $$$$

Lyden Gardens, 12. 215 E 64th St ☎ 355-1230. FAX 319-4230. $$

Lyden House, 55. 320 E 53rd St ☎ 888-6070. FAX 935-7690. $$

Madison Towers, 86. 22 E 38th St ☎ 685-3700. FAX 447-0747. $$

The Mark, 5. 25 E 77th St ☎ 744-4300. FAX 744-2749. $$$$

Marriott East Side, 58. 525 Lexington Ave ☎ 755-4000. FAX 751-3440. $$

Marriott Marquis, 72. 1535 B'way ☎ 398-1900. FAX 704-8930. $$$$

Mayfair, 10. 610 Park Ave ☎ 288-0800. FAX 737-0538. $$$$

Mayflower, 14. 15 Central Park W ☎ 265-0060. FAX 265-2026. $$$

Michelangelo, 50. 152 W 51st St ☎ 765-1900. FAX 541-7618. $$$$

Listed Alphabetically (cont.)

Milford Plaza, 71. 270 W 45 St ☎ 869-3600 FAX 944-8357. $

Millennium Hilton, 100. 55 Church St ☎ 693-2001. FAX 571-2317. $$$

Millennium Broadway, 73. 145 W 44th St ☎ 768-4400. FAX 768-0847. $$$

Morgans, 87. 237 Madison Ave ☎ 686-0300. FAX 779-8352. $$

NY Helmsley, 82. 212 E 42nd St ☎ 490-8900. FAX 936-4792. $$$$

NY Hilton, 45. 1335 Ave of the Americas ☎ 586-7000. FAX 315-1374. $$$$

NY Hotel Pennsylvania, 94. 401 Seventh Ave ☎ 736-5000. FAX 502-8799. $$

NY Palace, 51. 455 Madison Ave ☎ 888-7000. FAX 303-6000. $$$$

NY Vista, 99. 3 World Trade Ctr ☎ 938-9100. FAX 321-2107. $$$$

Novotel, 48. 226 W 52nd St ☎ 315-0100. FAX 765-5369. $$

Omni Berkshire Place, 43. 21 E 52nd St ☎ 800/262-9467. FAX 754-5020. $$$$

Omni Park Central, 31. 870 Seventh Ave ☎ 247-8000. FAX 484-3374. $$

Paramount, 70. 235 W 46th St ☎ 764-5500. FAX 354-5237. $

Park Lane, 22. 36 Central Park S ☎ 371-4000. FAX 319-9065. $$$$

Parker Meridien, 34. 118 W 55th St ☎ 245-5000. FAX 307-1776. $$$$

The Peninsula, 38. 700 Fifth Ave ☎ 247-2200. FAX 903-3949. $$$$

Pierre, 18. 2 E 61st St ☎ 838-8000. FAX 940-8109. $$$$

The Plaza, 20. Fifth Ave & 59th St ☎ 759-3000. FAX 546-5324. $$$$

Plaza Athénée, 11. 37 E 64th St ☎ 734-9100. FAX 772-0958. $$$$

Plaza Fifty, 53. 155 E 50th St ☎ 751-5710. FAX 753-1468. $$

Radisson Empire, 13. 44 W 63rd St ☎ 265-7400. FAX 245-3382. $

Regency, 17. 540 Park Ave ☎ 759-4100. FAX 826-5674. $$$$

Rihga Royal, 33. 151 W 54th St ☎ 307-5000. FAX 765-6530. $$$$

Ritz-Carlton, 25. 112 Central Park S ☎ 757-1900. FAX 757-9620. $$$$

Roger Smith Winthrop, 60. 501 Lex Ave ☎ 755-1400. FAX 319-9130. $

Roosevelt, 79. 45 E 45th St ☎ 661-9600. FAX 687-5064. $$

Royalton, 77. 44 W 44th St ☎ 869-4400. FAX 869-8965. $$$

St Moritz, 24. 50 Central Park S ☎ 755-5800. FAX 751-2952. $$$$

St Regis, 39. 2 E 55th St ☎ 753-4500. FAX 787-3447. $$$

Salisbury, 26. 123 W 57th St ☎ 246-1300. FAX 977-7752. $

Sheraton Centre, 46. 811 Seventh Ave ☎ 581-1000. FAX 262-4410. $$$

Sheraton Manhattan, 49. 790 Seventh Ave ☎ 581-3300. FAX 582-5489. $$

Sheraton Park Ave, 92. 45 Park Ave ☎ 685-7676. FAX 889-3193. $$$$

Sherry Netherland, 19. 781 Fifth Ave ☎ 355-2800. FAX 832-4845. $$$$

Shoreham, 37. 33 W 55th St ☎ 247-6700. FAX 957-8915. $$

SoHo Grand, 97. 310 W Broadway ☎ 965-3000 FAX 965-3200. $$$$

Southgate Tower, 95. 371 Seventh Ave ☎ 563-1800. FAX 643-8028. $$$

Stanhope, 4. 995 Fifth Ave ☎ 288-5800. FAX 517-0088. $$$$

The Surrey, 7. 20 E 76th St ☎ 288-3700. FAX 628-1549. $$$

Tudor, 83. 304 E 42nd St ☎ 986-8800. FAX 986-1758. $$$

UN Plaza, 80. 1 UN Plaza ☎ 758-1234. FAX 702-5051. $$$$

Waldorf-Astoria, 63. 301 Park Ave ☎ 355-3000. FAX 421-8103. $$$$

Warwick, 36. 65 W 54th St ☎ 247-2700. FAX 957-8915. $$$

Wellington, 32. 871 Seventh Ave ☎ 247-3900. FAX 581-1719. $

Westbury, 8. 15 E 69th St ☎ 535-2000. FAX 535-5058. $$$

Westpark Hotel, 28. 308 W 58th St ☎ 246-6440. FAX 246-3131. $

Wyndham, 23. 42 W 58th St ☎ 753-3500. FAX 754-5638. $

$$$$ = ***over $260*** $$$ = ***$200-$260*** $$ = ***$160-$200*** $ = ***under $160***

All prices are for a standard double room, excluding 13 1/4% city and state sales tax and $2 occupancy tax.

MAP 55 Performing Arts

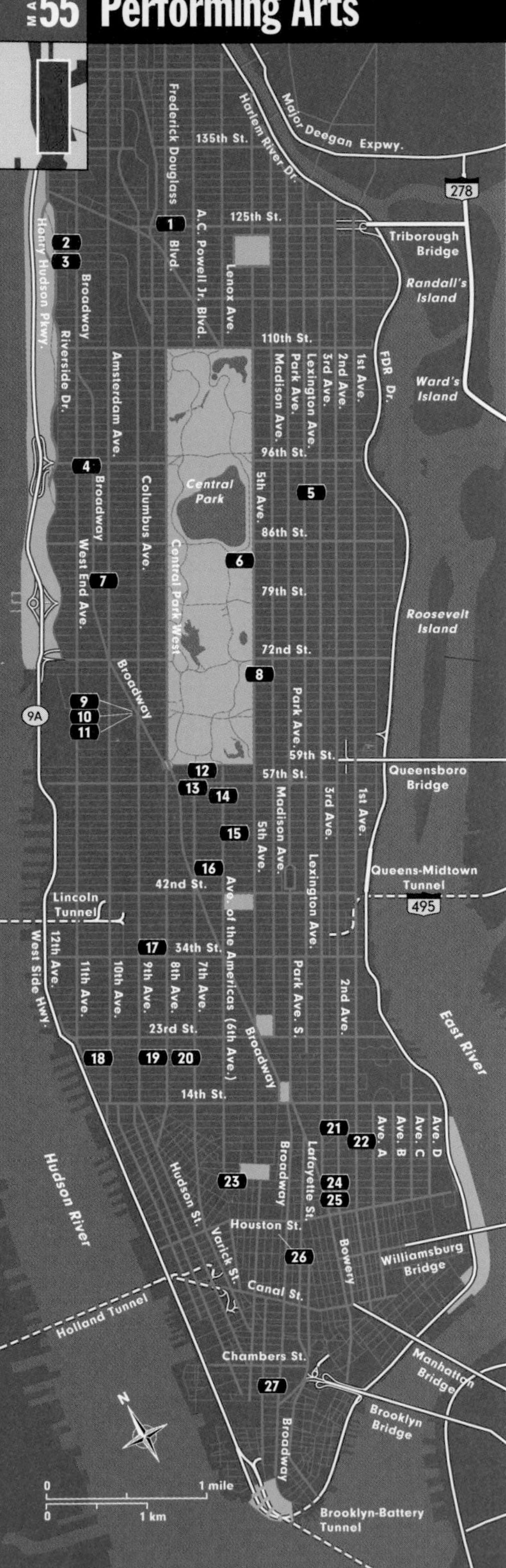

Listed by Site Number

1 Apollo Theater
2 Manhattan School of Music
3 Riverside Church
4 Symphony Space
5 Kaufman 92nd St YMCA
6 Grace Rainey Rogers Auditorium
7 Beacon Theater
8 Music Room
9 Juilliard School
10 Lincoln Center
11 Merkin Concert Hall
12 CAMI Hall
13 Carnegie Hall
14 City Center
15 Radio City Music Hall
16 Town Hall
17 Madison Square Garden
18 The Kitchen
19 Joyce Theater
20 Dance Theatre Workshop
21 St Mark's-in-the-Bowery
22 PS 122
23 Washington Square Church
24 La MaMa ETC
25 Amato Opera
26 New Museum of Contemporary Art
27 Warren St Performance Loft

Listed Alphabetically

Amato Opera, 25. 319 Bowery ☎ 228-8200

Apollo Theater, 1. 253 W 125th St ☎ 749-5838

Beacon Theater, 7. 2124 Broadway ☎ 496-7070

CAMI Hall, 12. 165 W 57th St ☎ 841-9650

Carnegie Hall, 13. 154 W 57th St ☎ 247-7800

City Center, 14. 131 W 55th St ☎ 581-7907

Dance Theatre Workshop, 20. 219 W 19th St ☎ 924-0077

Grace Rainey Rogers Auditorium, 6. Metropolitan Museum, 1000 Fifth Ave ☎ 570-3949

Joyce Theater, 19. 175 Eighth Ave ☎ 242-0800

Juilliard School, 9. 60 Lincoln Ctr Plaza ☎ 799-5000

Kaufman 92nd St YMCA, 5. 1395 Lexington Ave ☎ 415-5440

The Kitchen, 18. 512 W 19th St ☎ 255-5793

La MaMa ETC, 24. 74A E 4th St ☎ 475-7710

Lincoln Center, 10. Broadway & 64th St ☎ 875-5000

Madison Square Garden, 17. Seventh Ave & 32nd St ☎ 465-6000

Manhattan School of Music, 2. 120 Claremont Ave ☎ 749-2802

Merkin Concert Hall, 11. 129 W 67th St ☎ 362-8719

Music Room, 8. Frick Museum, 1 E 70th St ☎ 288-0700

New Museum of Contemporary Art, 26. 583 Broadway ☎ 219-1222

PS 122, 22. 150 First Ave ☎ 477-5288

Radio City Music Hall, 15. 1260 Sixth Ave ☎ 247-4777

Riverside Church, 3. 490 Riverside Dr ☎ 870-6700

St Mark's-in-the-Bowery, 21. Second Ave & 10th St ☎ 674-6377

Symphony Space, 4. 2537 Broadway ☎ 864-5400

Town Hall, 16. 123 W 43rd St ☎ 840-2824

Warren St Performance Loft, 27. 46 Warren St ☎ 732-3149

Washington Square Church, 23. 135 W 4th St ☎ 777-2528

Lincoln Center

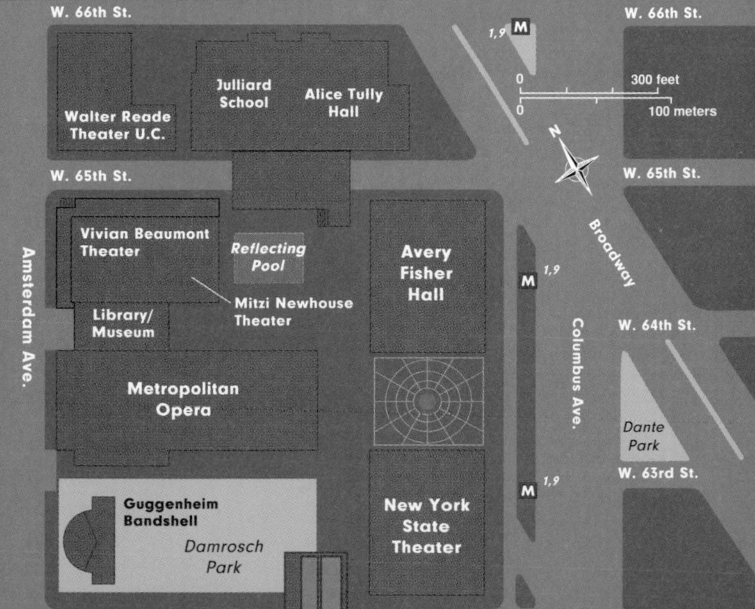

MAP 56 Theater District

Listed by Site Number

1 City Center Stage II
2 Theatre Four
3 Ensemble Studio Theatre
4 Broadway
5 Virginia
6 Neil Simon
7 Gershwin
8 Winter Garden
9 Circle in the Square
10 Ambassador
11 Eugene O'Neill
12 Longacre
13 Walter Kerr
14 Cort
15 Ethel Barrymore
16 Brooks Atkinson
17 Palace
18 Lunt-Fontanne
19 Roundabout
20 American Place
21 Richard Rogers
22 Imperial
23 Music Box
24 Criterion Center
25 Marquis
26 Lyceum
27 47th St
28 Martin Beck
29 Golden
30 Royale
31 Plymouth
32 Booth
33 Minskoff
34 Majestic
35 Broadhurst
36 Shubert
37 Belasco
38 St James
39 Helen Hayes
40 Lamb's
41 Westside Theatre
42 Kaufman
43 John Houseman
44 Nat Horne
45 Douglas Fairbanks
46 Judith Anderson
47 Playwrights Horizons
48 Harold Clurman
49 Samuel Beckett
50 New Victory
51 Nederlander

Listed Alphabetically

Ambassador, 10. 215 W 49th St ☎ 239–6200

American Place, 20. 111 W 46th St ☎ 840–2960

Belasco, 37. 111 W 44th St ☎ 239–6200

Booth, 32. 222 W 45th St ☎ 239–6200

Broadhurst, 35. 235 W 44th St ☎ 239–6200

Broadway, 4. 1681 Broadway ☎ 239–6200

Brooks Atkinson, 16. 256 W 47th St ☎ 719–4099

Circle in the Square, 9. 1633 Broadway ☎ 239–6200

City Center Stage II, 1. 131 W 55th St ☎ 581–1212

Cort, 14. 138 W 48th St ☎ 239–6200

Criterion Center, 24. 1530 Broadway ☎ 764–7903

Douglas Fairbanks, 45. 432 W 42nd St ☎ 239–4321

Ensemble Studio Theatre, 3. 549 W 52nd St ☎ 247–3405

Ethel Barrymore, 15. 243 W 47th St ☎ 239–6200

Eugene O'Neill, 11. 230 W 49th St ☎ 239-6200

47th St, 27. 304 W 47th St ☎ 239–6200

Gershwin, 7. 222 W 51st St ☎ 307–4100

Golden, 29. 252 W 45th St ☎ 239–6200

Harold Clurman, 48. 412 W 42nd St ☎ 594–2370

Helen Hayes, 39. 240 W 44th St ☎ 307–4100

Imperial, 22. 249 W 45th St ☎ 239–6200

John Houseman, 43. 450 W 42nd St ☎ 967-9077

Judith Anderson, 46. 412 W 42nd St ☎ 564-7853

Kaufman, 42. 534 W 42nd St ☎ 563–1684

Lamb's, 40. 130 W 44th St ☎ 997–1780

Longacre, 12. 220 W 48th St ☎ 239–6200

Lunt-Fontanne, 18. 205 W 46th St ☎ 307–4100

Lyceum, 26. 149 W 45th St ☎ 239–6200

Majestic, 34. 247 W 44th St ☎ 239–6200

Marquis, 25. 211 W 45th St ☎ 307–4100

Martin Beck, 28. 302 W 45th St ☎ 239-6200

Minskoff, 33. Broadway & 45th St ☎ 869–0550

Music Box, 23. 239 W 45th St ☎ 239–6200

Nat Horne, 44. Ninth Ave & 42nd St ☎ 279–4200

Nederlander, 51. 208 W 41st St ☎ 307–4100

Neil Simon, 6. 250 W 52nd St ☎ 307–4100

New Victory, 50. 209 W 42nd St ☎ 382–4000

Palace, 17. Broadway & 47th St ☎ 307–4100

Playwrights Horizons, 47. 416 W 42nd St ☎ 279–4200

Plymouth, 31. 236 W 45th St ☎ 239–6200

Richard Rogers, 21. 226 W 46th St ☎ 221–1211

Roundabout, 19. 1530 Broadway ☎ 869–8400

Royale, 30. 242 W 45th St ☎ 239–6200

St James, 38. 246 W 44th St ☎ 239-6200

Samuel Beckett, 49. 412 W 42nd St ☎ 307–4100

Shubert, 36. 225 W 44th St ☎ 239–6200

Theatre Four, 2. 424 W 55th St ☎ 489–7050

Virginia, 5. 245 W 52nd St ☎ 239-6200

Walter Kerr, 13. 219 W 48th St ☎ 239-6200

Westside Theatre, 41. 407 W 43rd St ☎ 239–6200

Winter Garden, 8. 1634 Broadway ☎ 239–6200

MAP 57 Theaters/The Village

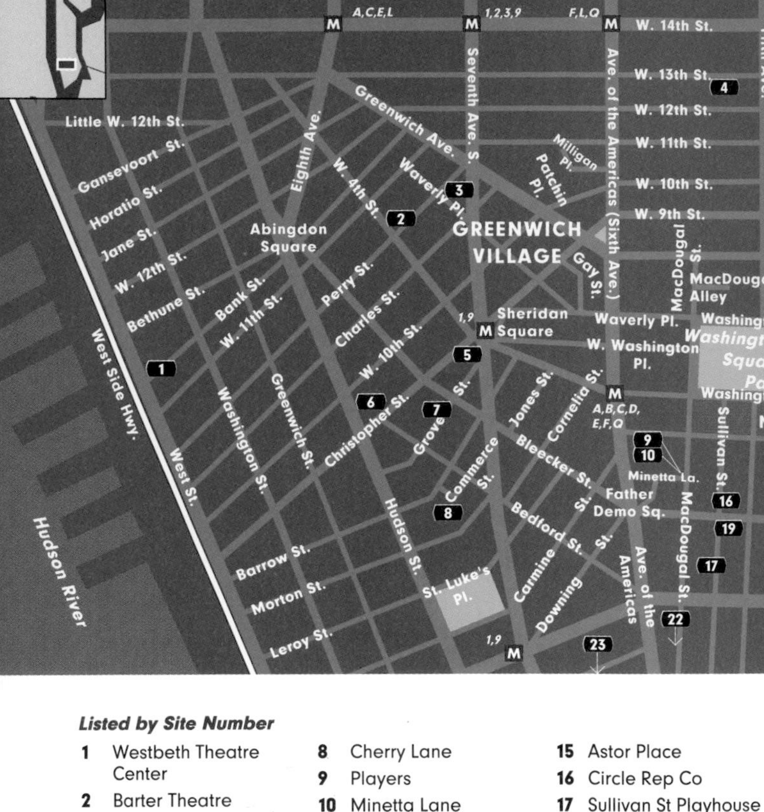

Listed by Site Number

1 Westbeth Theatre Center
2 Barter Theatre
3 Theatre Off Park
4 13th St
5 Actor's Playhouse
6 Lucille Lortel
7 Grove St Playhouse
8 Cherry Lane
9 Players
10 Minetta Lane
11 Classic Stage Company (CSC Rep)
12 Pearl Theatre Co
13 Orpheum
14 Public
15 Astor Place
16 Circle Rep Co
17 Sullivan St Playhouse
18 Jean Cocteau Rep
19 Duo Theatre
20 New York Theatre Workshop
21 La MaMa ETC

Listed Alphabetically

Actor's Playhouse, 5. 100 Seventh Ave S ☎ 463–0060

Astor Place, 15. 434 Lafayette St ☎ 254–4370

Barter Theatre, 2. 62 Perry St ☎ 741–9466

Cherry Lane, 8. 38 Commerce St ☎ 989–2020

Circle Rep Co, 16. 159 Bleecker St ☎ 254–6200

Classic Stage Company (CSC Rep), 11. 136 E 13th St ☎ 677–4210

Duo Theatre, 19. 62 E 4th St ☎ 598–4320

Grove Street Playhouse, 7. 39 Grove St ☎ 741-6436•

HERE, 22. 145 Ave of the Americas ☎ 647-0202

Jean Cocteau Rep, 18. 330 Bowery ☎ 677–0060

La MaMa ETC, 21. 74A E 4th St ☎ 475–7710

Lucille Lortel, 6. 121 Christopher St ☎ 239-6200

Minetta Lane, 10. 18 Minetta La ☎ 420–8000

New York Theatre Workshop, 20. 79 E 4th St ☎ 460–5475

Orpheum, 13. 126 Second Ave ☎ 477–2477

Pearl Theatre Co, Inc, 12. 80 St Marks Pl ☎ 598–9802

Listed by Site Number (cont.)

22 HERE

23 Soho Playhouse

24 Workhouse

Listed Alphabetically (cont.)

Players, 9. 115 MacDougal St
☎ 254-5076

Public, 14. 425 Lafayette St
☎ 539-8500

Soho Playhouse, 23. 15 Vandam St
☎ 691-1555

Sullivan St Playhouse, 17.
181 Sullivan St ☎ 674-3838

Theatre Off Park, 3. 224 Waverly Pl
☎ 627-2556

13th St, 4. 50 W 13th St
☎ 675-6677

Westbeth Theatre Center, 1.
151 Bank St ☎ 691-2272

Workhouse, 24. 41 White St
☎ 431-9220

MAP 58 Theaters/Other Locations

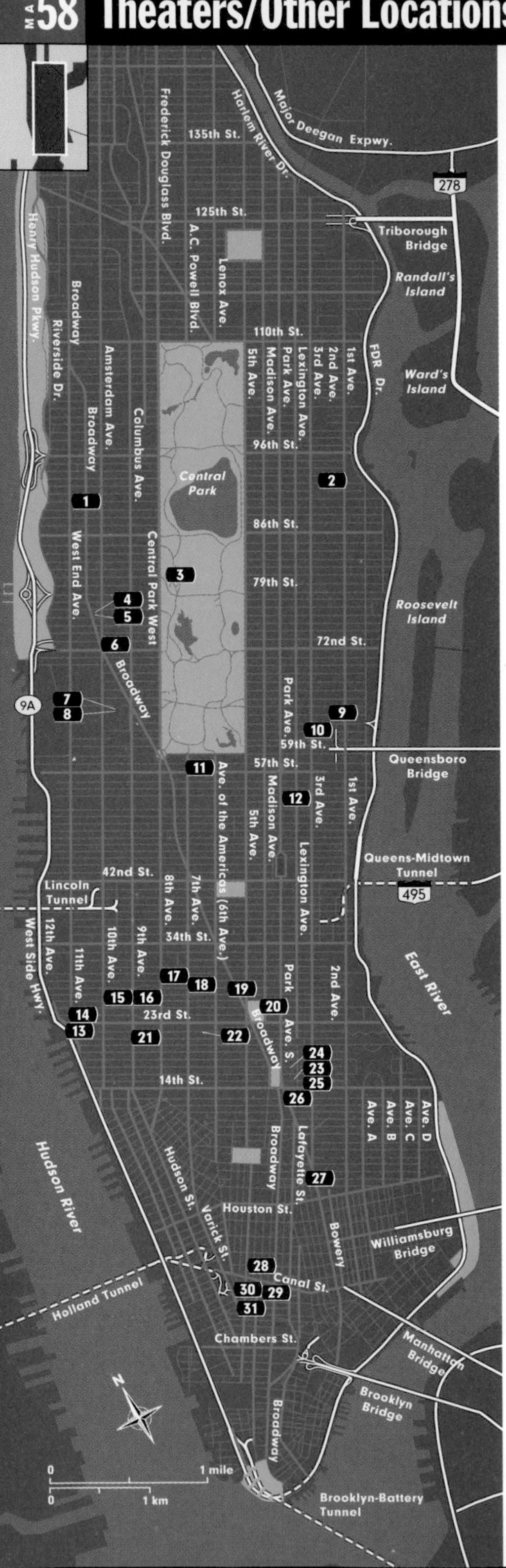

Listed by Site Number

1 Open Eye
2 Playhouse 91
3 Delacorte
4 Second Stage
5 Promenade
6 Triad
7 Mitzi Newhouse
8 Vivian Beaumont
9 Chicago City Limits
10 Theatre East
11 Manhattan Theatre Club
12 York
13 Sanford Meisner
14 WPA
15 Hudson Guild
16 Raymond J. Greenwald
17 29th St
18 TADA!
18 Manhattan Class Co
19 UBU Rep
20 Gramercy Arts
21 Atlantic Theater Company
22 Irish Repertory Theatre
23 Century Theater
24 Union Square Theatre
25 Vineyard Theatre
26 Variety Arts
27 Bouwerie Lane Theatre
28 Performing Garage
29 Franklin Furnace
30 SoHo Rep
31 One Dream

Listed Alphabetically

Atlantic Theater Company, 21. 336 W 20th St ☎ 645-1242

Bouwerie Lane Theatre, 27. 330 Bowery ☎ 677-0060

Century Theater, 23. 111 E 15th St ☎ 982-6782

Chicago City Limits, 9. 1105 1st Ave ☎ 888-5233

Delacorte, 3. 81st St in Central Park ☎ 861-7283

Franklin Furnace, 29. 112 Franklin St ☎ 925-4671

Gramercy Arts, 20. 138 E 27th St ☎ 889-2850

Hudson Guild, 15. 441 W 26th St ☎ 760-9800

Irish Repertory Theatre, 22. 133 W 22nd St ☎ 727-2737

Manhattan Class Co, 18. 120 W 28th St ☎ 727-7722

Manhattan Theatre Club, 11. 131 W 55th St ☎ 581-7907

Mitzi Newhouse, 7. Lincoln Center, Broadway & W 64th St ☎ 362-7600

One Dream, 31. 232 W B'way ☎ 274-1450

Performing Garage, 28. 33 Wooster St ☎ 966-3651

Playhouse 91, 2. 316 E 91st St ☎ 831-2000

Promenade, 5. 2162 Broadway ☎ 580-1313

Raymond J. Greenwald, 16. 307 W 26th St ☎ 633-9797

Sanford Meisner, 13. 164 Eleventh Ave ☎ 206-1764

Second Stage, 4. Broadway & 76th St ☎ 787-8302

SoHo Rep, 30. 46 Walker St ☎ 941-8632

TADA!, 18. 120 W 28th St ☎ 627-1732

Theatre East, 10. 211 E 60th St ☎ 838-9090

Triad, 6. 158 W 72nd St ☎ 362-2590

29th St, 17. 212 W 29th St ☎ 465-0575

UBU Rep, 19. 15 W 28th St ☎ 679-7562

Union Square Theatre, 24. 100 E 17th St ☎ 505-0700

Variety Arts, 26. Third Ave & 13th St ☎ 239-6200

Vineyard Theatre, 25 108 E 15th St ☎ 353-3366

Vivian Beaumont, 8. Lincoln Center, Broadway & W 64th St ☎ 362-7600

WPA, 14. 519 W 23rd St ☎ 206-0523

York, 12. 619 Lexington Ave ☎ 935-5820

Movies/Midtown & Uptown

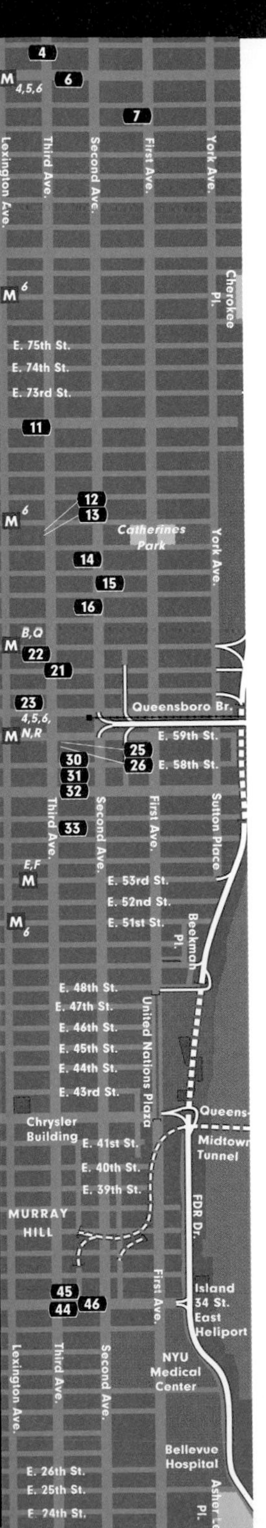

Listed by Site Number

1 Metro Cinema 1 & 2
2 Olympia I & II
3 84th St Sixplex
4 Orpheum VII
5 Park & 86th St Cinemas
6 86th St East Twin
7 United Artist East
8 Naturemax
9 Lincoln Square
10 Regency
11 Tower East
12 Whitney Museum
13 68th St Playhouse
14 Sony NY Twin
15 Beekman
16 United Artists 64th & 2nd Avenue (1–3)
17 Lincoln Plaza Cinemas (1–6)
18 Waltor Reade
19 62nd & Broadway
20 Columbus Circle
21 First & 62nd Cinemas (1–6)
22 Cinema 1, 2 & Cinema 3rd Ave
23 59th St East Cinema
24 Cinema 3
25 Baronet & Coronet
26 Manhattan Twin
27 Carnegie Hall
28 Carnegie Screening Room
29 Paris
30 Coronet Cinemas
31 Crown Gotham Cinema
32 Sutton 1 & 2
33 Eastside Playhouse
34 Ziegfeld Theatre
35 Mus of Modern Art
36 Worldwide Cinemas (1-6)
37 Radio City Music Hall
38 Guild
39 Sony State Theater
40 Embassy I
41 Embassy 2–4
42 Astor Plaza
43 Criterion Center (1–7)
44 Murray Hill Cinemas (1–4)
45 34th St Showplace
46 34th St East
47 23rd St West Triplex
48 Chelsea Cinemas (1–9)

Movies/Midtown & Uptown

Listed Alphabetically

Astor Plaza, 42. Broadway & 44th St ☎ 869-8340

Baronet & Coronet, 25. 993 Third Ave ☎ 355-1663

Beekman, 15. 1254 Second Ave ☎ 737-2622

Carnegie Hall Cinemas, 27. 887 Seventh Ave ☎ 265-2520

Carnegie Screening Room, 28. 887 Seventh Ave ☎ 265-2520

Chelsea Cinemas (1-9), 48. 260 W 23rd St ☎ 691-4744

Cinema 1, 2 & Cinema 3rd Ave, 22. Third Ave & 60th St ☎ 753-6022

Cinema 3, 24. 2 W 59th St ☎ 752-6453

Columbus Circle, 20. Broadway & 61st St ☎ 724-3700

Coronet Cinemas, 30. 993 Third Ave ☎ 355-1663

Criterion Center (1-7), 43. 1514 Broadway ☎ 354-0900

Crown Gotham Cinema, 31. 969 Third Ave ☎ 759-2262

Eastside Playhouse, 33. 919 Third Ave ☎ 755-3020

84th St Sixplex, 3. 2310 Broadway ☎ 877-3600

86th St East Twin, 6. 210 E 86th St ☎ 534-1880

Embassy I, 40. Broadway & 46th St ☎ 302-0494

Embassy 2-4, 41. 701 Seventh Ave ☎ 730-7262

59th St East Cinema, 23. 239 E 59th St ☎ 759-4630

First & 62nd Cinemas (1-6), 21. 400 E 62nd St ☎ 752-4600

Guild, 38. 33 W 50th St ☎ 757-2406

Lincoln Plaza Cinemas (1-6), 17. B'way & 63rd St ☎ 757-2280

Lincoln Square, 9. 1992 Broadway ☎ 336-5000

Manhattan Twin, 26. Third Ave & 59th St ☎ 935-6420

Metro Cinema 1 & 2, 1. Broadway & 99th St ☎ 222-1200

Murray Hill Cinemas (1-4), 44. 160 E 34th St ☎ 689-6548

Museum of Modern Art, 35. 11 W 53rd ☎ 708-9480

Naturemax, 8. American Museum of Natural History, Central Park W & 80th St ☎ 769-5650

Olympia I & II, 2. Broadway & 107th St ☎ 865-8128

Orpheum VII, 4. 1538 Third Ave ☎ 876-2400

Paris, 29. 4 W 58th St ☎ 688-3800

Park & 86th St Cinemas I & II, 5. 125 E 86th St ☎ 534-1880

Radio City Music Hall, 37. Sixth Ave & 50th St ☎ 247-4777

Regency, 10. 1987 Broadway ☎ 724-3700

68th St Playhouse, 13. Third Ave & 68th St ☎ 734-0302

62nd & Broadway, 19. Broadway & 62nd St ☎ 265-7466

Sony NY Twin, 14. 1271 Second Ave ☎ 744-7339

Sony State Theater, 39. Broadway & 46th St ☎ 391-2900

Sutton I & II, 32. Third Ave & 57th St ☎ 759-1411

34th St East, 46. Second Ave & 34th St ☎ 683-0255

34th St Showplace, 45. Third Ave & 34th St ☎ 532-5544

Tower East, 11. Third Ave & 72nd St ☎ 879-1313

23rd St West Triplex, 47. 333 W 23rd St ☎ 989-0060

United Artist East, 7. First Ave & 85th St ☎ 249-5100

United Artists 64th Street, 16 Second Ave and 64th St ☎ 832-1670

Walter Reade Theater, 18. 165 W 65th St ☎ 875-5600

Whitney Museum, 12. Third Ave & 68th St ☎ 570-3600

Worldwide Cinemas (1-6), 36. Eighth Ave & 50th St ☎ 246-1583

Ziegfeld Theatre, 34. Sixth Ave & 54th St ☎ 765-7600

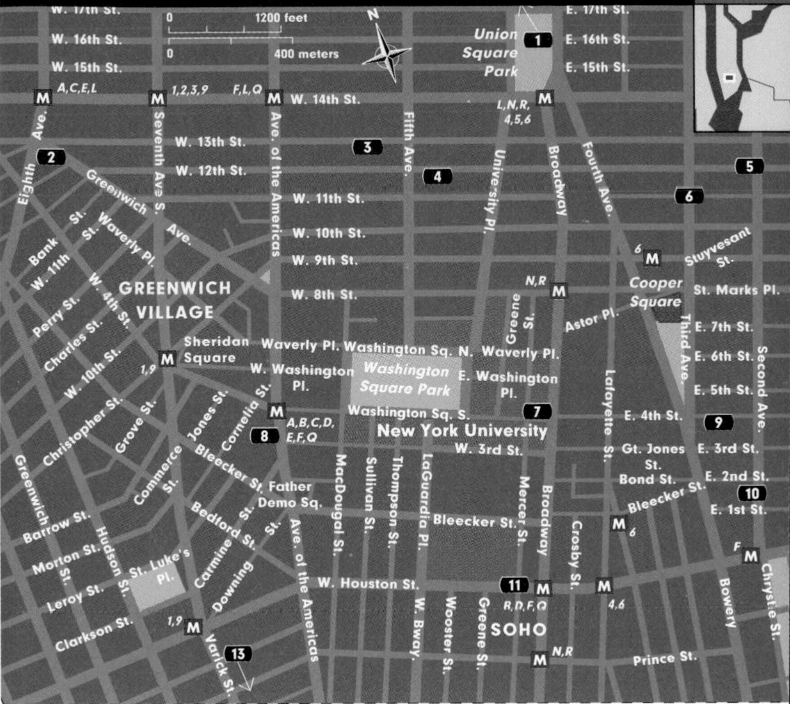

Listed by Site Number

1 19th St East (1–6)
2 Art Greenwich Twin
3 Quad Cinema (1–4)
4 Cinema Village
5 Village East Cinemas (1–7)
6 Village Theatre VII (1–7)
7 Women Make Movies
8 Waverly 1 & 2
9 Millennium Film Workshop
10 Anthology Film Archives
11 Angelika Film Center (1–6)
12 Film Forum (1–3)
13 The Screening Room

Listed Alphabetically

Angelika Film Center (1–6), 11. 18 W Houston St ☎ 995-2000

Anthology Film Archives, 10. 32–34 Second Ave ☎ 505-5181

Art Greenwich Twin, 2. 97 Greenwich Ave ☎ 929-3350

Cinema Village, 4. 22 E 12th St ☎ 924-3363

Film Forum (1–3), 12. 209 W Houston St ☎ 727-8110

Millennium Film Workshop, 9. 66 E 4th St ☎ 673-0090

19th St East (1–6), 1. Broadway & E 19th St ☎ 260-8000

Quad Cinema (1–4), 3. 34 W 13th St ☎ 255-8800

The Screening Room, 13. 54 Varick St ☎ 334-2100

Village East Cinemas (1–7), 5. Second Ave & 12th St ☎ 529-6799

Village Theatre VII (1–7), 6. Third Ave & 11th St ☎ 982-0400

Waverly 1 & 2, 8. Sixth Ave & W 3rd St ☎ 929-8037

Women Make Movies, 7. 462 Broadway ☎ 925-0606

Nightlife/Uptown

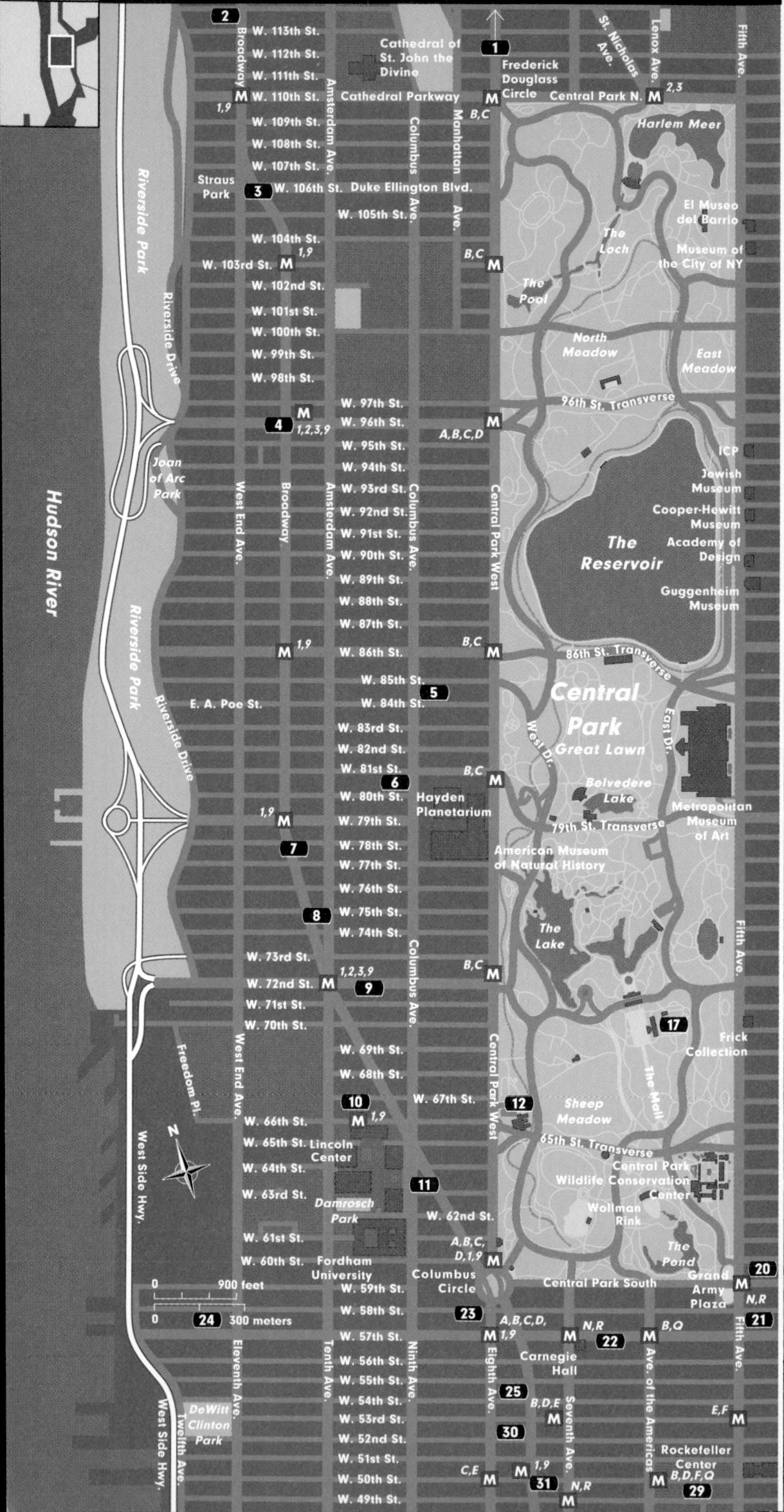

2
W. 113th St.
W. 112th St.
W. 111th St.
W. 110th St.
Cathedral of St. John the Divine
1
Frederick Douglass Circle
St. Nicholas Ave.
Lenox Ave.
Fifth Ave.
Cathedral Parkway
Central Park N.
2,3
1,9
B,C
Harlem Meer
W. 109th St.
W. 108th St.
W. 107th St.
Amsterdam Ave.
Columbus Ave.
Manhattan Ave.
Straus Park
3
W. 106th St. Duke Ellington Blvd.
W. 105th St.
El Museo del Barrio
The Loch
W. 104th St.
1,9
W. 103rd St.
B,C
Museum of the City of NY
W. 102nd St.
The Pool
W. 101st St.
W. 100th St.
North Meadow
East Meadow
W. 99th St.
W. 98th St.
Riverside Park
Riverside Drive
W. 97th St.
96th St. Transverse
4
1,2,3,9
W. 96th St.
A,B,C,D
W. 95th St.
ICP
W. 94th St.
Jewish Museum
Joan of Arc Park
W. 93rd St.
West End Ave.
Broadway
Amsterdam Ave.
Columbus Ave.
Central Park West
W. 92nd St.
Cooper-Hewitt Museum
W. 91st St.
The Reservoir
Academy of Design
W. 90th St.
Hudson River
W. 89th St.
W. 88th St.
Guggenheim Museum
W. 87th St.
1,9
W. 86th St.
B,C
86th St. Transverse
W. 85th St.
5
E. A. Poe St.
W. 84th St.
Central Park
Riverside Park
Riverside Drive
W. 83rd St.
West Dr.
East Dr.
W. 82nd St.
Great Lawn
W. 81st St.
B,C
6
Belvedere Lake
W. 80th St.
Hayden Planetarium
Metropolitan Museum of Art
1,9
W. 79th St.
79th St. Transverse
7
W. 78th St.
American Museum of Natural History
W. 77th St.
W. 76th St.
8
W. 75th St.
The Lake
W. 74th St.
Fifth Ave.
W. 73rd St.
1,2,3,9
B,C
W. 72nd St.
9
W. 71st St.
Columbus Ave.
17
W. 70th St.
Frick Collection
Freedom Pl.
W. 69th St.
The Mall
W. 68th St.
10
W. 67th St.
12
Sheep Meadow
West End Ave.
Central Park West
W. 66th St.
1,9
W. 65th St.
Lincoln Center
65th St. Transverse
W. 64th St.
Central Park Wildlife Conservation Center
West Side Hwy.
11
W. 63rd St.
Damrosch Park
Wollman Rink
W. 62nd St.
W. 61st St.
A,B,C,D,1,9
The Pond
W. 60th St.
Fordham University
Columbus Circle
20
0 900 feet
Central Park South
Grand Army Plaza
W. 59th St.
N,R
W. 58th St.
23
0 24 300 meters
A,B,C,D,1,9
N,R
B,Q
21
W. 57th St.
22
Fifth Ave.
Carnegie Hall
Eleventh Ave.
Tenth Ave.
Ninth Ave.
Eighth Ave.
W. 56th St.
W. 55th St.
25
W. 54th St.
B,D,E
Seventh Ave.
Ave. of the Americas
DeWitt Clinton Park
W. 53rd St.
E,F
30
W. 52nd St.
West Side Hwy.
Twelfth Ave.
W. 51st St.
Rockefeller Center
C,E
1,9
W. 50th St.
31
B,D,F,Q
N,R
29
W. 49th St.

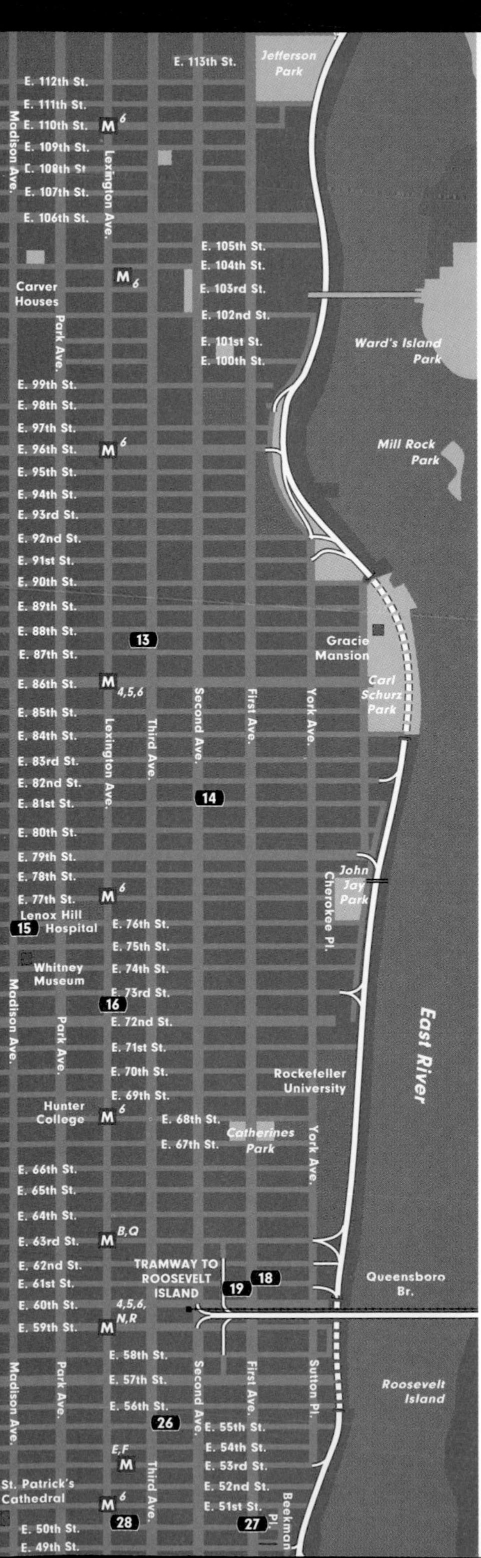

Listed by Site Number

1 Apollo Theatre
2 West End Gate
3 Augie's Pub
4 Latin Quarter
5 Venue
6 The Works
7 Stand Up NY
8 China Club
9 Triad
10 Off Center
11 Iridium
12 Tavern on the Green
13 Manny's Car Wash
14 Comic Strip
15 Bemelmans Bar/Café Carlyle
16 Lexington Bar & Books
17 Central Park Summer Stage
18 Dangerfield's
19 Chicago City Limits
20 Café Pierre
21 5757
22 Russian Tea Room
23 Le Bar Bat
24 Copacabana
25 Ed Sullivan's
26 Michael's Pub
27 Beekman Bar and Books
28 Tatou
29 Rainbow & Stars
29 Rainbow Room

Nightlife/Midtown & Downtown

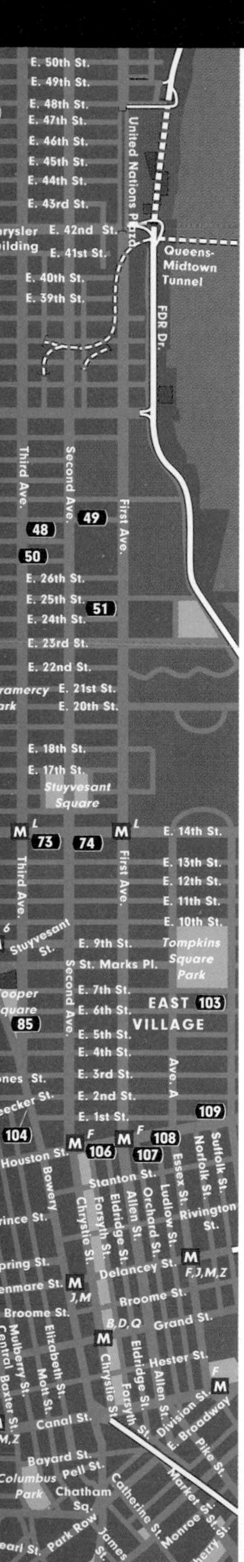

Listed by Site Number

30 Roseland
31 Caroline's
32 Otis
33 Don't Tell Mama
34 Danny's Skylight Room
35 Supper Club
36 Whiskey
37 Sound Factory
38 Birdland
39 West Bank Cafe
40 Sardi's
41 O'Lunney's
42 Laura Belle's
43 Judy's
44 Algonquin
45 Denim 'n Diamonds
46 Stella Del Mare
47 Hideaway
48 Dakota
49 Paddy Reilly's
50 Rodeo Bar
51 NY Comedy Club
52 Improvisation
53 Chelsea Commons
54 The Eagle
55 The Kitchen
56 Roxy
57 Gotham Comedy Club
58 Les Poulets
59 Cheetah
60 Tramps
61 Stringfellows
62 Splash
63 Irving Plaza
64 Palladium
65 Mother
66 Cooler
67 Rebar
68 Cajun
69 Chicago Blues
70 Nell's
71 Zinno
72 Smalls
73 Beauty Bar
74 Flamingo East
75 Webster Hall
76 System
77 Village Vanguard
78 Henrietta Hudson
79 Eighty-Eights
80 Duplex
81 The Monster
82 Sweet Basil
83 Cornelia Street Café
84 Knickerbocker
85 Continental
86 Bottom Line
87 Visiones
88 Blue Note
89 Mostly Magic
90 Comedy Cellar
91 Café Wha
92 Mondo Cane
93 Back Fence
94 Kenny's Castaways
95 Boston Comedy Club
96 Rock 'n Roll Café
96 Terra Blues
97 Bitter End
98 Life
99 SOB's
100 Ear Inn
101 Don Hill's
102 Spy
103 Sidewalk Cafe
104 CBGB & OMFUG
105 Time Café/Fez
106 Sapphire Bar
107 Mercury Lounge
108 The Bank
109 Meow Mix
110 Wetlands
111 New Music Cafe
112 Windows on the World
113 Knitting Factory

Nightlife

Listed Alphabetically

Algonquin, 44. 59 W44th St ☎ 840-6800. Cabaret

Apollo Theatre, 1. 253 W 125th St ☎ 749-5838. Concert Hall

Augie's Pub, 3. 2751 Broadway ☎ 864-9834. Jazz/Blues/R&B

Back Fence, 93. 155 Bleecker St ☎ 475-9221. R&R/Folk

The Bank, 108. 225 E Houston St ☎ 505-5033. Dance Club

Beauty Bar, 73. 231 E 14th St ☎ 539-1389 Bar Music

Beekman Bar and Books, 27. 889 First Ave ☎ 980-9314. Jazz

Bemelman's Bar/Café Carlyle, 15. 35 E 76th St ☎ 744-1600. Bar Music

Birdland, 38. 315 W 44th St ☎ 581-3080. Jazz

Bitter End, 97. 147 Bleecker St ☎ 673-7030. Jazz/Blues/R&B

Blue Note, 88. 131 W 3rd St ☎ 475-8592. Jazz/Blues/R&B

Boston Comedy Club, 95. 82 W 3rd St ☎ 477-1000. Comedy

Bottom Line, 86. 15 W 4th St ☎ 228-6300. Folk/Rock

Café Pierre, 20. 2 E 61st St ☎ 940-8185. Cabaret

Café Wha, 91. 115 MacDougal St ☎ 254-3706. Comedy/Jazz

Cajun, 68. 129 Eighth Ave ☎ 691-6174. Jazz

Caroline's, 31. 1626 Broadway ☎ 757-4100. Comedy

CBGB & OMFUG, 104. 315 Bowery ☎ 982-4052. Punk/Rock/Dance

Central Park Summer Stage, 17. Central Park at 72nd St ☎ 360-2777. Pop/Rock/Folk/Jazz

Cheetah, 59. 12 W 21st St ☎ 206-7770. Dance Club

Chelsea Commons, 53. 242 10th Ave ☎ 929-9424. Rock/Folk

Chicago Blues, 69. 73 Eighth Ave ☎ 924-9755. Blues/Jazz

Chicago City Limits,19. 1105 First Ave☎ 888-5233. Comedy

China Club, 8. 2130 Broadway ☎ 877-1166. Rock/Dance Club

Comedy Cellar, 90. 117 MacDougal St ☎ 254-3480. Comedy

Comic Strip, 14. 1568 Second Ave ☎ 861-9386. Comedy

Continental, 85. 25 Third Ave ☎ 529-6924. Rock Club

Cooler, 66. 416 W 14th St ☎ 229-0785.

Copacabana, 24. 617 W 57th St ☎ 582-2672. Dance Club

Cornelia Street Cafe, 83. 29 Cornelia St ☎ 989-9318. Jazz

Dakota, 48. 405 Third Ave ☎ 684-8376. Gay

Dangerfield's, 18. 1118 First Ave ☎ 593-1650. Comedy

Danny's Skylight Room, 34. 346 W 46th St ☎ 265-8130. Cabaret

Denim 'n Diamonds, 45. 511 Lexington Ave ☎ 371–1600. Country

Don Hill's, 101. 511 Greenwich Ave. ☎ 334-1390. Rock

Don't Tell Mama, 33. 343 W 46th St ☎ 757-0788. Cabaret

Duplex, 80. 61 Christopher St ☎ 255-5438. Cabaret/Piano

The Eagle, 54. 142 Eleventh Ave ☎ 691-8451. Gay

Ear Inn, 100. 326 Spring St ☎ 226-9060. Rock/Blues

Ed Sullivan's, 25. 1697 Broadway ☎ 541-1697. Cabaret

Eighty Eight's, 79. 228 W 10th St ☎ 924-0088. Cabaret

5757, 21. 57 E 57th St ☎ 758-5700. Piano Bar

Flamingo East, 74. 219 Second Avenue ☎ 533-2860. Rock/Funk

Gotham Comedy Cub, 57. 34 W 22nd St ☎ 367-9000. Comedy

Henrietta Hudson, 78. 448 Hudson St ☎ 924–3347. Lesbian

Hideaway, 47. 32 W 37th St ☎ 947-8940. Ballroom/Variety

Improvisation, 52. 433 W 34th St ☎ 279-3446. Comedy

Iridium, 11. 48 W 63rd St ☎ 582-2121. Jazz

Irving Plaza, 63. 17 Irving Place ☎ 777-6800. Swing

Judy's, 43. 49 W 44th St ☎ 764-8930. Piano

Kenny's Castaways, 94. 157 Bleecker St ☎ 473-9870. Rock

The Kitchen, 55. 512 W 19th St ☎ 255-5793. Jazz/Performance

Knickerbocker, 84. 33 University Pl ☎ 228-8490. Jazz

Knitting Factory, 113. 74 Leonard St ☎ 219-3055. Rock/Jazz

Latin Quarter, 4. 2551 Broadway ☎ 864-7600. Latin

Laura Belle's, 42. 120 W 43rd St ☎ 819-1000. Dance/Supper Club

Le Bar Bat, 23. 311 W 57th St ☎ 307-7228. Dance Club

Les Poulets, 58. 16 W 22nd St ☎ 229-2000. Rock

Listed Alphabetically (cont.)

Lexington Bar & Books, 16. 1020 Lexington Ave ☎ 717-3902. Jazz

Life, 98. 158 Bleecker St ☎ 420-1999. Dance Club

Manny's Car Wash, 13. 1558 Third Ave ☎ 369-2583. Blues

Michael's Pub, 26. 211 E 55th St ☎ 758-2272. Piano Bar/Jazz

Mondo Cane, 92. 205 Thompson St ☎ 254-5166. Blues/Jazz

Monster, 81. 80 Grove St ☎ 924-3557. Gay/Disco

Mostly Magic, 89. 55 Carmine St ☎ 924-1472. Comedy/Magic

Meow Mix, 109. 269 Houston St ☎ 334-7474. Lesbian

Mercury Lounge, 107. 217 E Houston St ☎ 260-4700. Rock

Mother, 65. 432 W 14th St ☎ 366-5680. Performance Art

Nell's, 70. 246 W 14th St ☎ 675-1567. Dance Club

New Music Cafe, 111. 285 W Broadway ☎ 941-1019. Reggae/Rock

New York Comedy Club, 51. 241 E 24th St ☎ 696-5233. Comedy

Off Center, 10. 148 W 67th St ☎ 724-6643. Comedy

O'Lunney's, 41. 204 W 43rd St ☎ 840-6688. Country/Folk

Otis, 32. 754 Ninth Ave ☎ 246-4417. Pop/Rock

Palladium, 64. 126 E 14th St ☎ 473-7171. Dance Club

Paddy Reilly's, 49. 519 Second Ave ☎ 686-1210. Irish

Rainbow Room, 29. 30 Rockefeller Plz ☎ 632-5000. Ballroom/Cabaret

Rainbow & Stars, 29. 30 Rockefeller Plz ☎ 632-5000. Cabaret

Rebar, 67. Eighth Ave & 16th St ☎ 627-1680. Comedy

Red Blazer Too, 32. 349 W 46th St ☎ 262-3112. Jazz/Blues/Swing

Rock 'n Roll Café, 96. 149 Bleecker St ☎ 677-7630. Rock

Rodeo Bar, 50. 375 Third Ave ☎ 683-6500. Country/Rockabilly/Blues

Roseland, 30. 239 W 52nd St ☎ 247-0200. Ballroom/Rock

Roxy, 56. 515 W 18th St ☎ 645-5156. Dance Club

Russian Tea Room, 22. 150 W 57th St ☎ 265-0947. Cabaret

Sapphire Bar, 106. 249 Eldridge St ☎ 777-5153. Funk/Soul

Sardi's, 40. 234 W 44th St ☎ 221-8444. Cabaret

Sidewalk Café, 103. 94 Ave A ☎ 473-7373. Jazz/Rock

Smalls, 72. 183 W 10th St ☎ 929-7565. Jazz

SOB's, 99. 204 Varick St ☎ 243-4940. Brazilian/Reggae/Jazz

Sound Factory, 37. 618 W 46th St ☎ 643-0728. Dance Club

Splash, 62. 50 W 17th St ☎ 691-0073. Gay

Spy, 102. 101 Greene St ☎ 343-9000. Bar/Lounge

Stand Up NY, 7. 236 W 78th St ☎ 595-0850. Comedy

Stella Del Mare, 46. 346 Lexington Ave ☎ 687-4425. Piano Bar

Stringfellows, 61. 35 E 21st St ☎ 254-2444. Adult Entertainment

Supper Club, 35. 240 W 47th St ☎ 921-1940. Dance/Supper Club

Sweet Basil, 82. 88 Seventh Ave S ☎ 242-1785. Jazz/Swing/Fusion

System, 76. 76 E 13th St ☎ 388-1060. Dance Club

Tatou, 28. 151 E 50th St ☎ 753-1144. Dance/Supper Club

Tavern on the Green, 12. Central Park at W 67th St ☎ 873-3200. Jazz

Terra Blues, 96. 149 Bleecker St ☎ 777-7776. Blues

Time Café/Fez, 105. 380 Lafayette St ☎ 533-2680. Lounge/Cabaret/Jazz

Tramps, 60. 51 W 21st St ☎ 727-7788. Blues/Country/Rock

Triad, 9. 158 W 72nd St ☎ 362-2590. Comedy

Venue, 5. 505 Columbus Ave ☎ 579-9463. Dance Club

Village Vanguard, 77. 178 Seventh Ave S ☎ 255-4037. Jazz/Blues

Visiones, 87. 125 MacDougal St ☎ 673-5576. Blues/Jazz/R&B

Webster Hall, 75. 125 E 11th St ☎ 353-1600. Dance Club

West Bank Café, 39. 407 W 42nd St ☎ 695-6909. Comedy/Music

West End Gate, 2. 2911 Broadway ☎ 662-8830. Rock/Jazz

Wetlands, 110. 161 Hudson St ☎ 966-5244. Psychedelic Rock

Whiskey, 36. 235 W 46th St ☎ 819-0404. Bar Music

Windows on the World, 112. 1 World Trade Ctr ☎ 938-1111. Jazz/Dinner

The Works, 6. 428 Columbus Ave ☎ 799-7365. Gay

Zinno, 71. 126 W 13th St ☎ 924-5182. Blues/Jazz/R&B

Notes